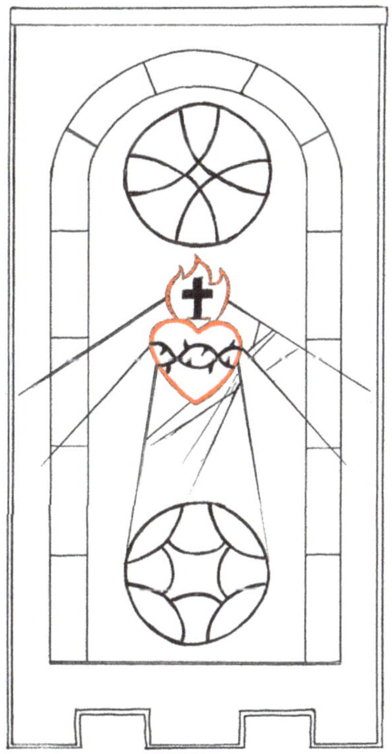

Stefan Salinas

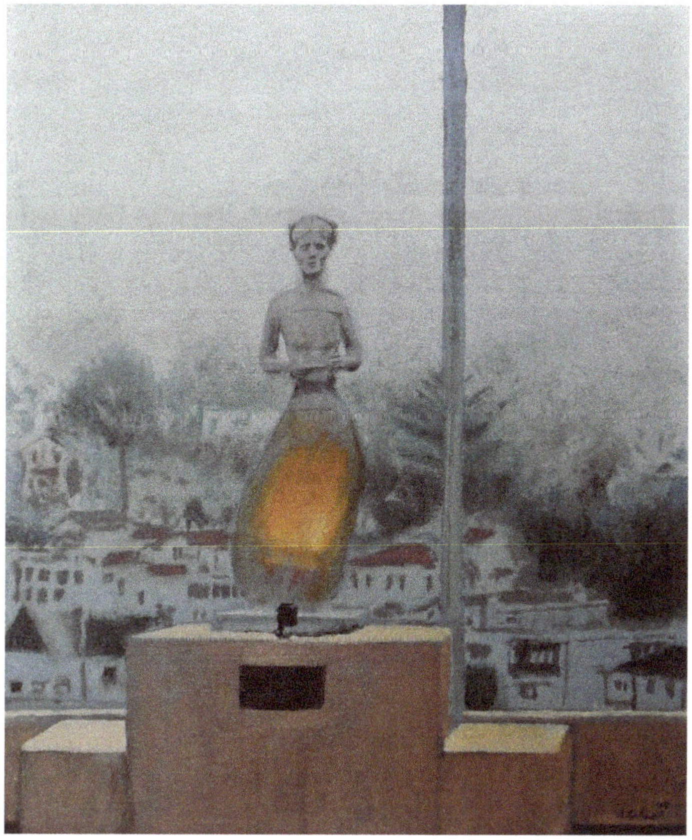

Works on Canvas, on Paper, in Churches, and in Books

Camelopardalis
SAN FRANCISCO

Editor: Robert Savigny

ISBN: 978-0-9986088-6-0
Library of Congress Control Number: 2021909621

Art on pages 118 & 119 from *The Jesuit Post: #Faith #God #Frontiers #Culture #Mystery #Love*. New York, Orbis Books, 2014.
Art on pages 122 & 123 from *Afterlife, Interrupted, Book Two*. Tucson, Fluid Creations, Inc., 2020.

Camelopardalis / Stefan Salinas
PO Box 470041, San Francisco, CA 94147 USA
https://www.stefansalinas.com

Printed on acid-free paper by IngramSpark in Australia/Canada/Germany/USA/UK.

Front cover: **Christ the Monarch**, 2018, Acrylic, pencil, ink, and gold leaf on fabric and paper, 12"h x 9"w
St. Francis and the Wolf of Gubbio, 2014, Stained glass
Half-title page: Sketch for **Most Holy Redeemer processional banner**, 2018
Title page: **Florence Nightingale**, 2015, Oil on canvas, 12"h x 10"w, (sculpture by David Edstrom, 1937)
Back cover: **The Visitation (Inner Cosmos)** (detail), 2015, Acrylic, ink and gold leaf on cork
St. Luke panel, altar rails, 2014, oak, acrylic and gold leaf on linen
Leaning (detail), 2003, Oil on canvas, 24"h x 18"w

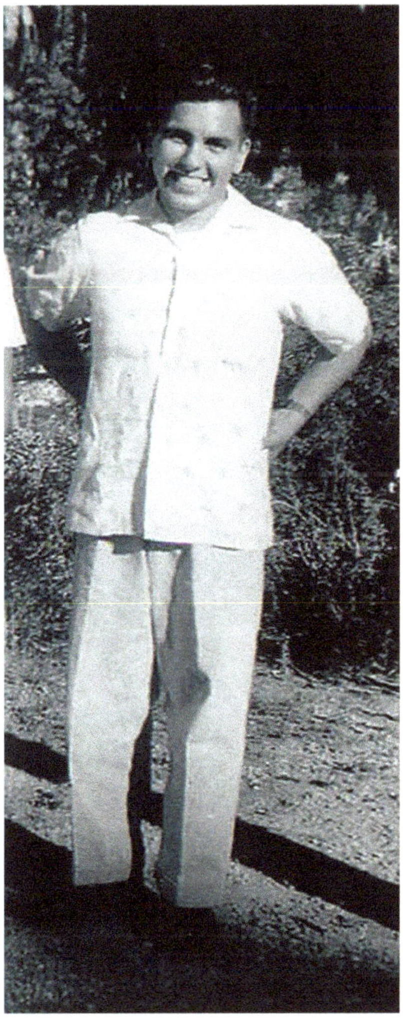

In memory of

&

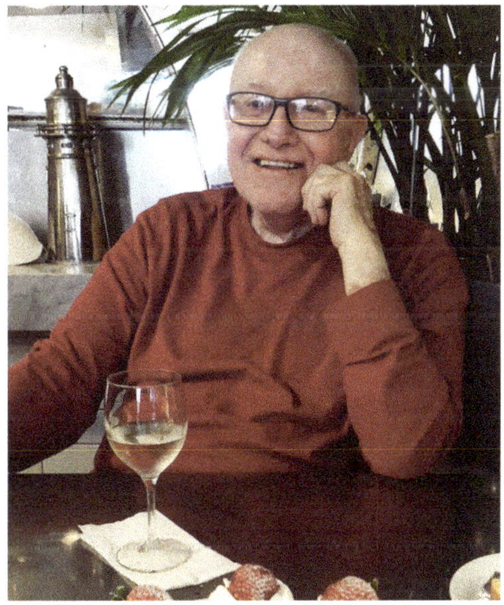

William John Mathews

1931-2021
Dearest friend, religious guide,
and favorite art patron

Great Uncle Jesse Acosta Almazán

1938-2002
One of the founders of ***Con Safo***,
San Antonio's first
Chicano art collective

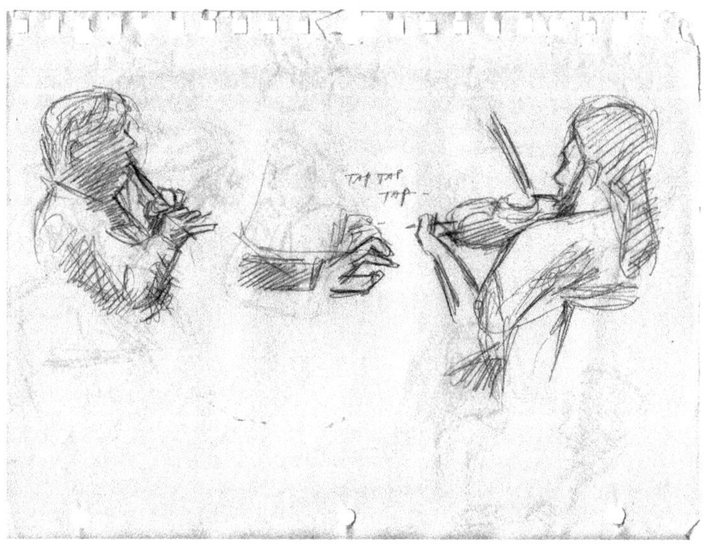
TAP TAP
TAP

Table of Contents

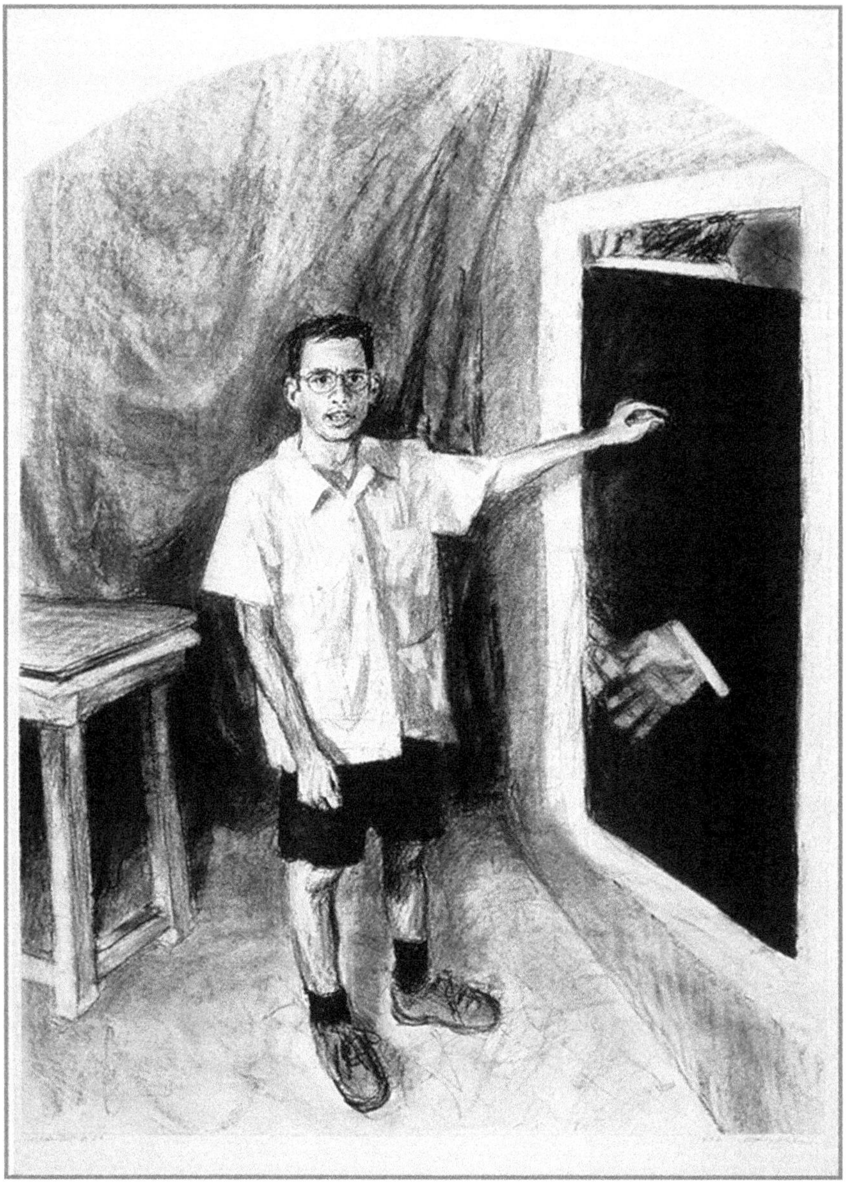

Self-Portrait, 1998
Charcoal on paper

Early Life and Influences

My parents placed a variety of visual books around the household for an artistic mind to dive into. A world atlas, a book on the art of Mexico, a Time-Life collection of European masters provided by my paternal grandmother, and one of my favorites: an edition of *10,000 Dreams Interpreted*, which featured hundreds of paintings, prints and drawings from museums in Europe and America. I spent hours upon hours looking at those illustrations. There was also a book by fantasy painter Bruce Pennington, inspired by Nostradamus' prophecies. What kid growing up in the '70s did not study their favorite bands' album covers? The Beatles and Pink Floyd's cover art made me want to one day design some myself. My mother allowed me to pick out a poster when I was around eight, but forbid me from hanging it in my shared bedroom. As it was a creepy fantasy scene of old ruins made up of a skeleton, pipes, machinery, stone and human anatomy, by H.R. Geiger, it was permitted to live under my bed. To me it was as fascinating as Hieronymus Bosch's works, like *The Garden of Earthly Delights*, when I first saw those in books. There were bedsheets with detailed Noah's Ark scenes and wallpaper with vintage cars. How important these simple sources were for a budding creative's eyes.

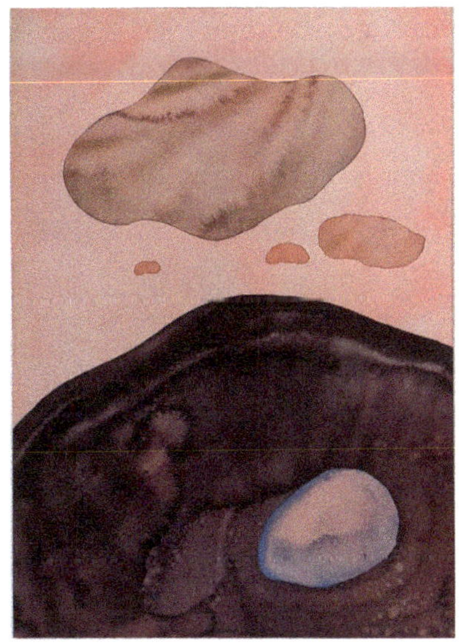

Landscape by Jesse Acosta Almazán
21.5"h x 15.5"w

Adorning the walls of my childhood home hung prints and posters featuring artists like Will Barnet, Mark Rothko, and Marc Chagall. Abstracts and impressionism. The most important pieces in the house were three by my Great Uncle Jesse Almazán. When I was young, looking up at his art - specifically one of a hill, and lake - took me into another world. Knowing he was a relative guided me. I, too,could follow this calling. He may have paid my parents a visit when I was an infant, or perhaps the art was acquired before then. I drove to see him and his wife twice in the 1990s, the second time to attend one of his last art openings. He lived in San Antonio, where during the '60s, he co-founded *Con Safo*, San Antonio's first Chicano art collective. I treasure my memory of visiting a museum with him, listening to his explanations of how John Singer Sargent painted undercoats of color, and seeing the variety of plants at the botanical gardens there, through his eyes. It was a marvel, the volume of chalk pastels he whipped out just before my visit, him trying out the medium for the first time. He had the forever-young spark of life in his eyes.

That same spark I now see in the eyes of photos of an artist whose sculptures I encountered when I moved to San Francisco: Beniamino "Benny" Bufano. A statue by him of Saint Francis, with Inuit art-inspired facial features, outstretched arms to reference the crucifix, and a mosaic set on his body with a tree filled with birds, stands outside the Mondavi Winery in Napa Valley. Looking at it, a bright energy shook within my body. Benny's vision, particularly the bold eyes staring straight at us, like those found in funerary portraits from Roman-era Egypt and early Coptic Christian manuscripts, have found their way into my own handiwork.

My father would take us to international festivals, African cultural events, Chinese New Year's celebrations, car shows - I loved them all. It helped to be in a family of many talents, skills and interests. An older sister was drawn to the medical field. An older brother who was the family DJ went on to teach mathematics, a fraternal twin who played flute in the school band explored photography and later became an engineer. All strong forces of nature, headed in different directions, not unlike our parents. Good times, bad times, conflict, sadness, love, divorce, achievements, creativity – much of it went in the pot of soup I am stirring, and keep adding ingredients to.

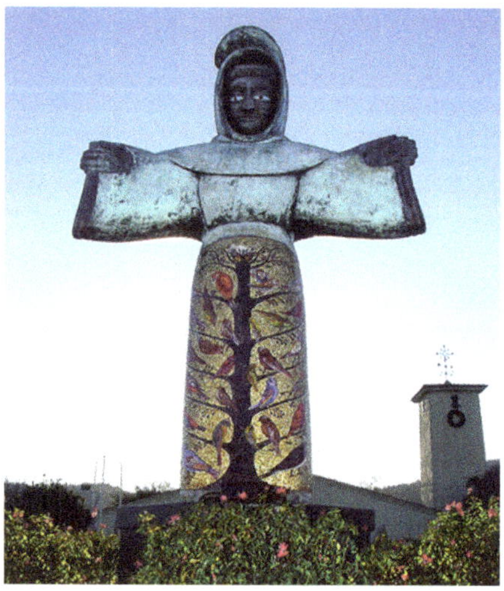

Saint Francis, Benny Bufano, 1939
Ceramic mosaic on bronze

Movies also fed my storytelling and paintings. Filmmakers like Martin Scorsese, Peter Greenaway, Alfred Hitchcock, Terry Gilliam, Hayao Miyazaki, Jim Henson, Stanley Kubrick, and David Lynch, just to name a few. Science fiction and fantasy stories occupied my young imagination. Like many kids from my generation, I wanted to be the next George Lucas. Playing with action figures, inspired by the religious elements within *Star Wars* and other sci-fi films, I would make up elaborate hero's journey plots. For the stories, I sketched creatures, costumes, ships, alien written languages - whole worlds. One story in particular had to do with the afterlife, in which the souls of all living beings from different planets arrive, mixed together, in the same plane of existence. A book involving religion and science fiction may be in my future.

In Houston, the main art museums brought in a bountiful array of artists. I especially liked the vibrations within the Menil Collection. Two structures that I cannot thank Dominique de Menil enough for are the Rothko Chapel (a space with a dual nature, museum and inter-faith prayer chapel) and her gift to St. Thomas University's campus: St. Basil Chapel. Both were designed by Philip Johnson. During my high school and college years, artists who invigorated my creative juices included Mel Chin, Cindy Sherman, James Whistler, Marcel Duchamp, and Gilbert & George. Genres and realms that captivated me were Inuit paintings and sculptures, Persian illuminated manuscripts, Les Nabi (a French post-Impressionist group), Orthodox Christian icons, Turkmen weavings, most of the European Renaissance, Gothic art, Tiffany glass, Tibetan scroll paintings, architecture old and new, any stained

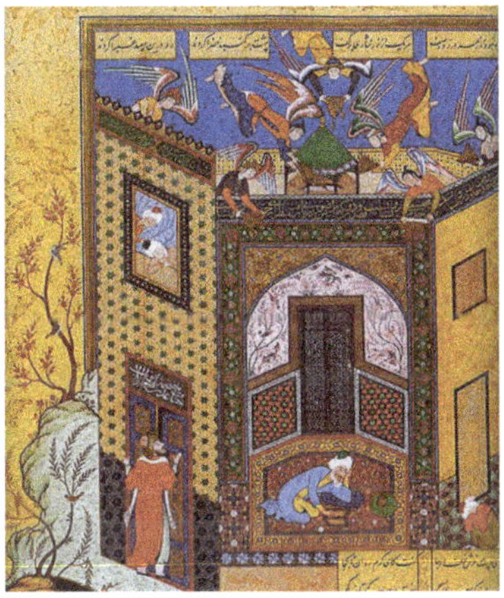 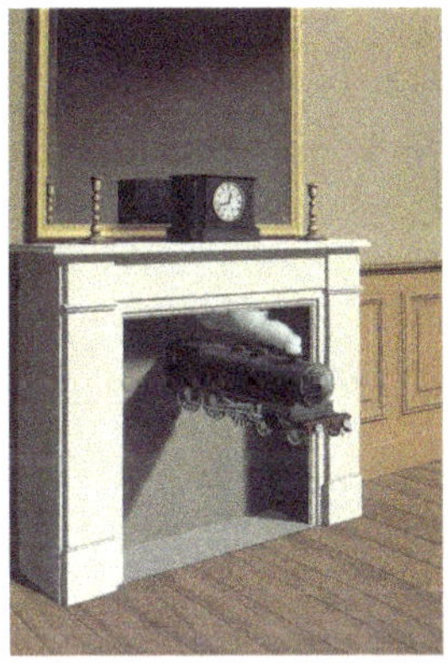 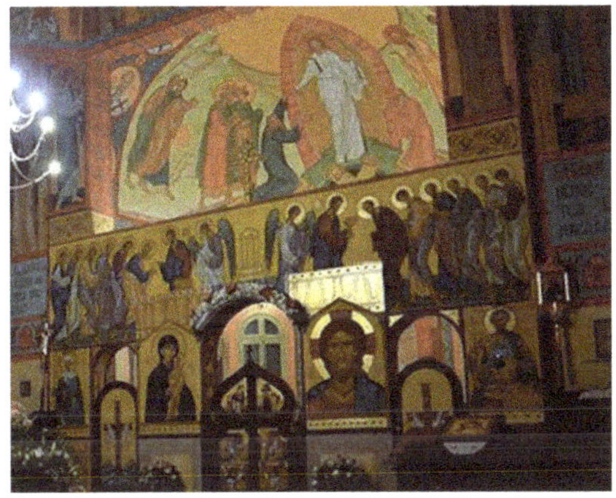

glass windows, surrealism, and Islamic calligraphy and design. Illustrators that immediately come to mind: Chris Van Allsburg, Beatrix Potter, William Steig, Ezra Jack Keats' *The Snowy Day*, Dr. Seuss' *The Sneetches and Other Stories*, Maurice Sendak, Peter Sís, Maira Kalman, Lane Smith, Ed Young, and Norman Rockwell. Comic book artists include Lynda Barry, the genius Chris Ware, Alison Bechdel, Marjane Satrapi, Patrick McDonnell, and Gary Larson.

Studio artists I keep returning to for inspiration include: Ben Shahn, Pieter Bruegel, George Tooker, Mary Cassatt, Benny Bufano, Henri de Toulouse-Lautrec, Édouard Vuillard, Maurice Denis, Stuart Davis, Käthe Kollwitz, Georgia O'Keeffe, Katsuyuki Nishijima, Diego Rivera, Georges de La Tour, Max Ernst, Odilon Redon, R.B. Kitaj, George Grosz, Gustav Klimt (if you have never seen his landscapes, you simply MUST), David Hockney, Hilma af Klint, M.C. Escher, and Dale Chihuly.

Dreams must be mentioned here. They, too, have been a creative influence. I have

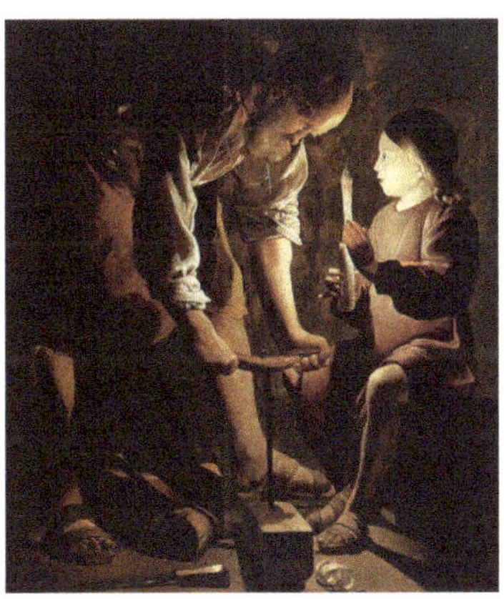 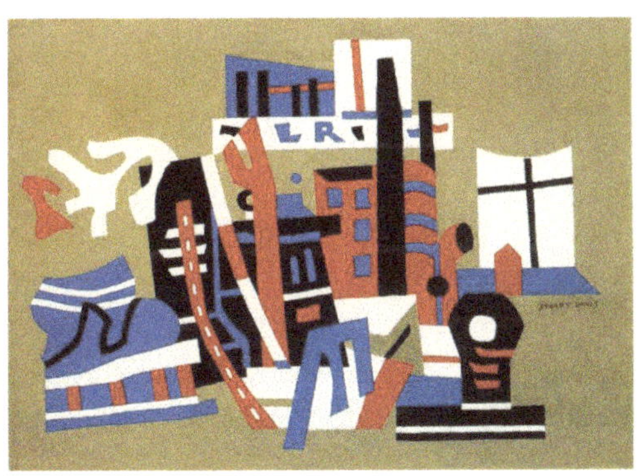 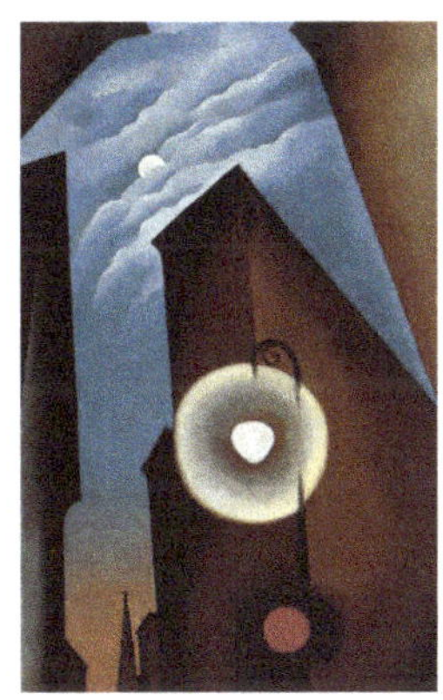

Top: Persian Miniature, 1553 *Time Transfixed*, Rene Magritte, 1938 Russian Orthodox church
Bottom: *Joseph the Carpenter*, Georges de la Tour, 1642 *New York Waterfront*, Stuart Davis, 1938 *New York with Moon*, Georgia O'Keeffe, 1926

been blessed with having the ability to remember long, intricate ones, and my poor siblings and parents cursed for having to hear me retell them! Some notable dreams have even "informed" me of my deeper self and the road being traveled on. Did some contain messages from the subconscious? My higher Self, busy performing his nightly housekeeping?

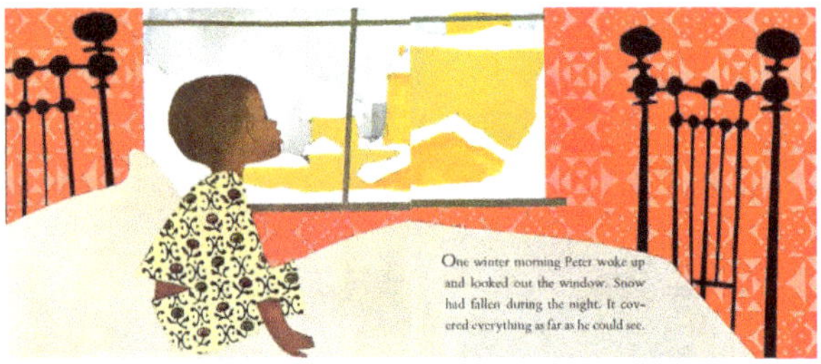

From *The Snowy Day*, Ezra Jack Keats, 1962

An ancestor? God? Without them, I would not have made the leap to convert to Catholicism in 2011. During the early production of both my first graphic novel and webcomic, "people" in dreams pressed me to continue working on them, pointing out how important it was to birth them into this world.

Music has also played an important part in my life. For years I was a baritone in choirs and an occasional soloist. How can an artist work without listening to music, at least not half of the time? Songs have filtered into my webcomic. I hope to explore music more and even collaborate with musicians in the future.

During the first few years in grammar school, I was placed in a class for "slow learners." The culprit was daydreaming more than anything. Concerned, my mother took me to a therapist to assess my skills. The therapist saw my artistic abilities and suggested I attend a magnet (charter) school for the arts. It was the best decision they made on my behalf. The rules for attending one meant sustaining a decent grade point average and excellent conduct. I am grateful for receiving instruction and guidance from several art teachers. Thank you for the lighthouse that is Dr. Patsy Menefee. She was my first art teacher during 4th and 5th grade, then, she taught at my junior high. The time she led the classes to learn calligraphy, I was NOT an enthused pupil. Mrs. Menefee, mea culpa! Years later we reconnected, and are friends through today.

I had a love for acting as well as art, so at the High School for the Performing and Visual Arts (now the Kinder School), I auditioned for the theater department first. The second year I transferred to the visual arts and was fortunate to have learned under David Sheard, Eileen Montgomery, John Halaka, Bill Frazier, Lisa Hardaway, and Lorena Cook. Rix Jennings was also a high school teacher, but I learned a lot more in two summer classes he taught at his studio. During breaks, he would read us passages from The Inner Game of Tennis.

At the University of Houston: Derek Boshier, Rachel Hecker, David Hickman, Al Souza, Gail Stack, Richard Stout† (step-by-step oil painting instructor, bar-none), and Liz Ward (printmaker extraordinaire). From the bottom of my heart, I thank you all.

It is also helpful to have honest colleagues around, with whom to bounce ideas off and exchange critiques of each other's work. I am eternally grateful to Willy Golden, a friend since the sixth grade. He is an accomplished musician, film and video editor, and a sculptor to boot. Willy can be the devil's advocate like no one else, and we know each other well enough to ask tough questions and make honest remarks. Eric Langhirt, a former choir buddy, doesn't just think outside the box; he thinks outside the space those who think outside the box stand in. William Mathews† and William Dohar have also patiently listened to my ideas for years, sharing their knowledge, and asking probing questions along the way. Thanks to Janine Reed, for her expert advice.

Thanks to the individuals who modeled for paintings and illustrations: Wendell Butterfield†, Liz Co, Kay Dunn, Myrna Frankel†, Robert Giesberg, María C. González, Joe Harris†, Michael Higgins, William Howland, Sara Hron, Eric Langhirt, John Lind, Dan Linder, Robert Megna, Elen Nettlebeck, Leoni and Matthew Nguyen, Trevor Phillips, Robert Porter†, Jack Ronan, David Ruettiger, Erin Stephanie, Kelsey Walsh, Charles Westphal†, and Richard Woo.

Thank you Nick Andrade, Bernard Brennan†, Sabrina DeCarolis, Vicki Fowler, Christina Gray, Thuan V. Hoang, Laurie Kimball, Tony LaTorre, Robert Lynn, Stephanie Martin†, Nancy O'Connor, Sia Piroozfar†, Bob Savigny, the Warren family, Edževit Winkler-Žepčanin, Rose Zimbardo†, and many other associates, peers and friends.

And of course, my parents† (Jimmy Salinas† and Paola Pagliotti†), siblings (Patricia, Loris and Marc) and extended family, for all their support and encouragement.

Thank you, Lord, for placing me on this beautiful, winding path,
lined with all of these colorful gardens and wildflowers.

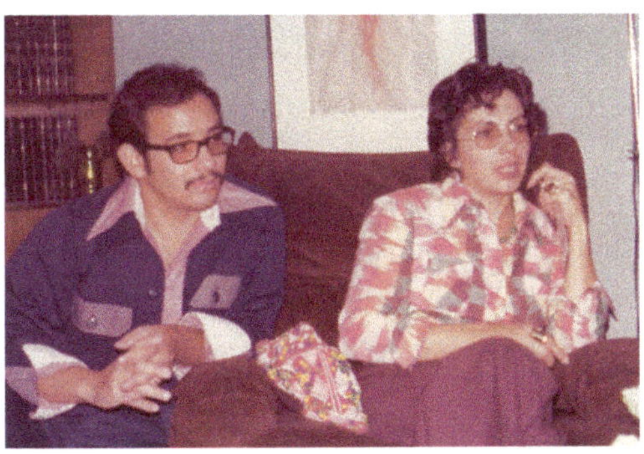

Parents: Jimmy Salinas & Paola Pagliotti

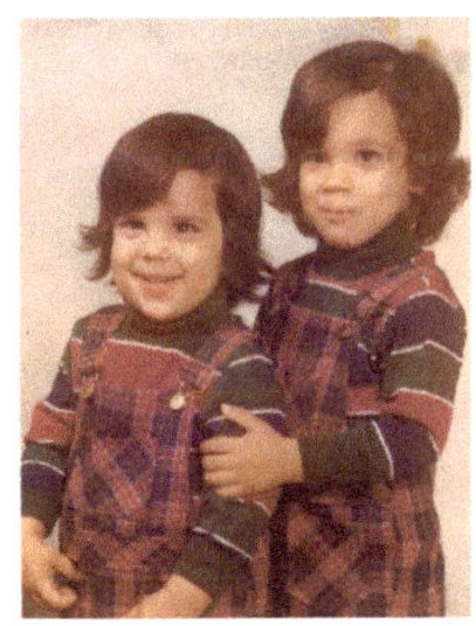

Twins Marc & Stefan, 2 years of age

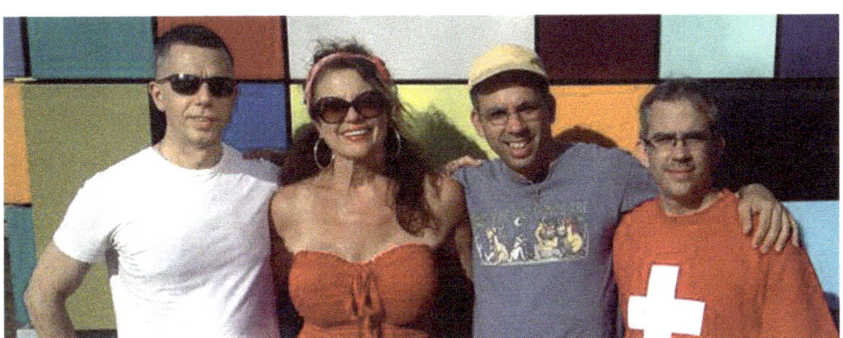

Siblings: Loris, Patricia, Stefan & Marc, 2014

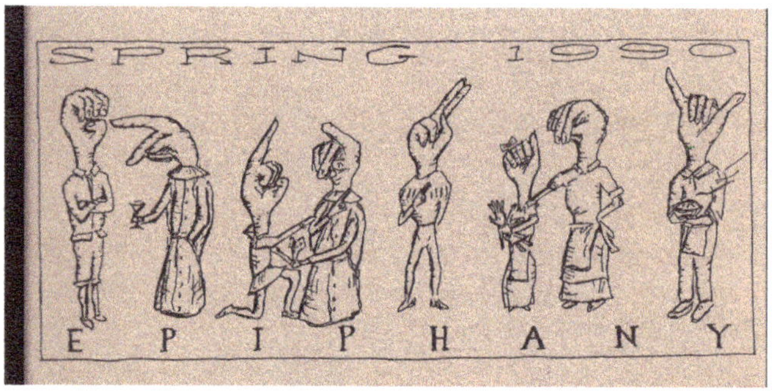

Cover for a high school arts magazine, 1990, Pen on paper

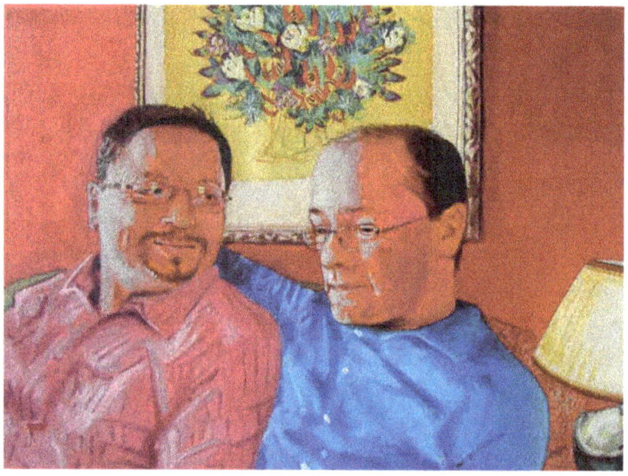

I dabbled into portraiture of people and pets. One has to make money aside from the day jobs: telemarketing, food store, antique shop, sales, hotels, etc.

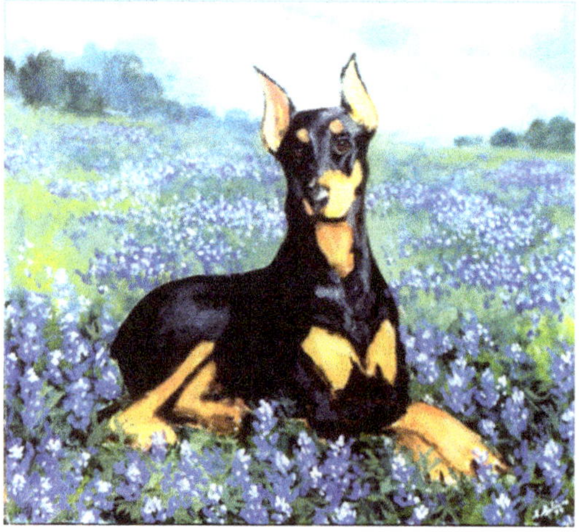

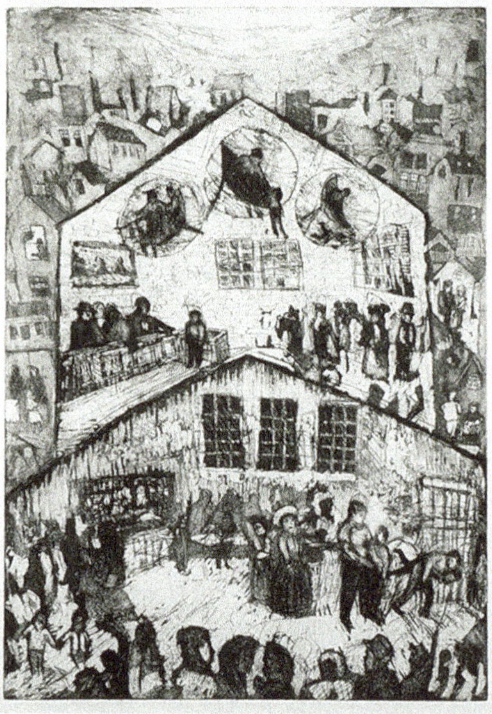

Peter Grimes (Prologue & Act 1), 1995
Intaglio print

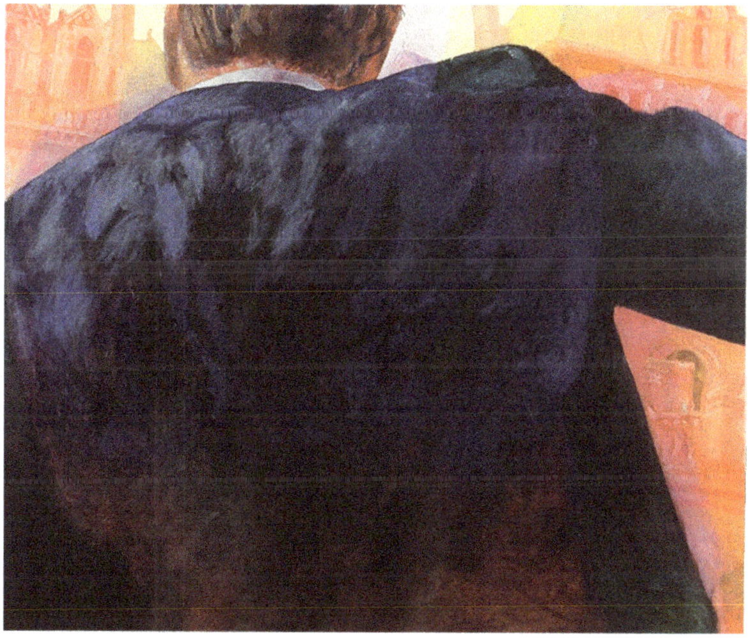

Man Pointing, 1996, Acrylic on unstretched canvas

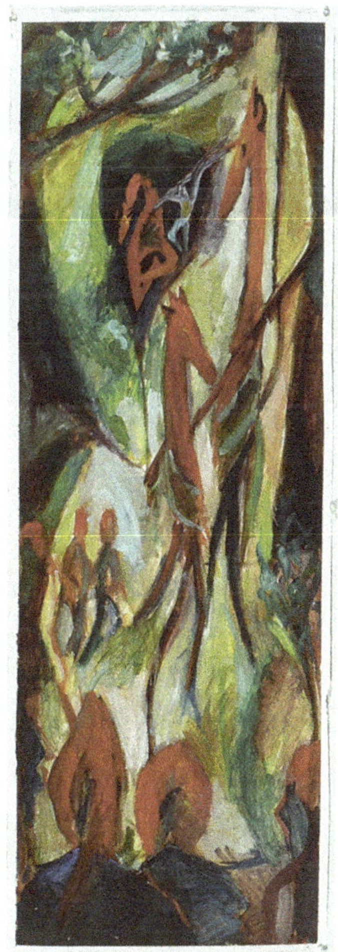

Giraffe Dance, 1993
Acrylic on paper

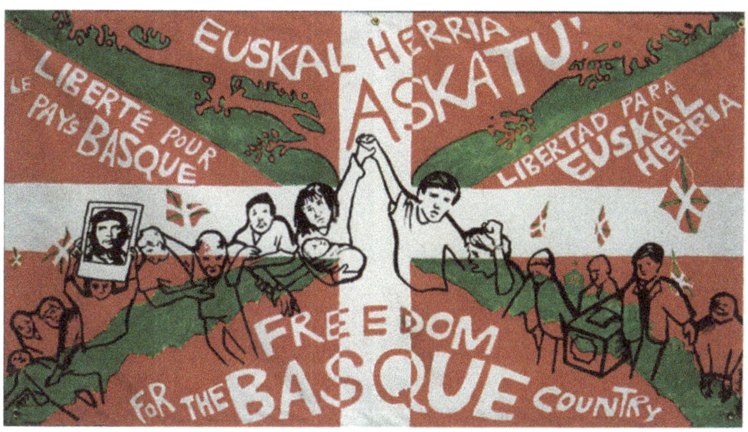

Protest banner for the Basque people, 1995
Enamel on vinyl, 7'h x 4'w

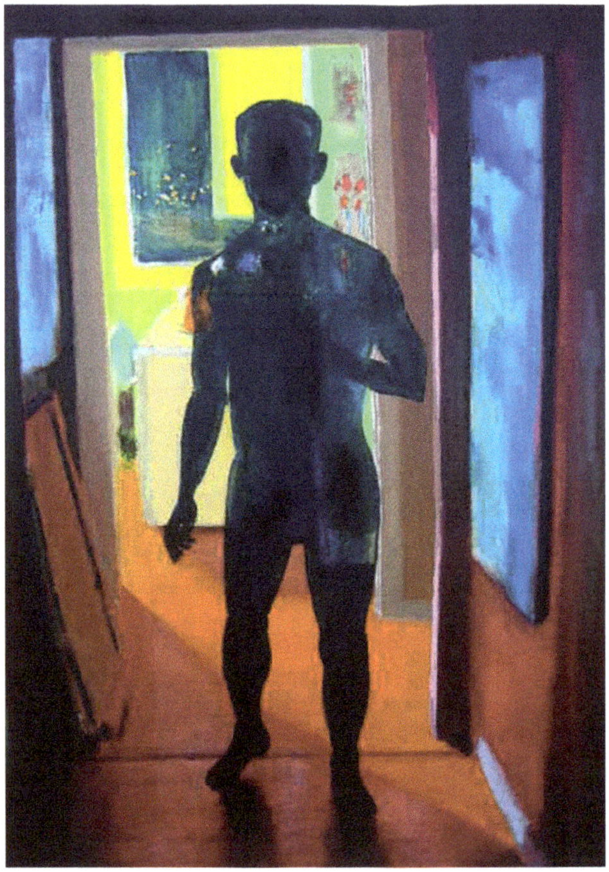

Presence (Stepping Forth), 2002
Oil on canvas

Paintings

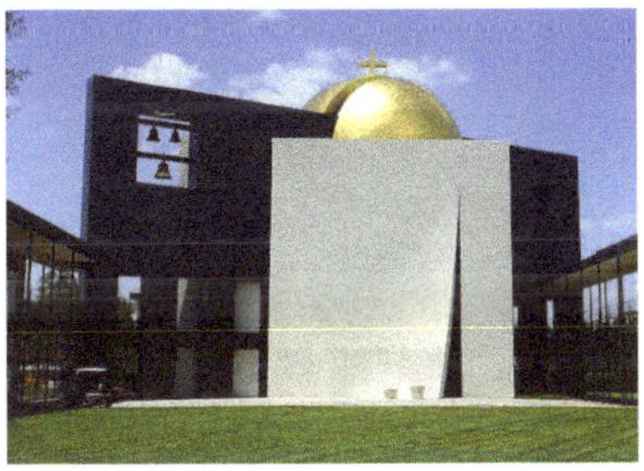
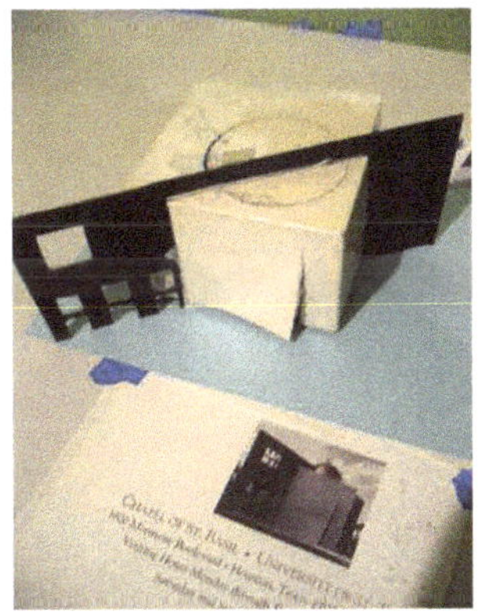
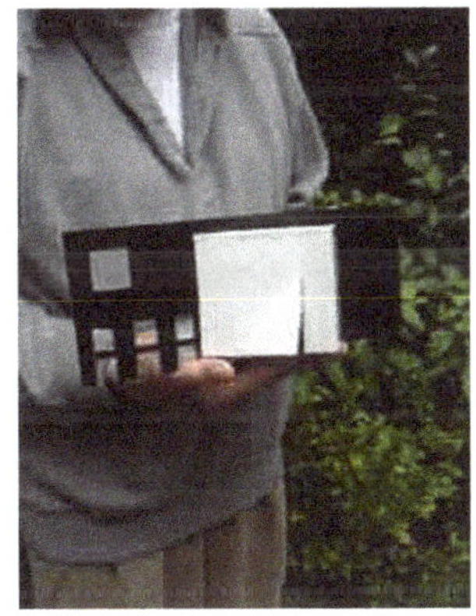
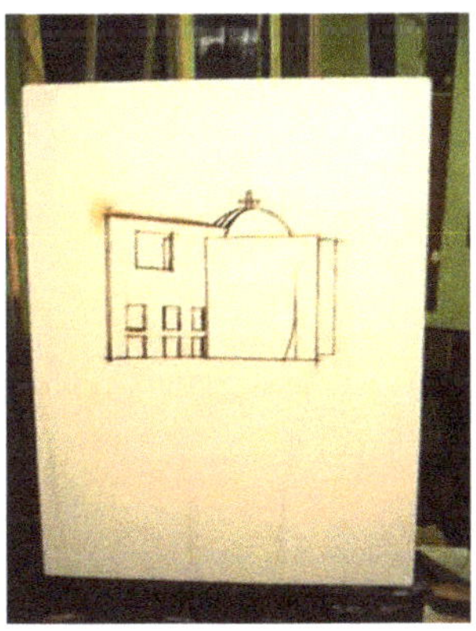
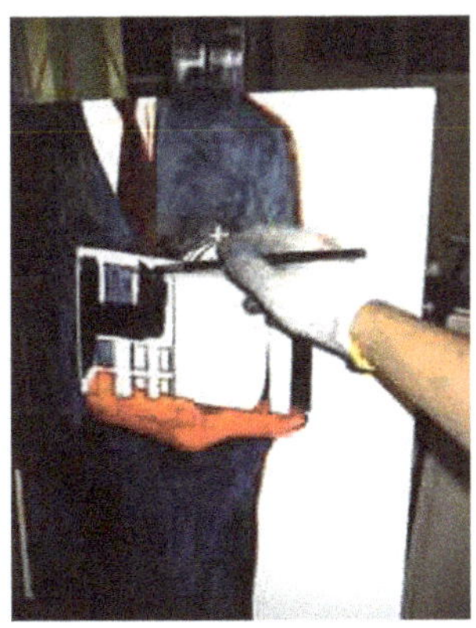
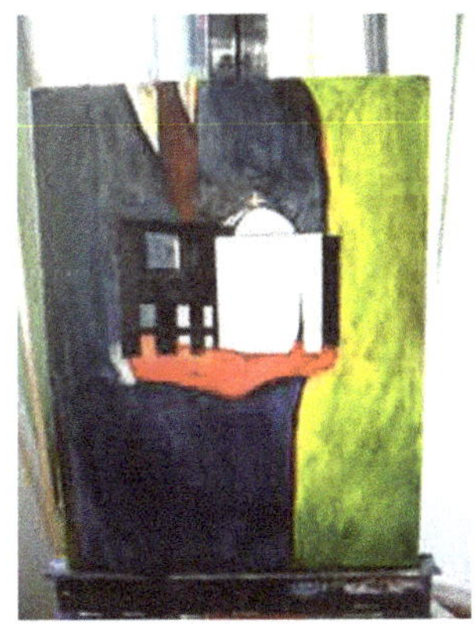
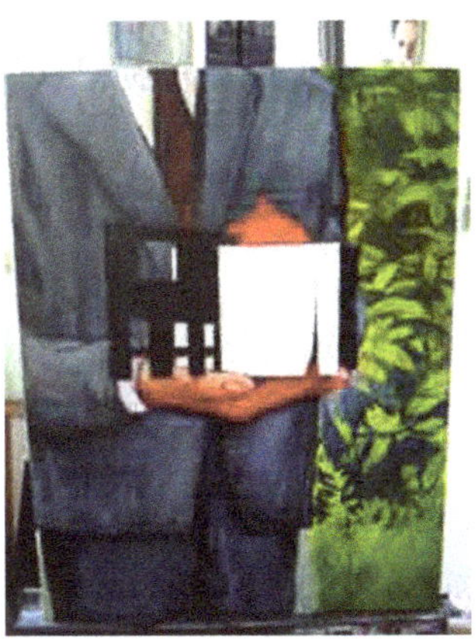
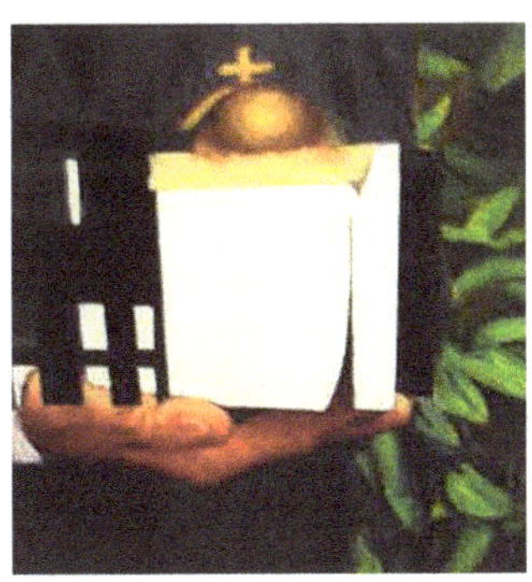
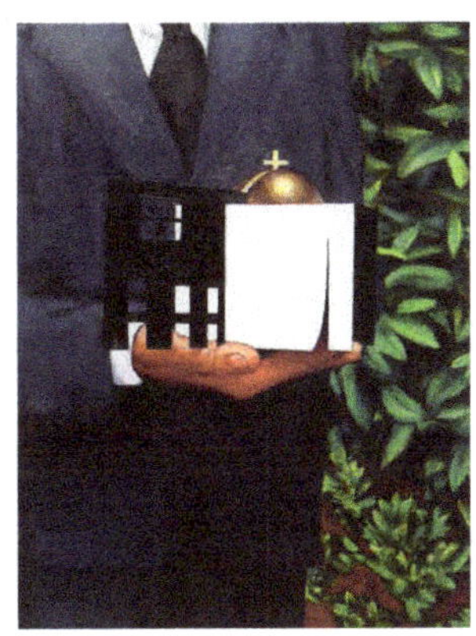

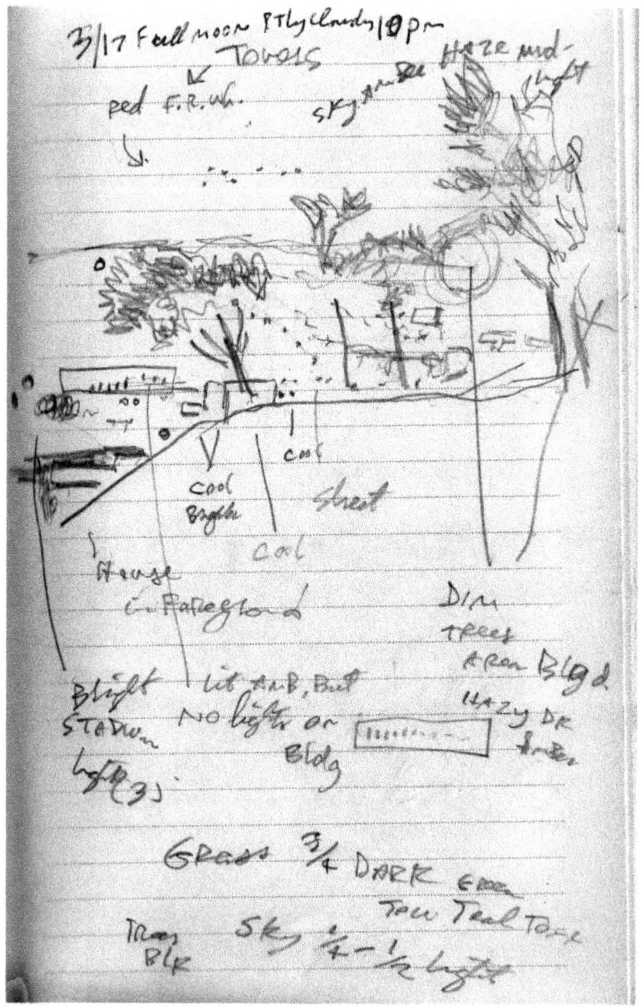
3/17 Full moon Ptly cloudy 10pm
Towers
Red
cool
cool
street
cool
House
Foreground
Dim
trees
Bldg.
Hazy
Bright
STADIUM
lights (3)
NO lights on
Bldg
Grass 3/4 DARK
Sky 1/4 – 1/2 light

When I attended the University of Houston, there seemed to be two schools of thought in the art department: figurative and representational art versus abstract forms that resembled single-celledorganisms and Pop Art collage. I was one of the few figurative painters, the minority group.

In the '90s, I was asked to create political banners, including one large wooden sign for a front yard in a wealthy neighborhood, protesting America's lack of involvement in helping the Bosnian Muslims in what was then Yugoslavia. The style I employed in my studio art was basically impressionistic, but in those signs, I used a rougher, cartoon look. Those simpler forms worked into my paintings but then left them and became the language of my books and graphic art. The paintings went back to impressionism, and then towards realism.

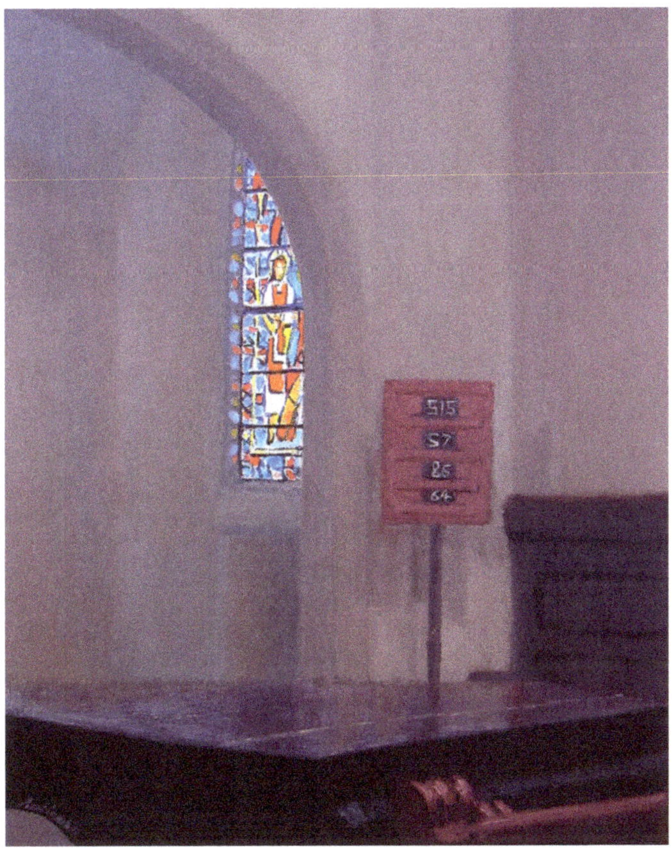

Portrait of Young Jesus, 2011
Oil on canvas

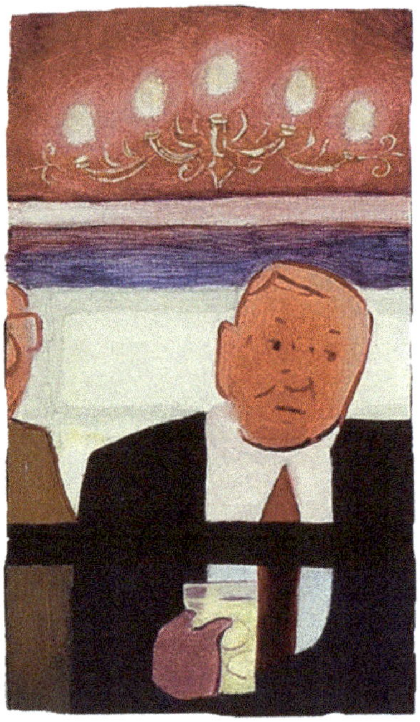

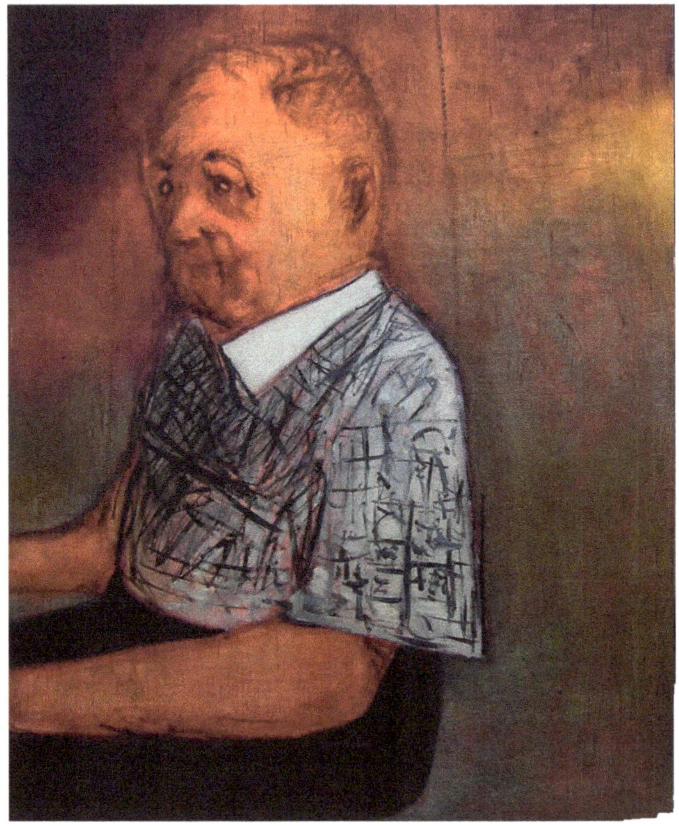

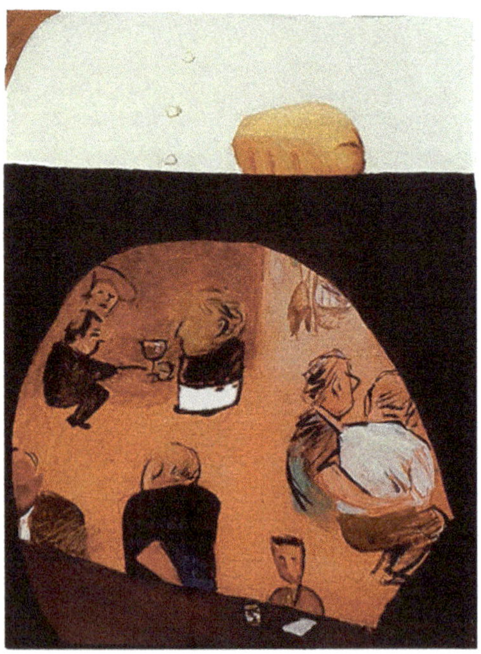

The Man Who Sits and Waits, 1997
Oil on wood, 24"h x 19"w

Two paintings from the series:
A Den of Comfort, 1998, Oil on wood

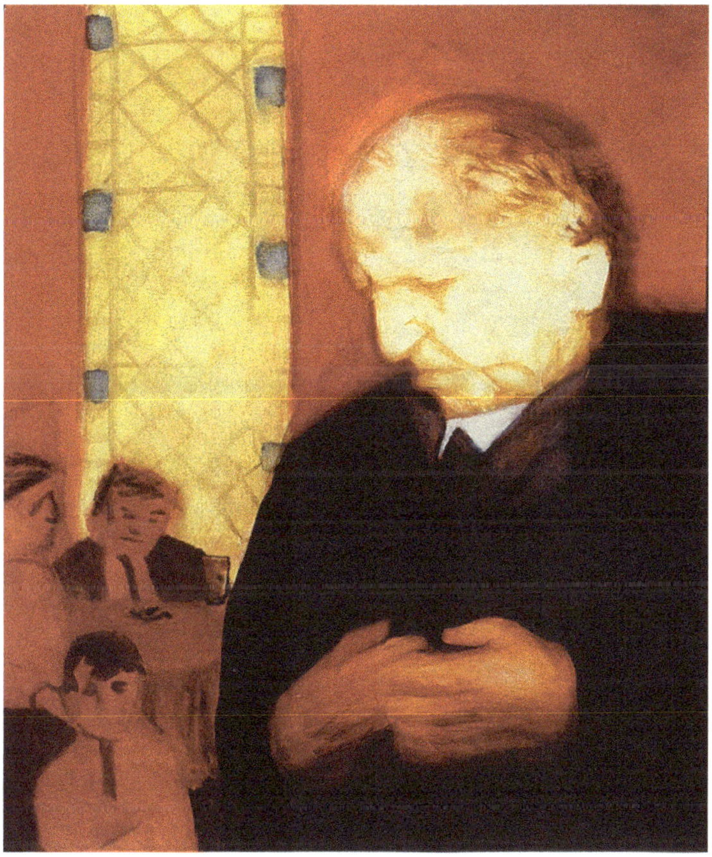

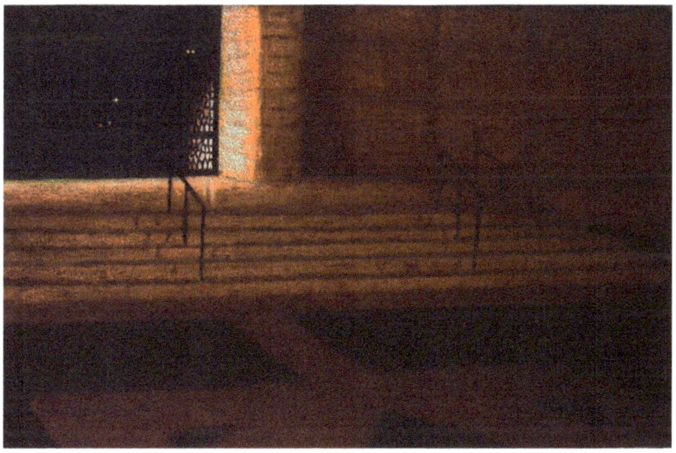

The Man I Mistook for God, 1998, Oil on wood, 24"h x 18"w
Saint Mary's Steps, 2011, Oil on canvas, 8"h x 12"w

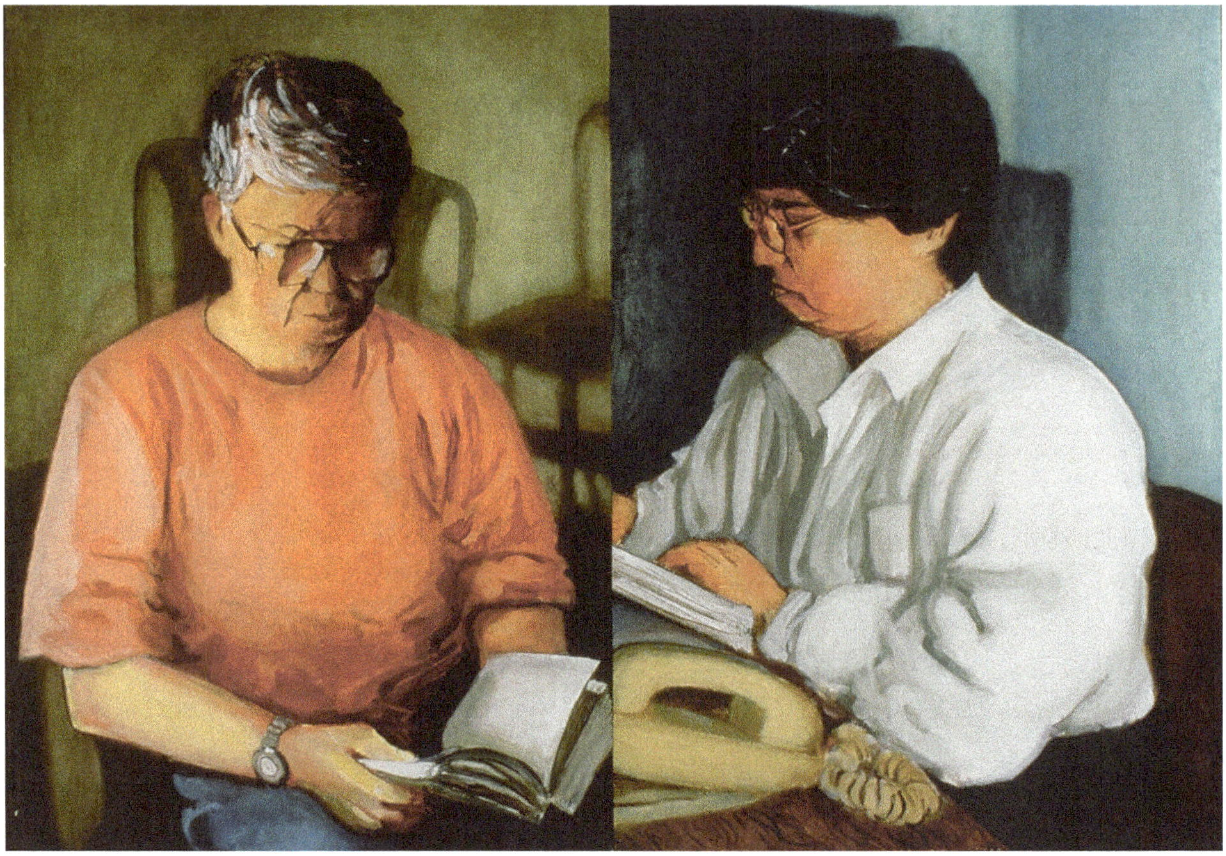

Reading, 1999, Oil on wood

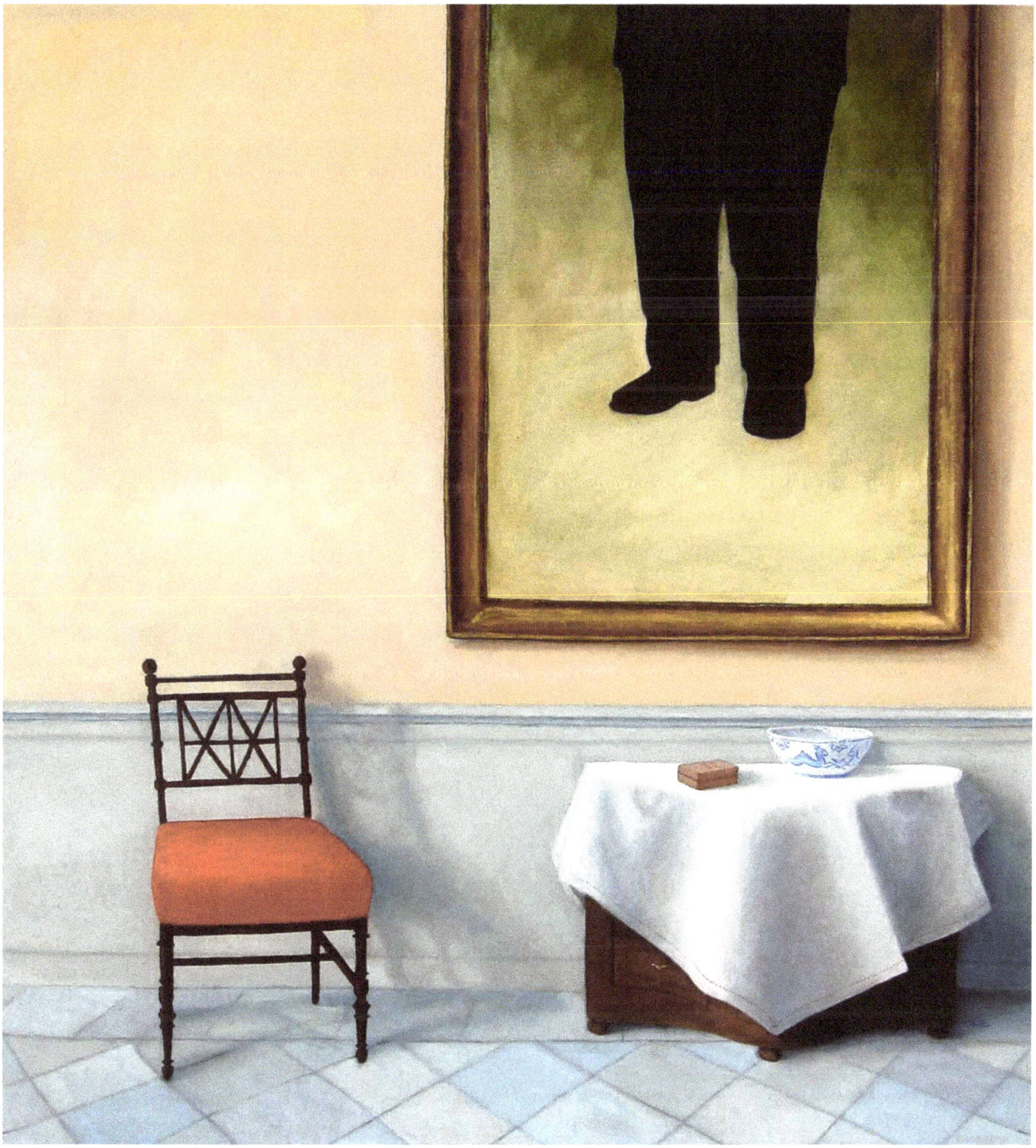

Portrait, Chair and Chest, 2001
Oil on canvas, 33"h x 30"w

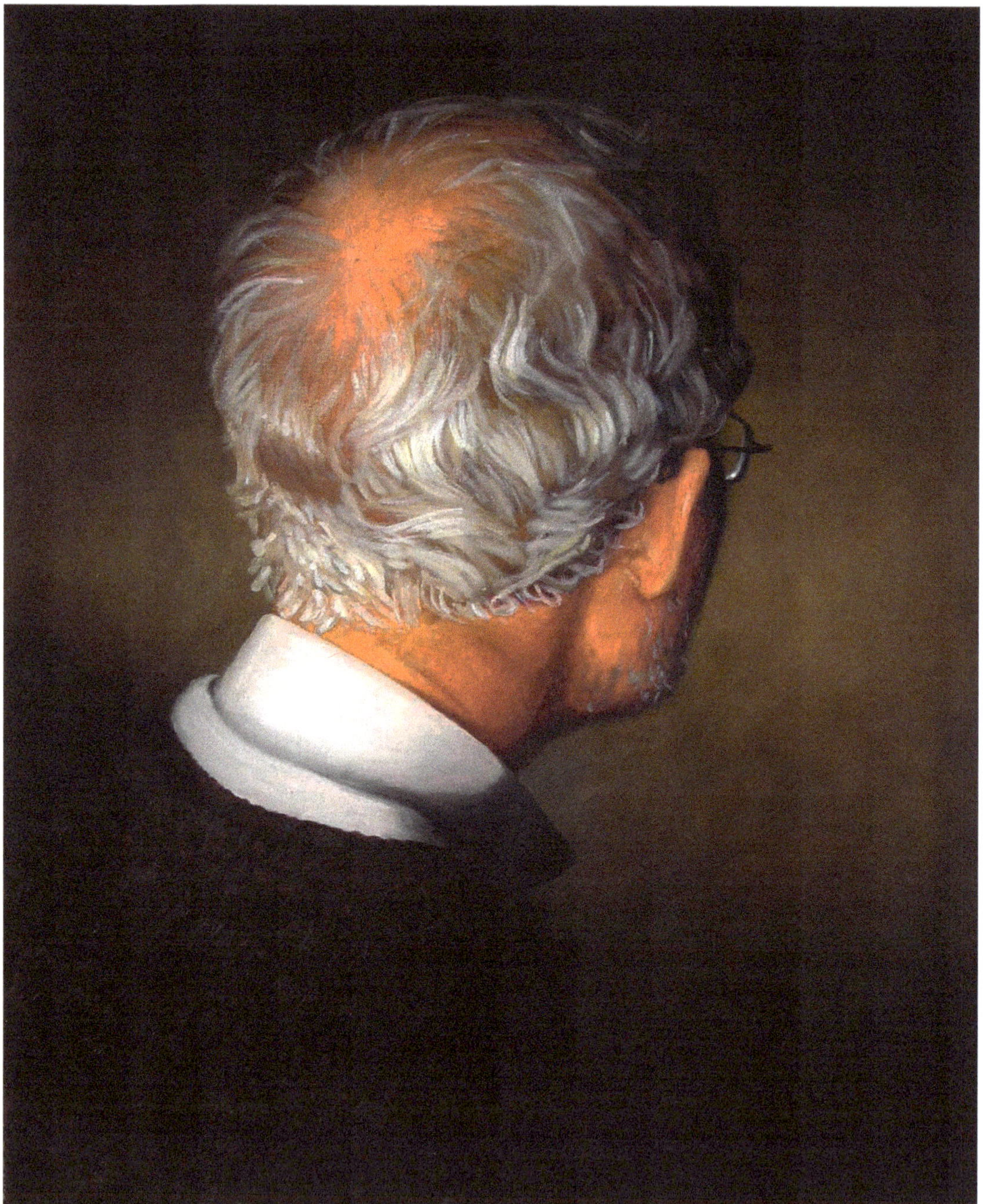

Jack: Turning Away, 2002
Oil on canvas, 30"h x 24"w

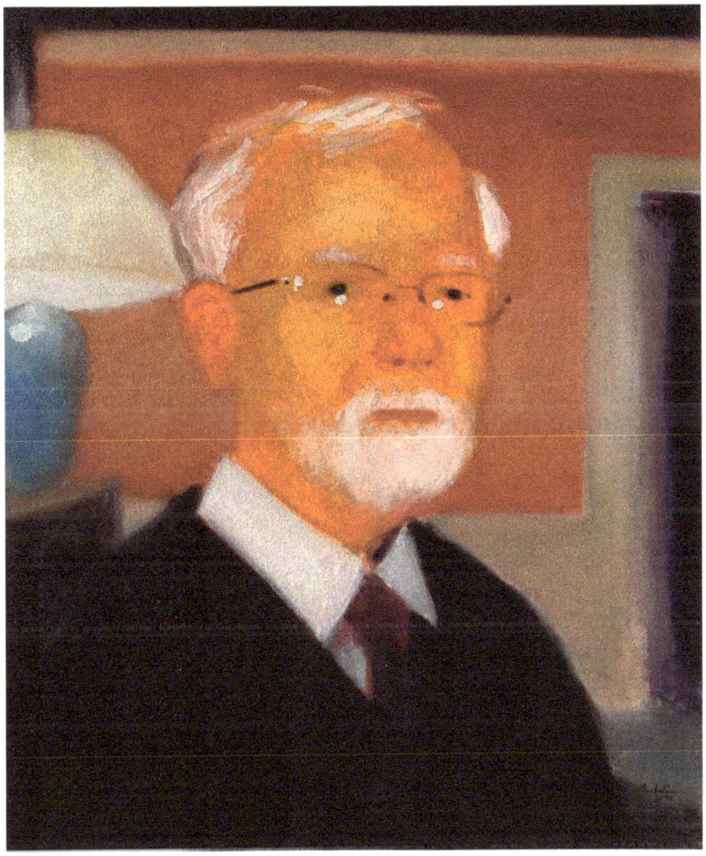

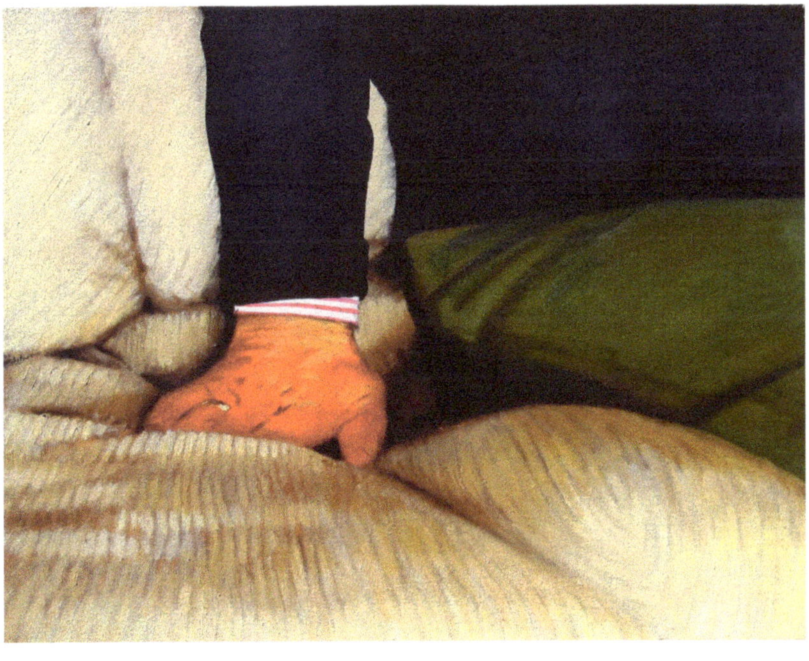

Jack: Red Room, 2002, Oil on canvas, 22"h x 18"w **Hand on Couch**, 2002, Oil on Canvas, 16"h x 20"w

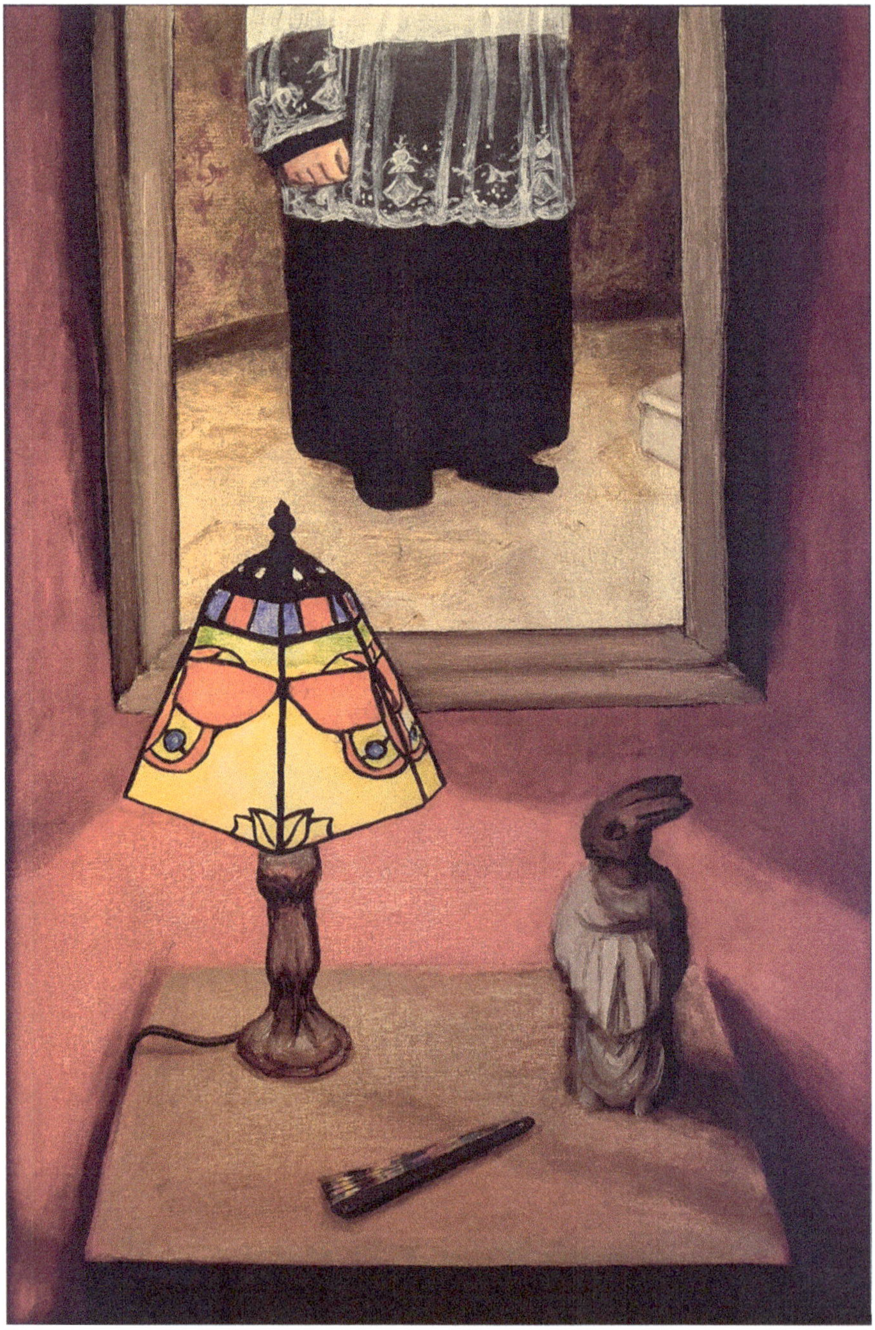

Portrait, Lamp and Zodiac Figure, 2003
Oil on canvas, 18"h x 12"w

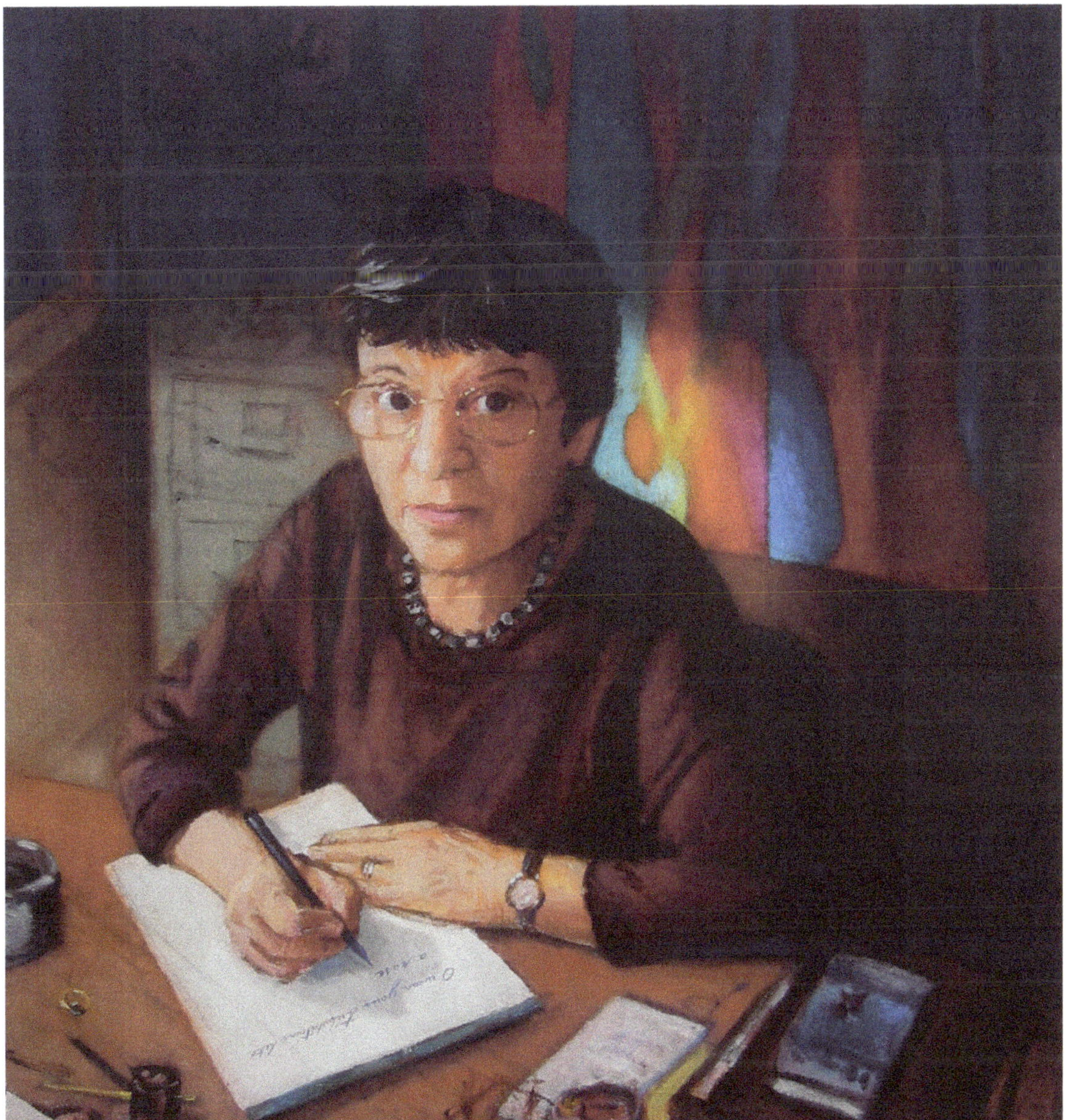

At Her Desk, 2002
Oil on canvas, 22"h x 20"w

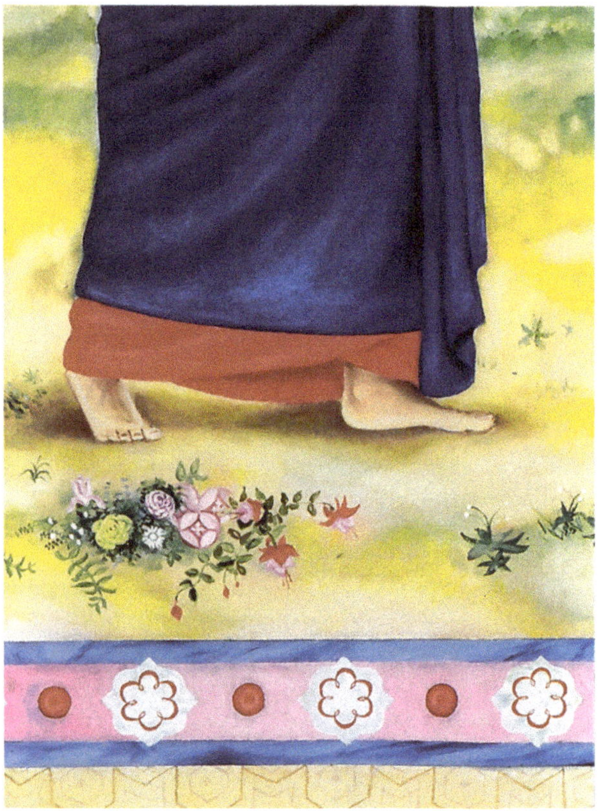

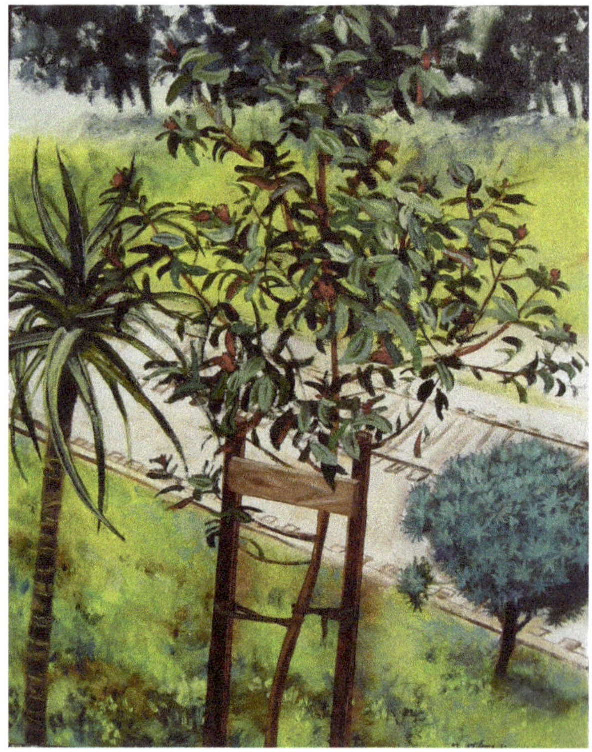

Walking Figure with Flowers, 2003, Oil on canvas, 26" x 19"
With Support, 2003, Oil on canvas

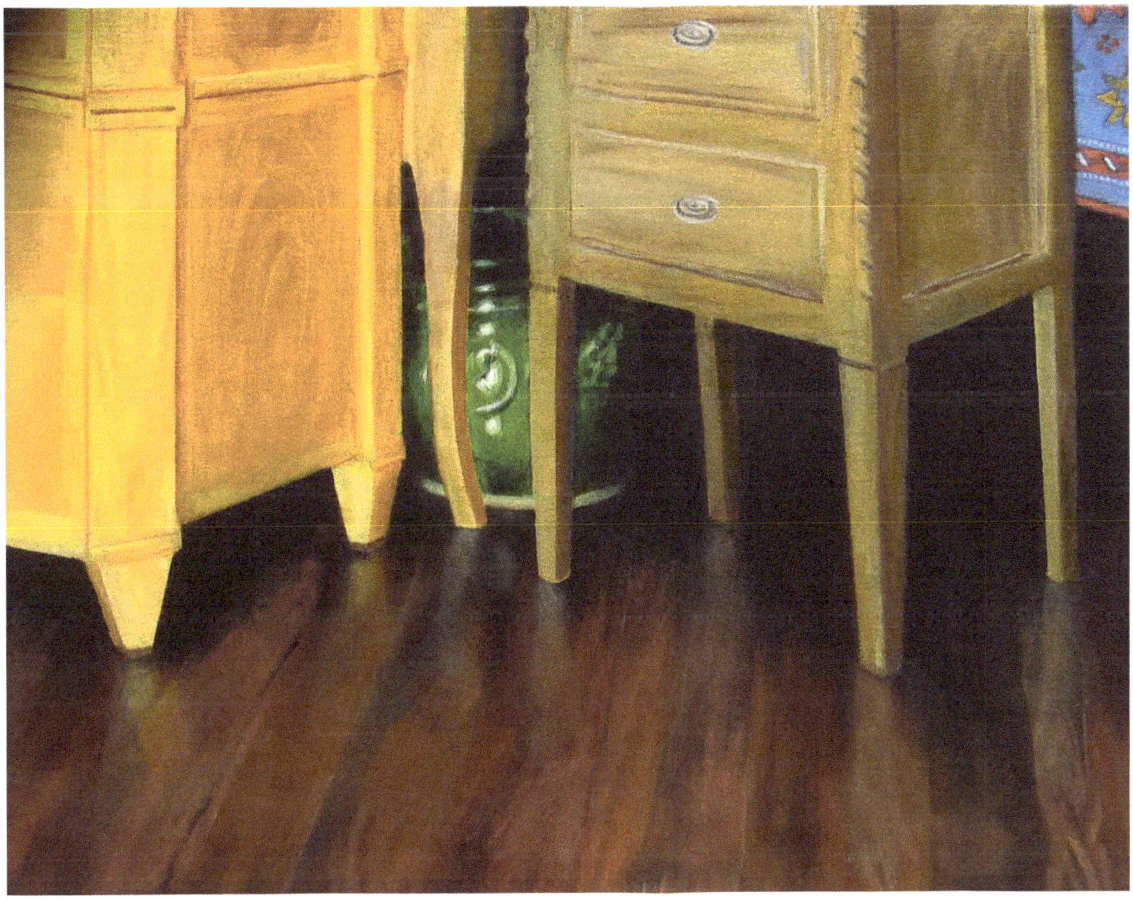

T. Reggiardo Antiques, 2003
Oil on canvas, 16"h x 20"w

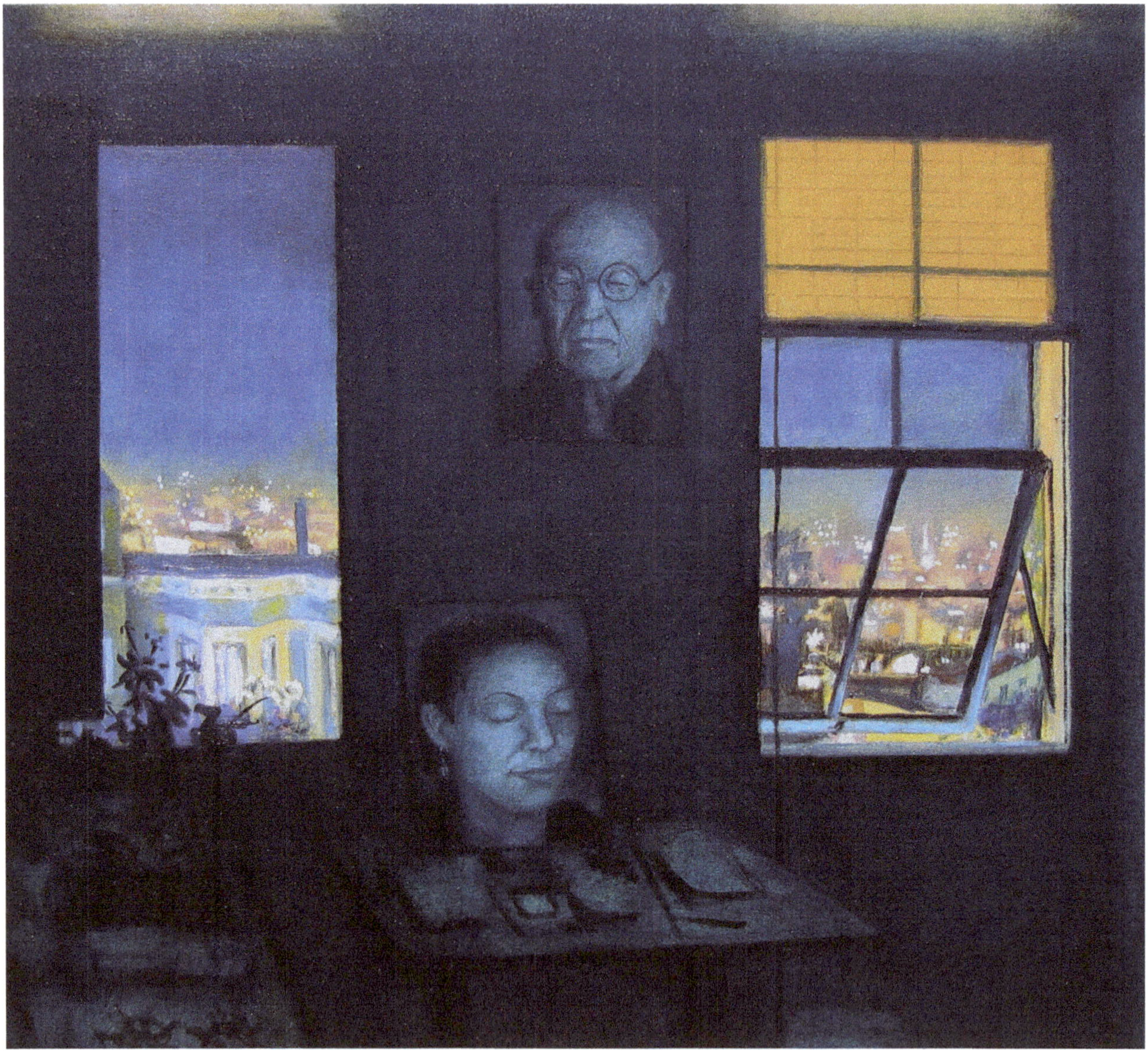

Windows, 2003
Oil on canvas

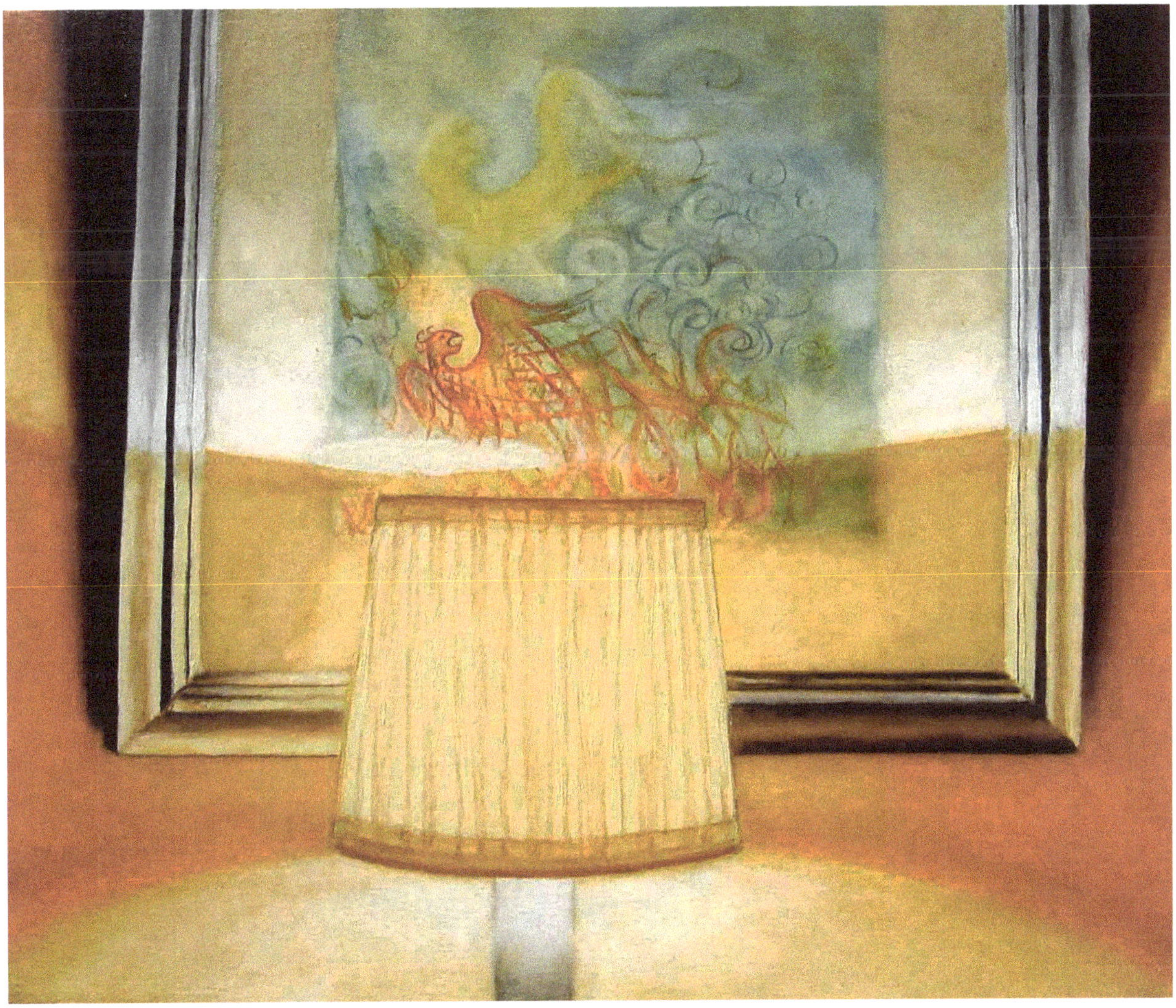

The Phoenix, 2004
Oil on canvas, 18"h x 21"w

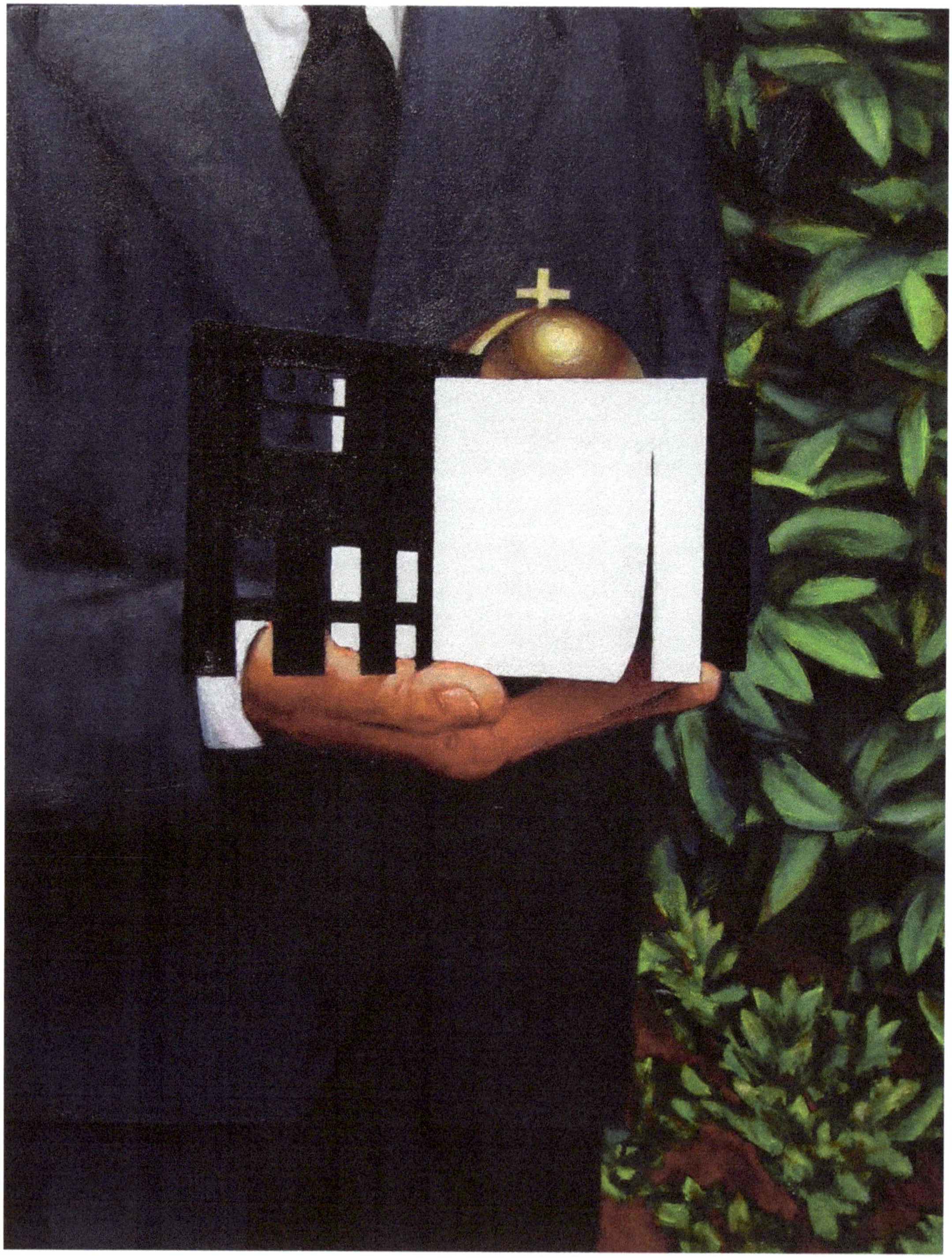

Philip Johnson's Chapel of St. Basil, 2004, Oil on canvas, 12"h x 10"w

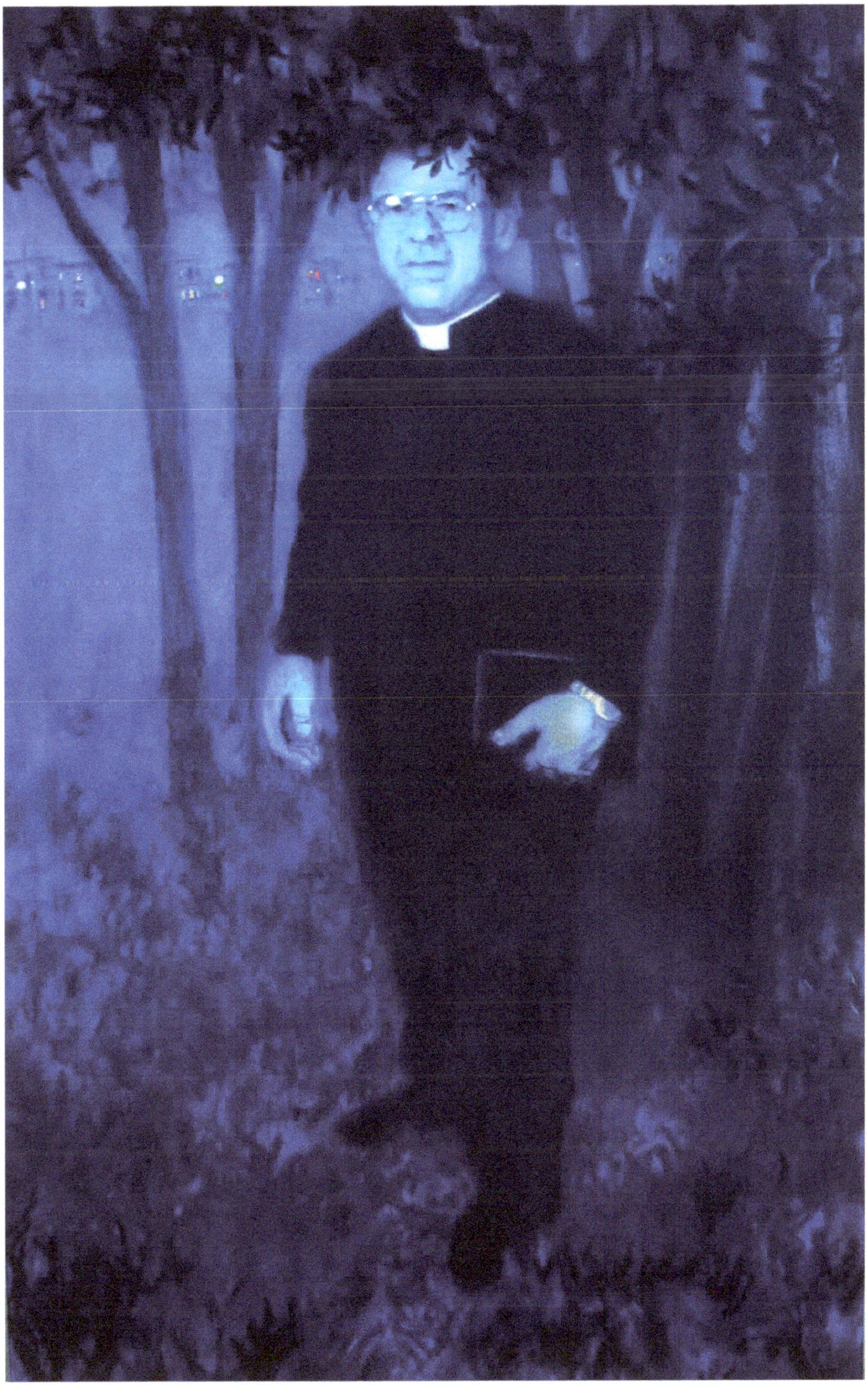

Priest in the Night, 2004, Oil on canvas, 42"h x 26"w

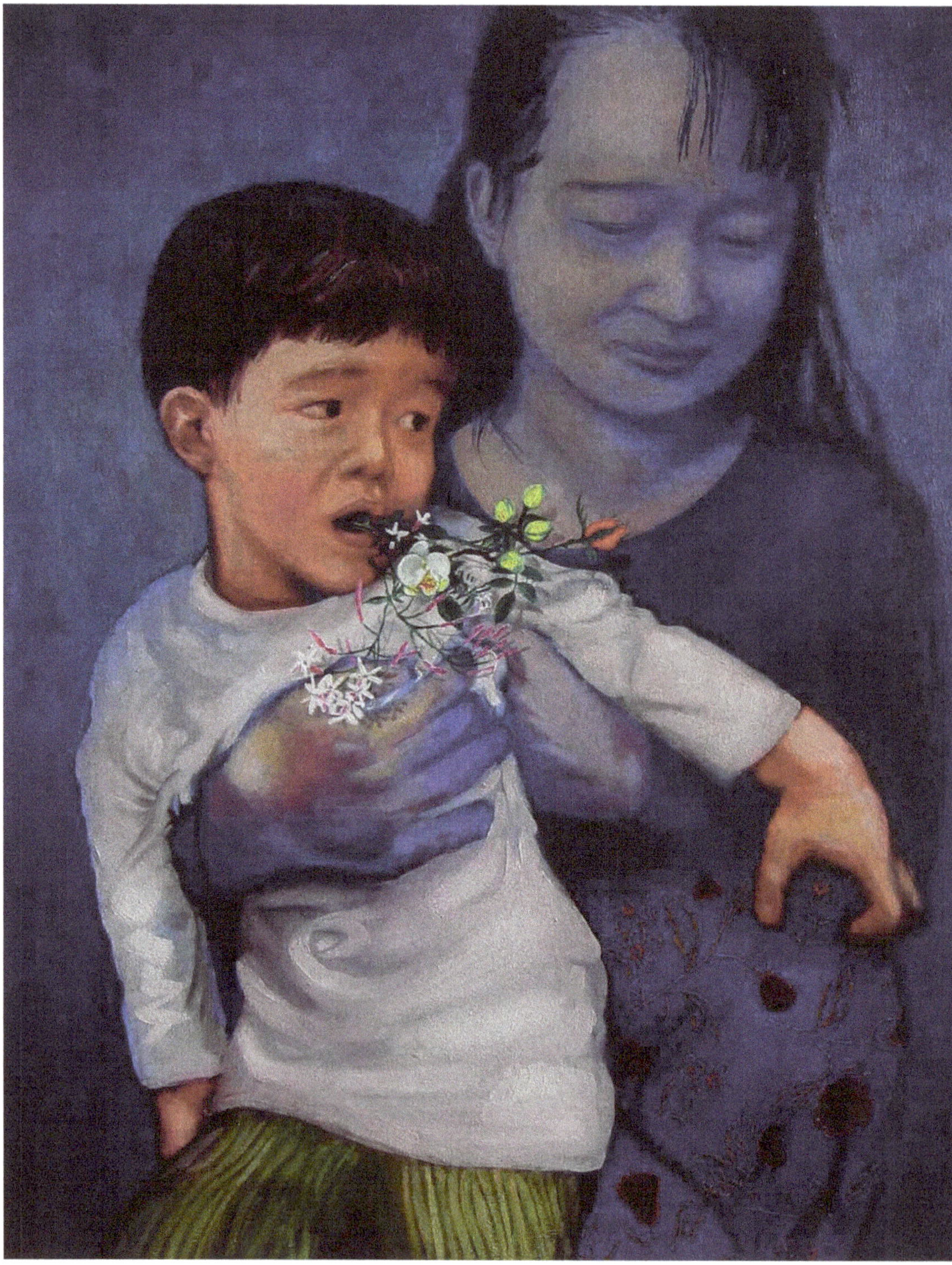

Mourning, 2005, Oil on canvas, 32"h x 24"w

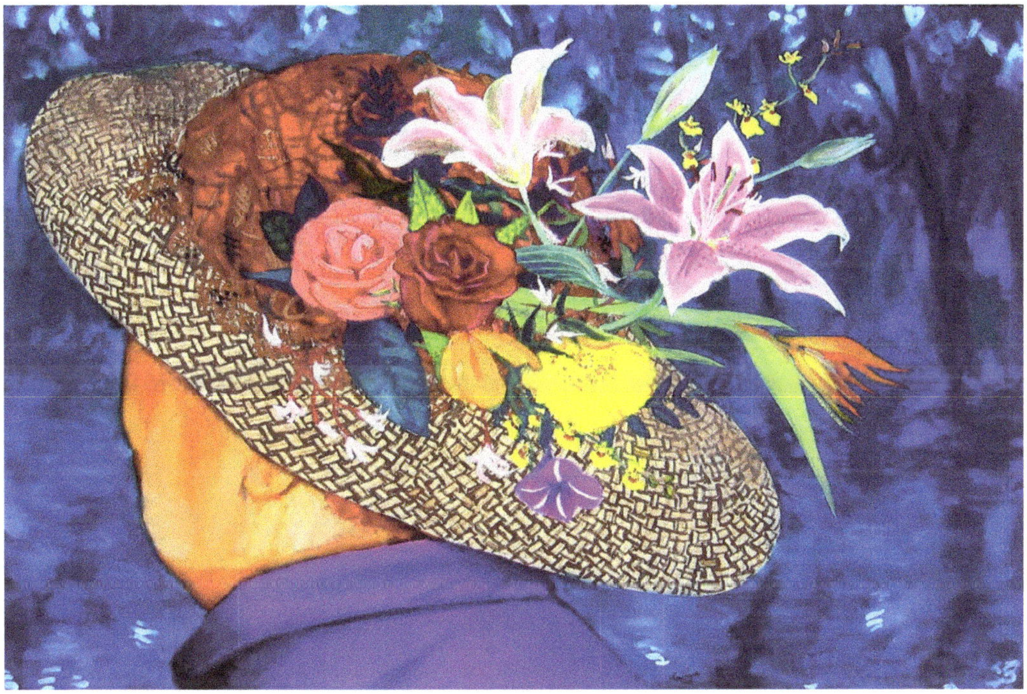

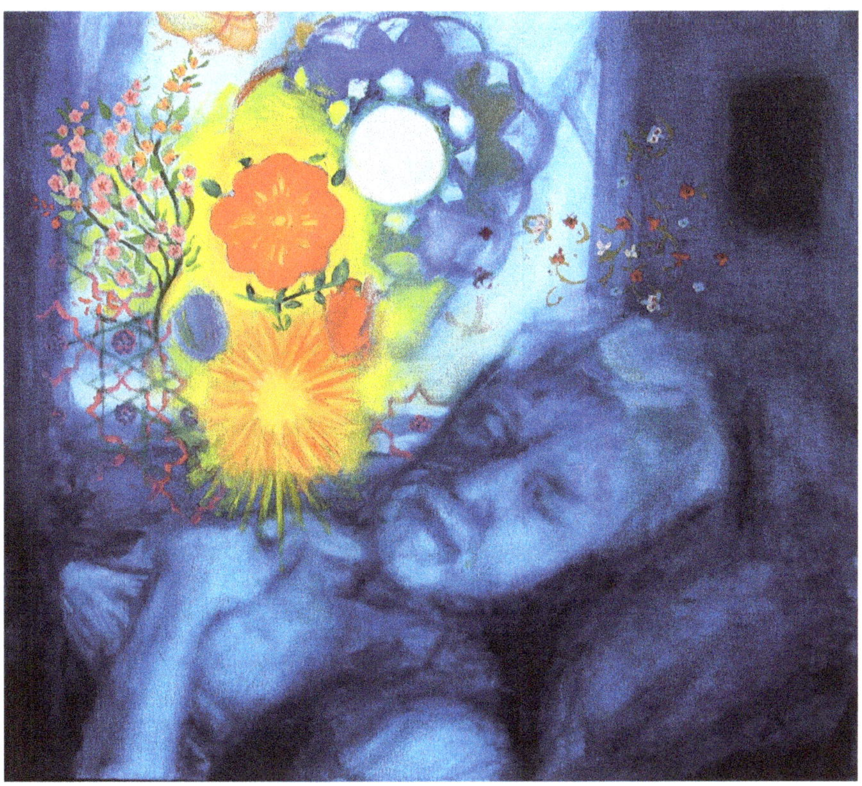

The Hat and the Spirit, 2004, Oil on canvas **Renaissance**, 2005, Oil on canvas, 18"h x 20"w

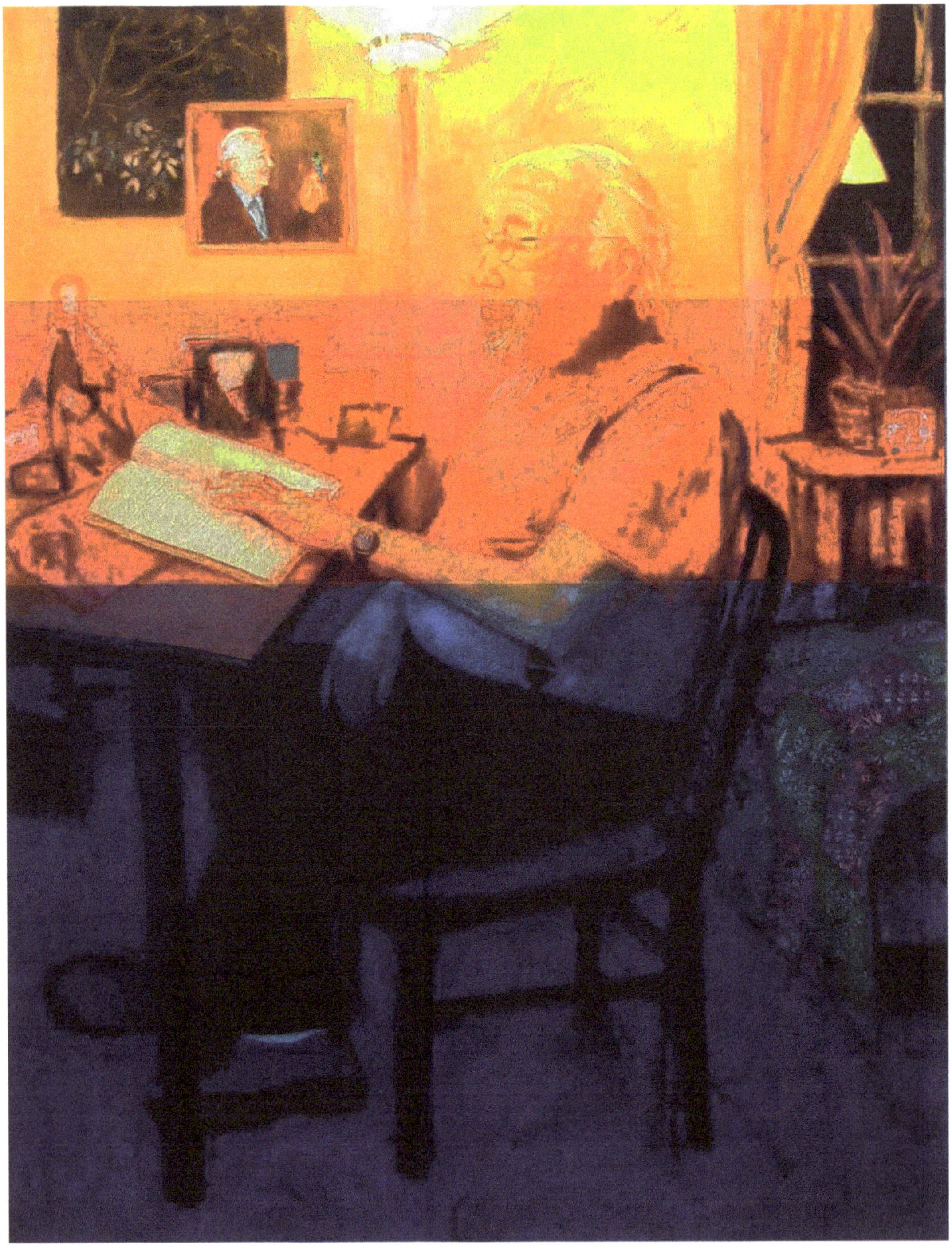

Portrait in Three Levels, 2005
Oil on canvas, 32"h x 24"w

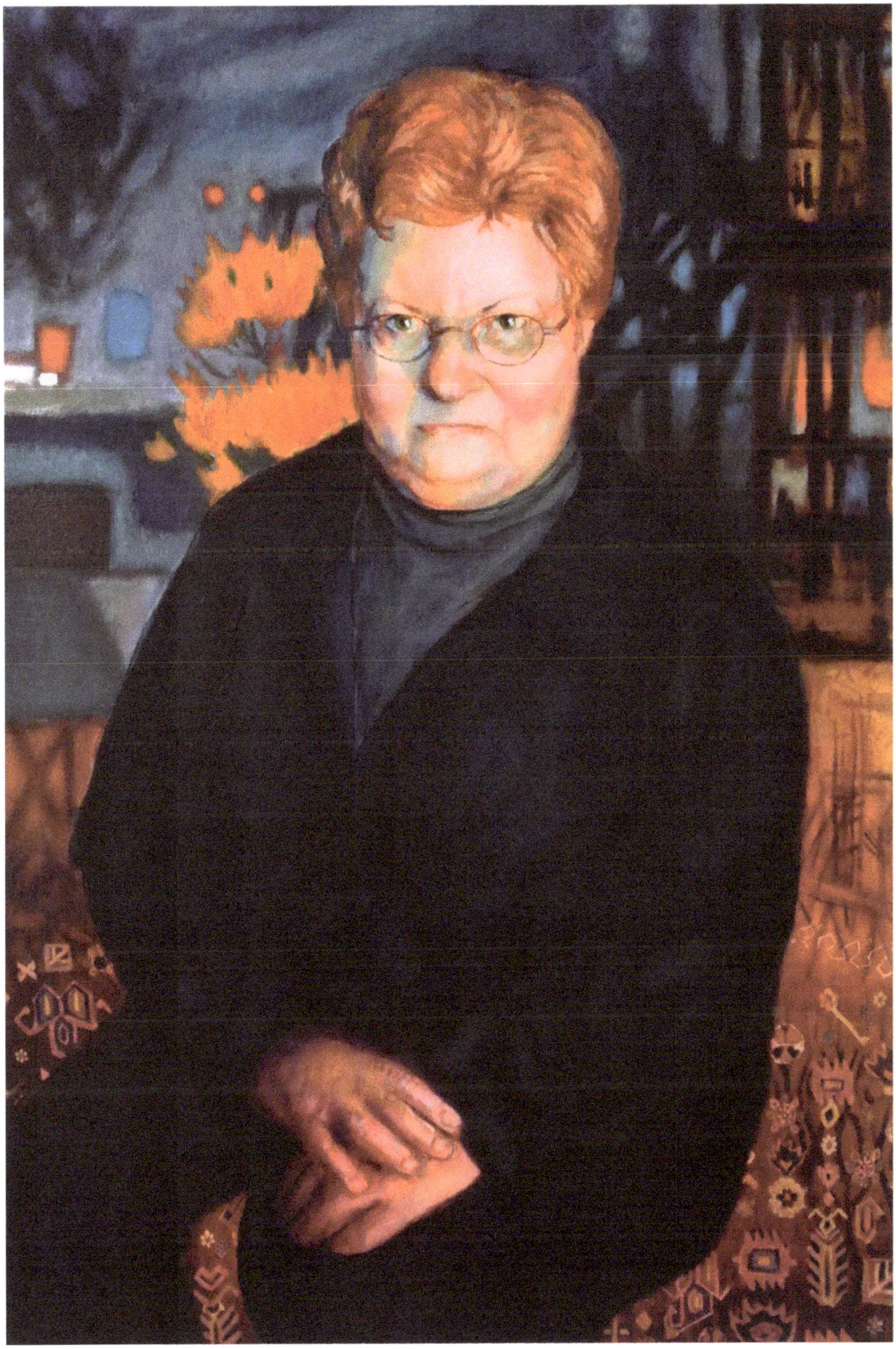

Her Vision Pierces Through, 2002, Oil on canvas, 30"h x 20"w

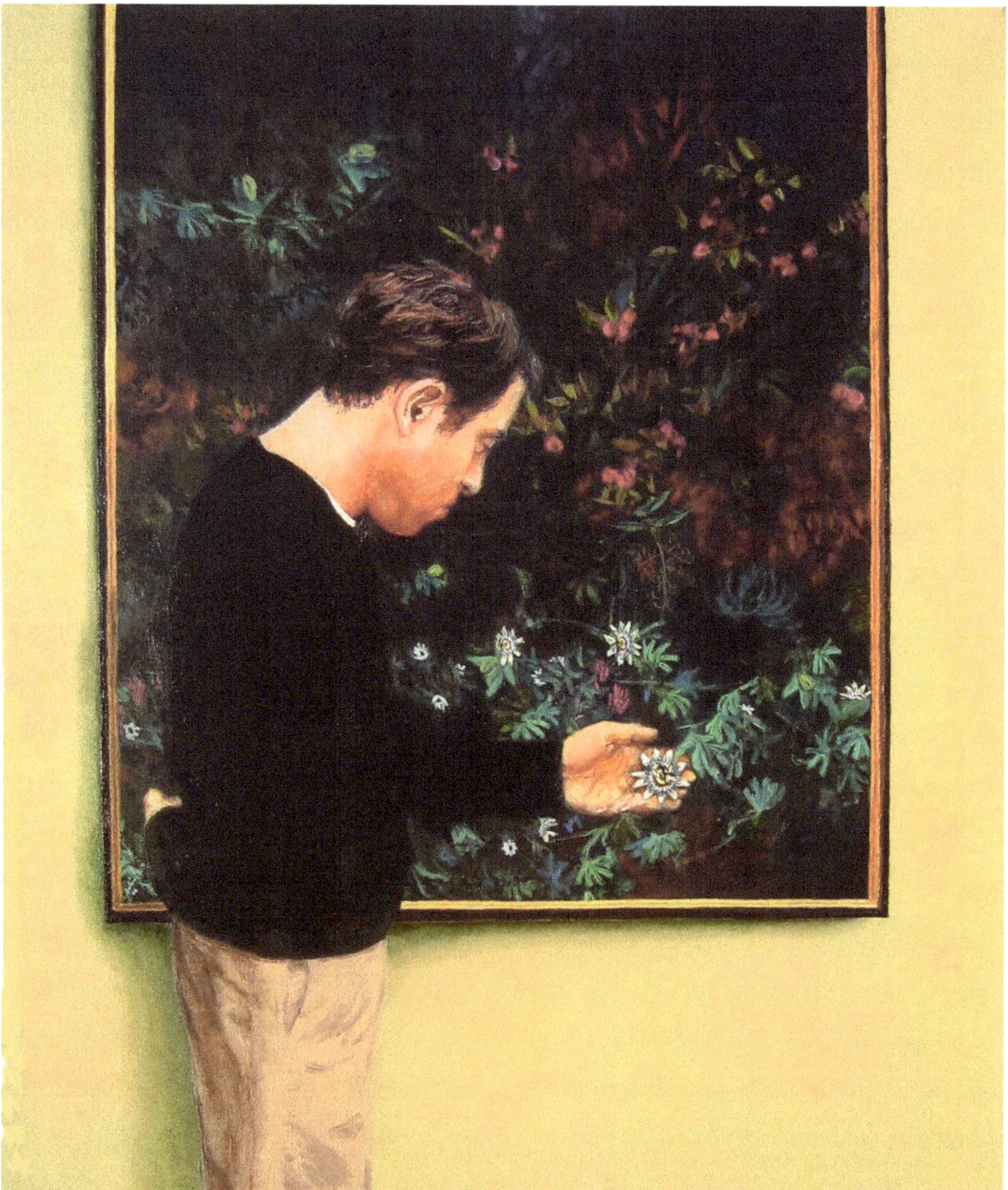

Passion Flower, 2006, Oil on canvas, 32"h x 26"w

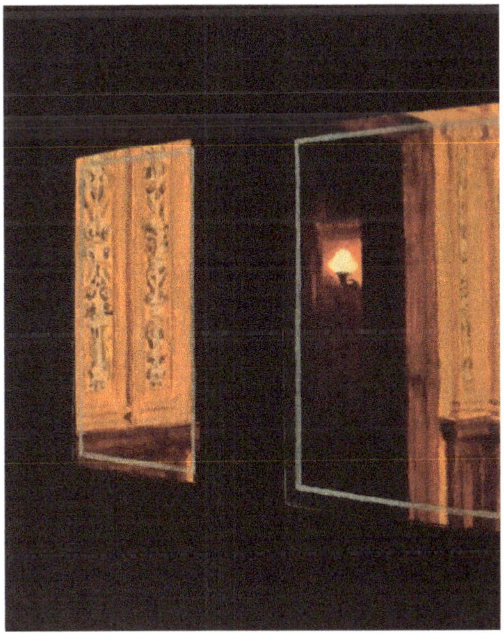

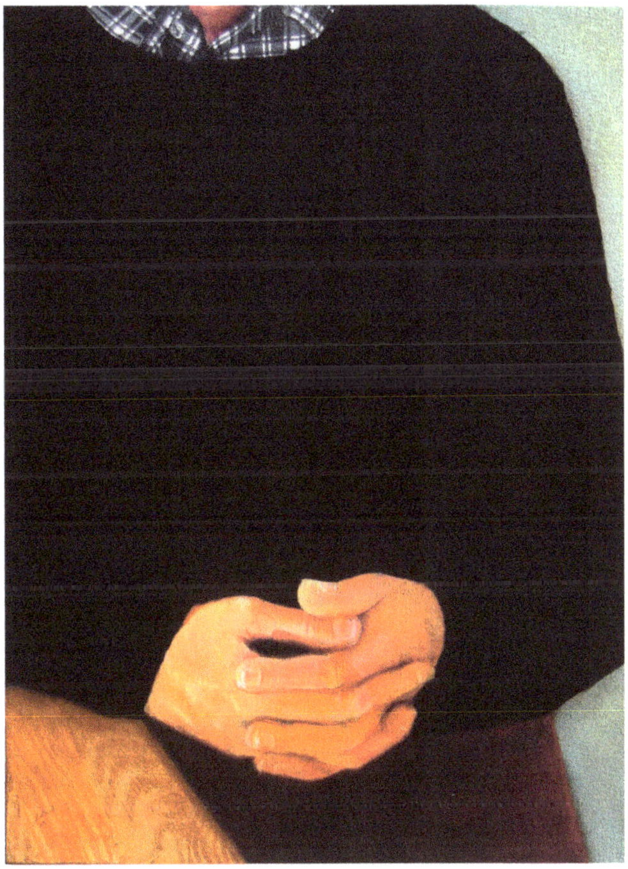

Narthex, St. Ignatius, 2015
Oil on canvas, 10"h x 8"w

Leaning, 2003
Oil on canvas, 24"h x 18"w

St. Francis, Fisherman's Wharf
2015, Oil on canvas, 8"h x 10"w
(sculpture by Benny Bufano, 1928)

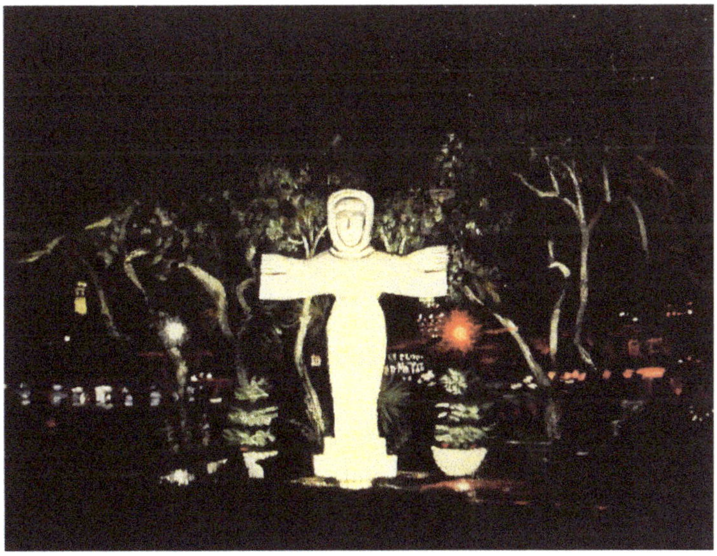

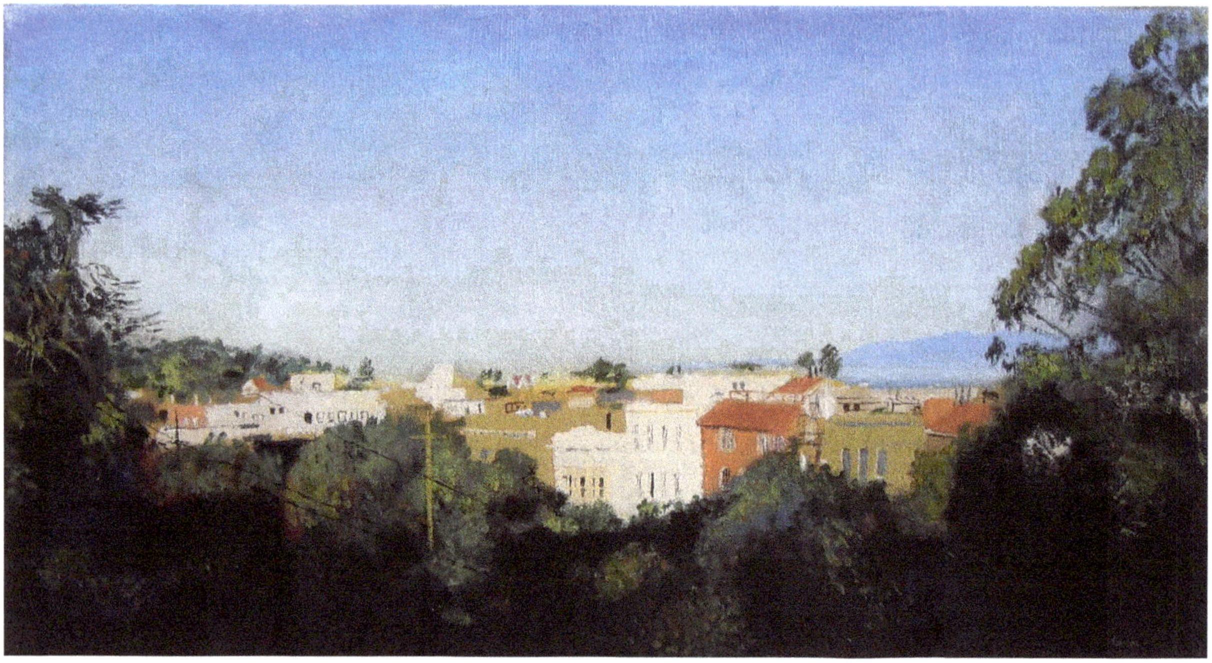

Golden Gate Park, Facing North, 2010, Oil on canvas, 10"h x 18"w
Kalmanovitz Hall, USF, 2015, Oil on canvas, 14"h x 18"w

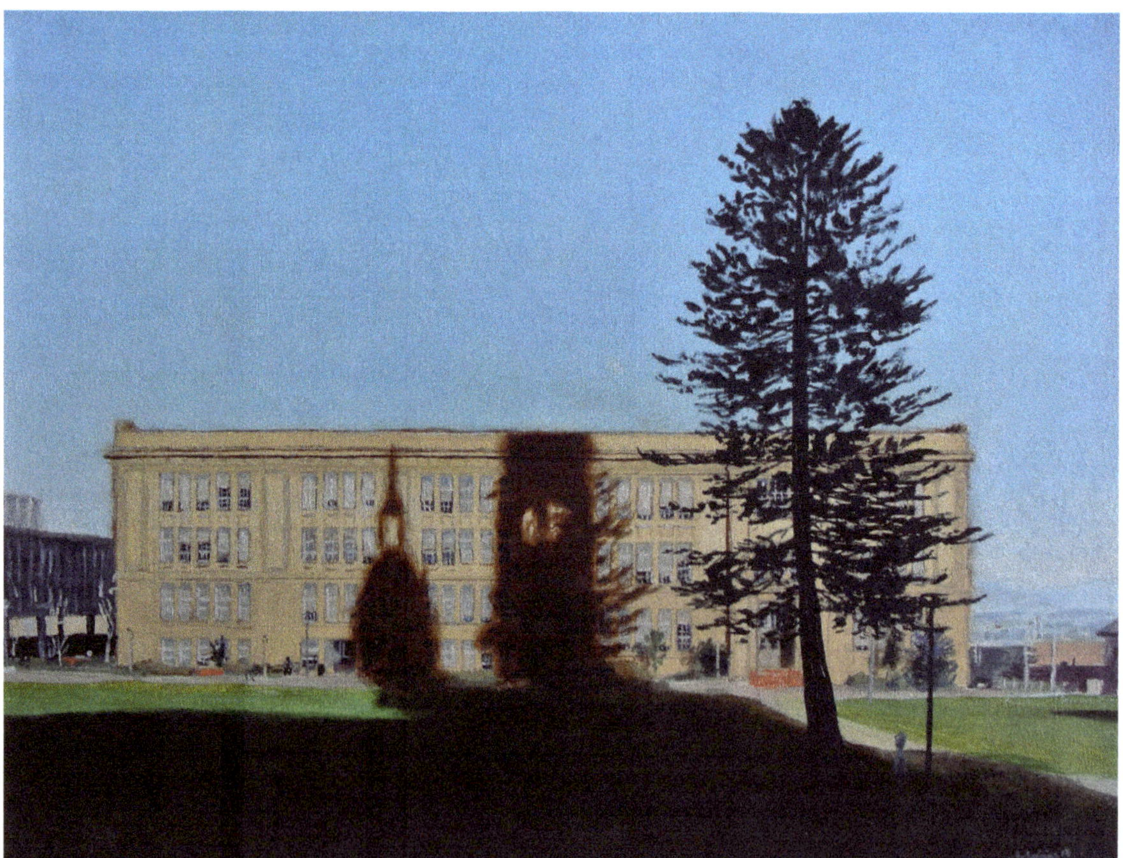

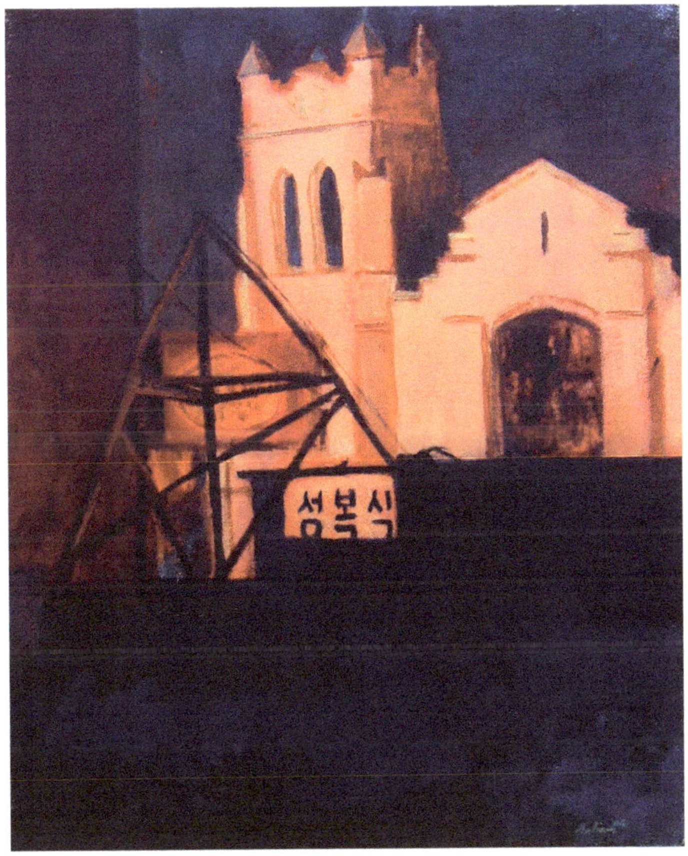

Park Presidio United Methodist Church, 2006, Oil on canvas, 14"h x 10"w
Pacific Heights Nocturne, 2011, Oil on canvas, 10"h x 12"w

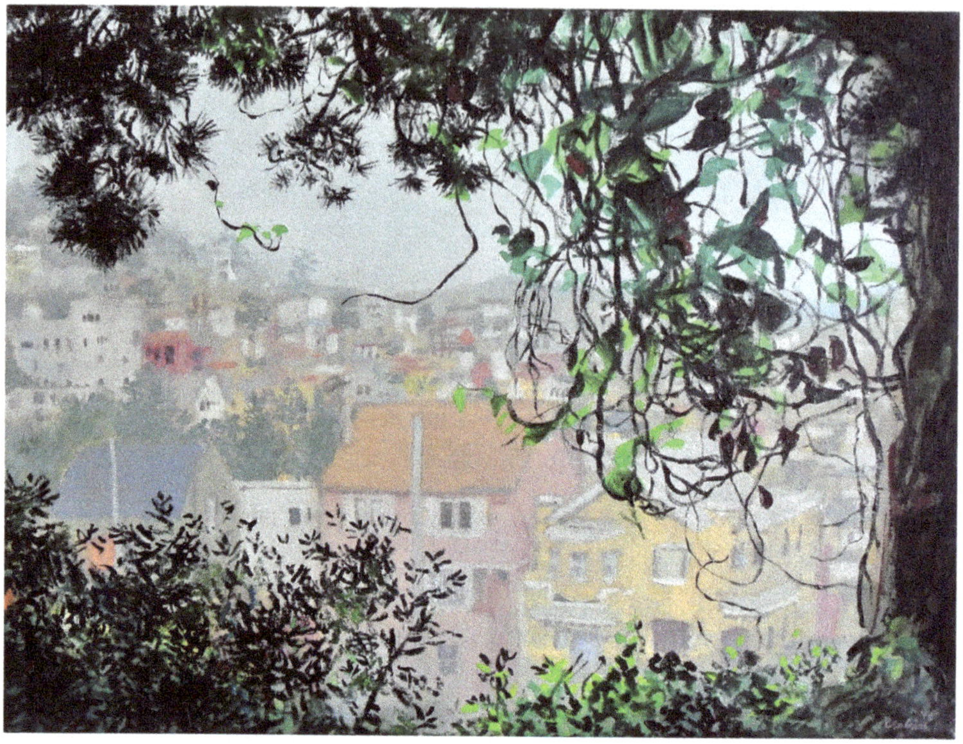

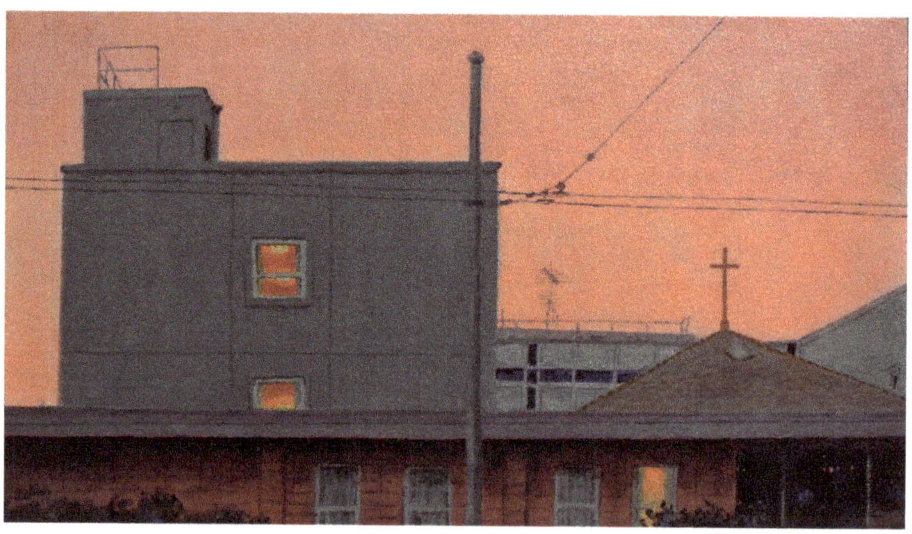

Clayton and Market, 2015, Oil on canvas, 13"h x 17"w
PBVM Motherhouse at Dusk, 2017, Oil on canvas, 8"h x 14"w

Works on Paper

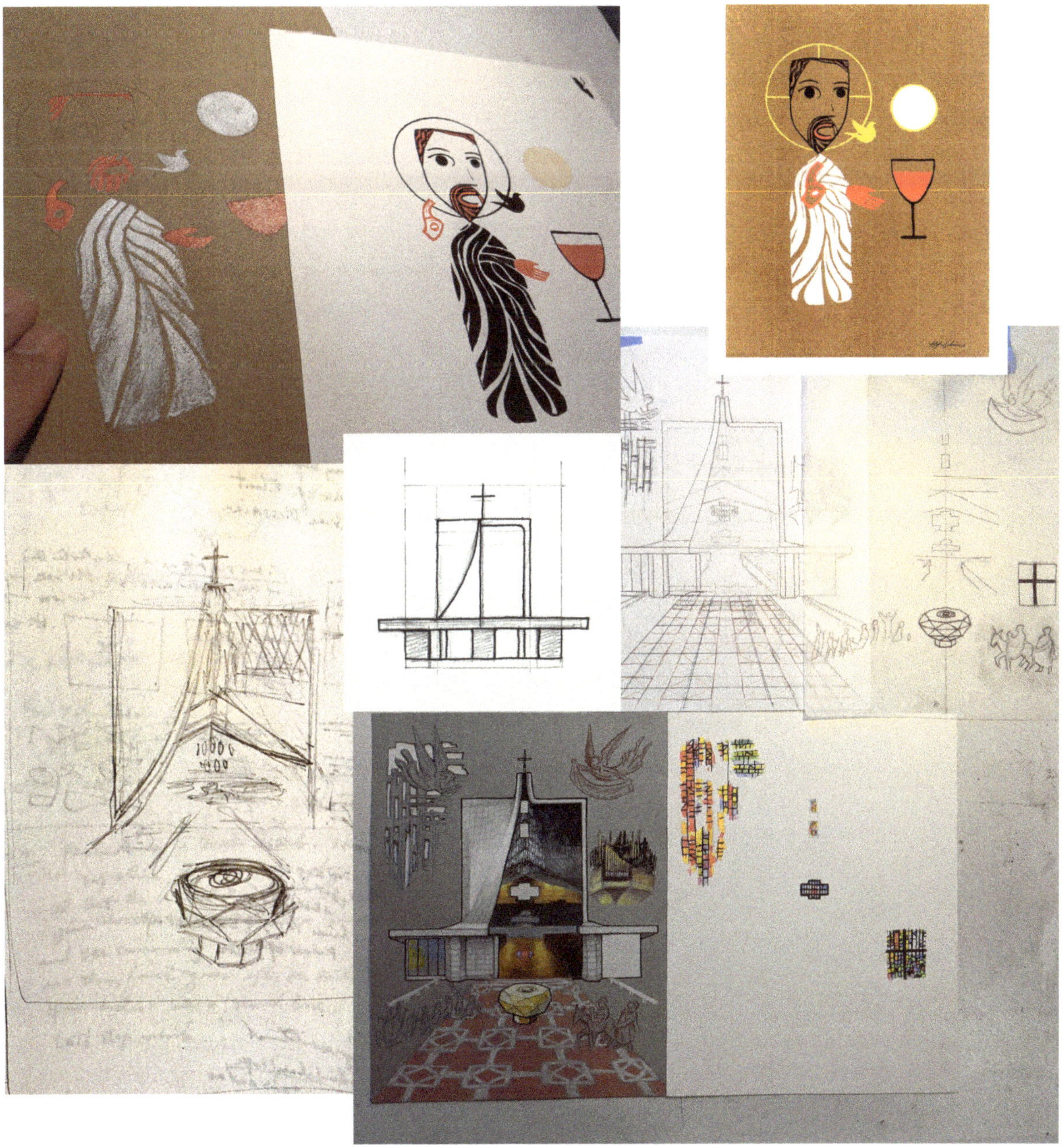

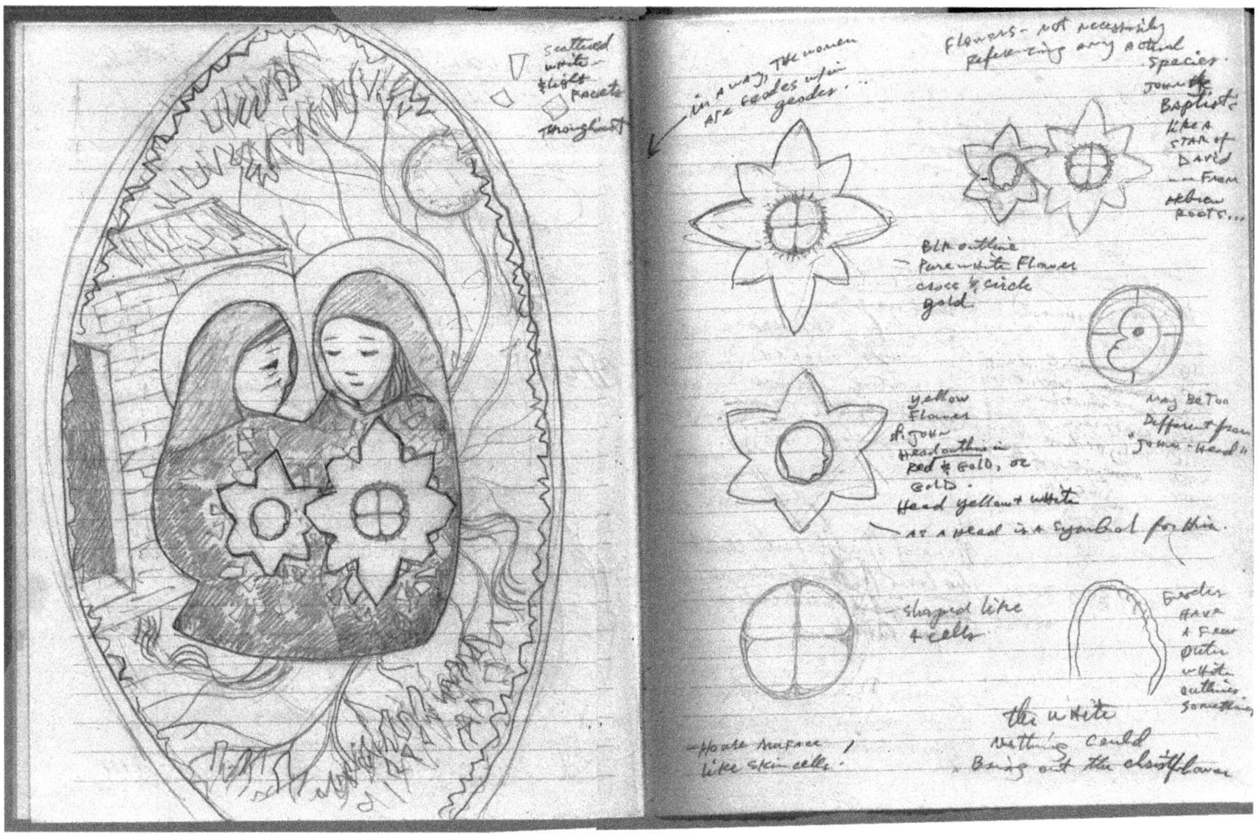
Scattered white & light facets throughout
in a way, the women are geodes w/in geodes...
Flowers - not necessarily referencing any actual species.
John the Baptist's like a Star of David -- from Hebrew roots...
Blk outline
Pure white flower
cross & circle gold
yellow flower
st. John
Head outline in red & gold, or gold.
Head yellow & white
may be too different from "John-Head"
as a head is a symbol for this.
shaped like 4 cells
Geodes have a few outer white outlines something
the white netting could bring out the christ flower
House surface like skin cells!

Aside from the art created before 2015, most of the selections in this chapter were compositions created with the intention of being mechanically reproduced. The first ones here were printed, then embellished with gold paint and mounted on varnished wood panels. Later, I found Print Salon, a shop in Wisconsin, to make giclée prints on 100% cotton rag. Their production and service quality is impeccable. Unlike standard dye-based ink printing with four colors, giclées involve eight to twelve color passes, with archival pigment-based ink. Most of the images are scanned straight from the original illustration, with minimal digital adjustments here and there (sometimes done to ensure the print came out as close to the original, the way the human eye sees it).

Some of them were put together from layers, and a few are photographs of three-dimensional pieces. Like the art I have done in churches, the icons included here were made with focus and care to assist the viewer in prayer. In each, my aim was to carry forth a deeper truth from above/within the heart/beyond the veil.

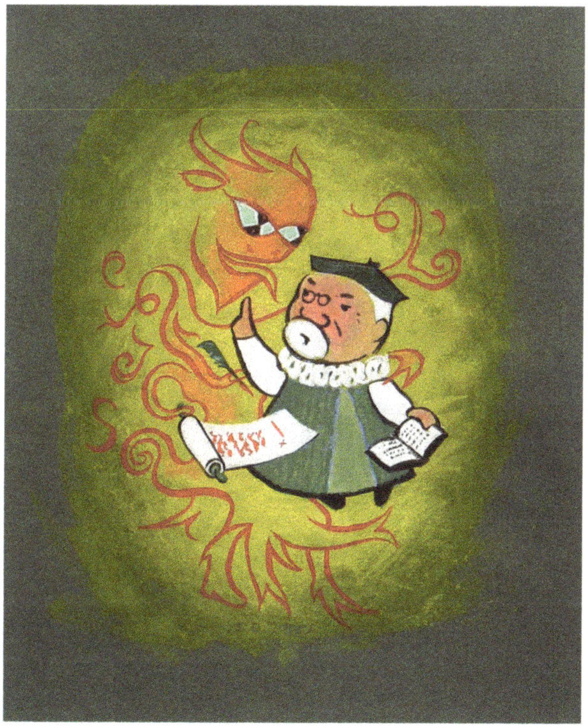

Doctor Faust, 2005, Acrylic on paper, 10"h x 8"w

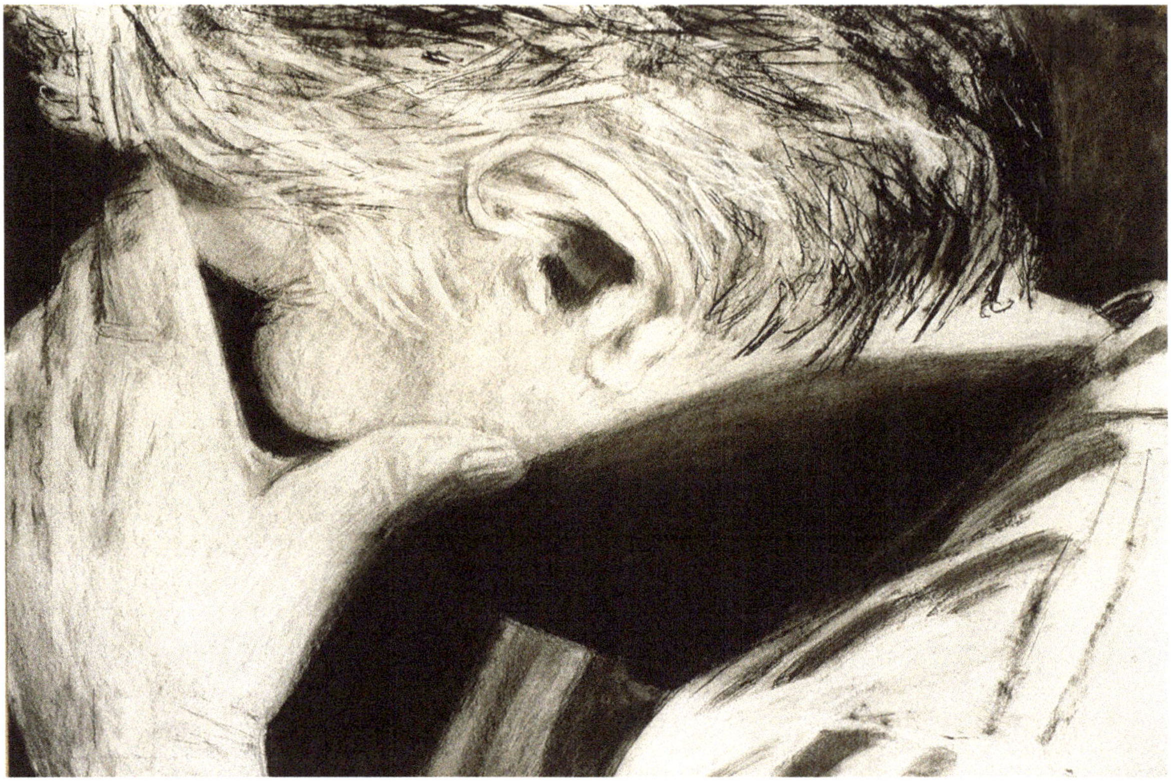

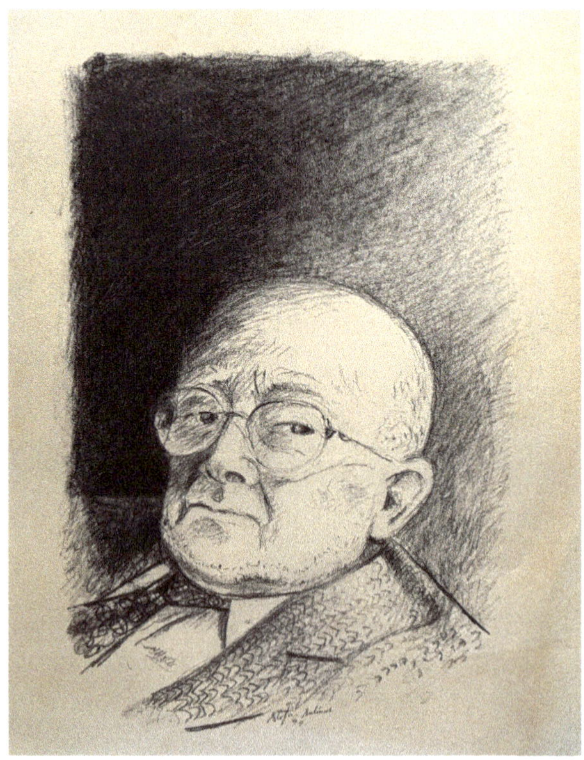

Kay: Hand on Face, 1999
Charcoal on paper, 30"h x36"w

Robert Giesberg, 1999
Charcoal on paper, 14"h x10"w

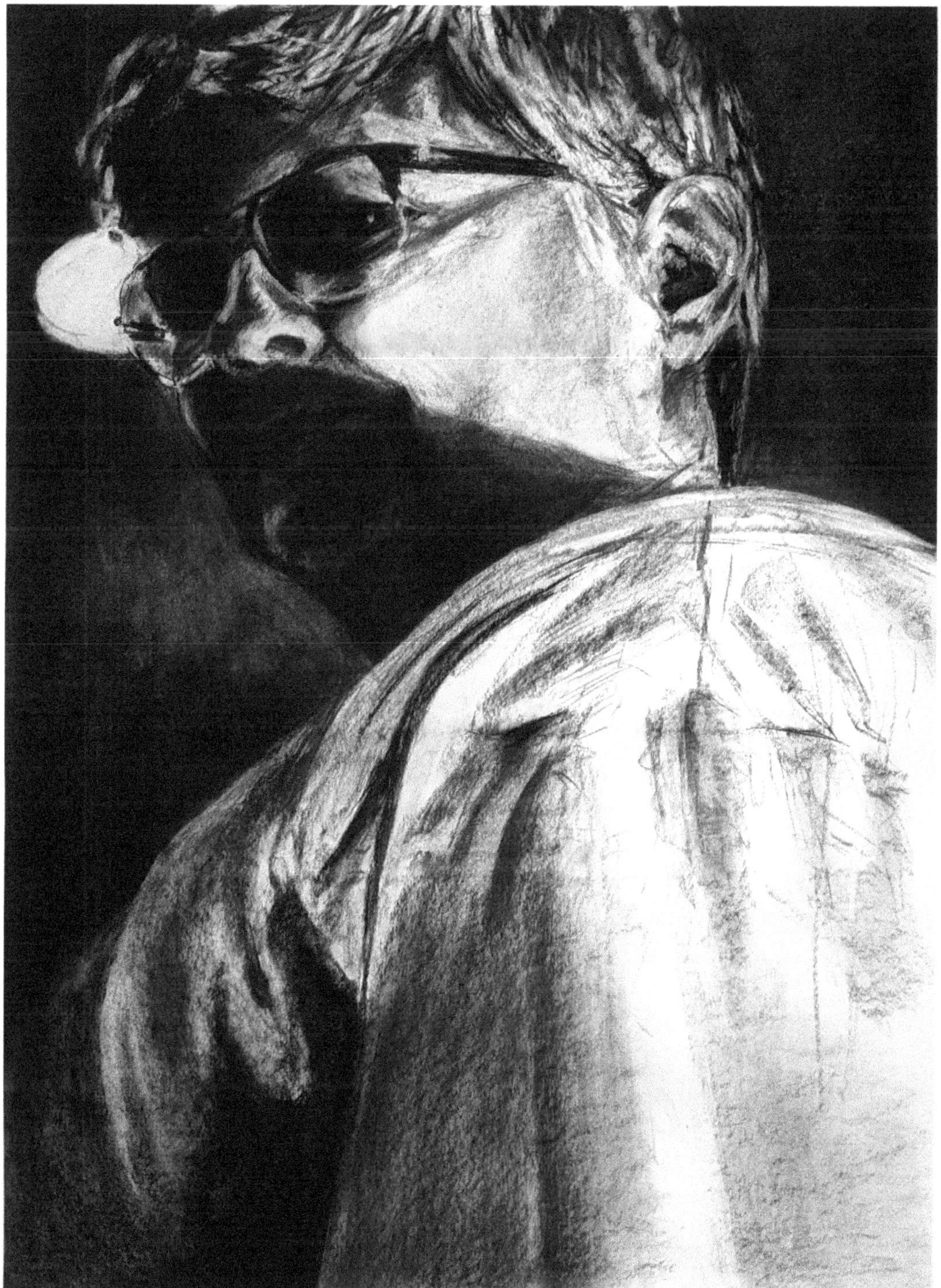

Kay, 1997, Charcoal on paper, 50"h x 38.5"w

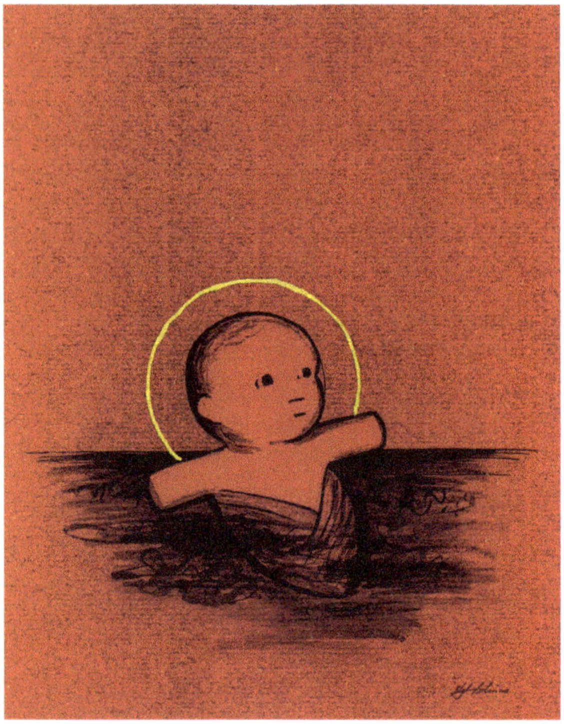

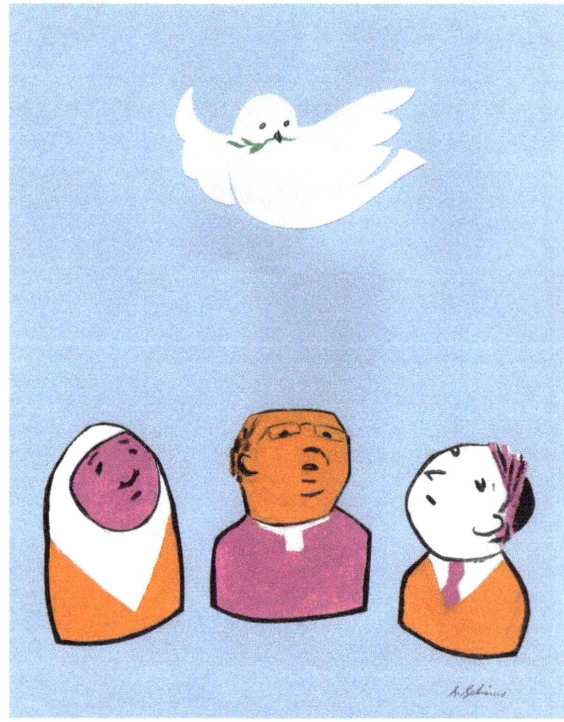

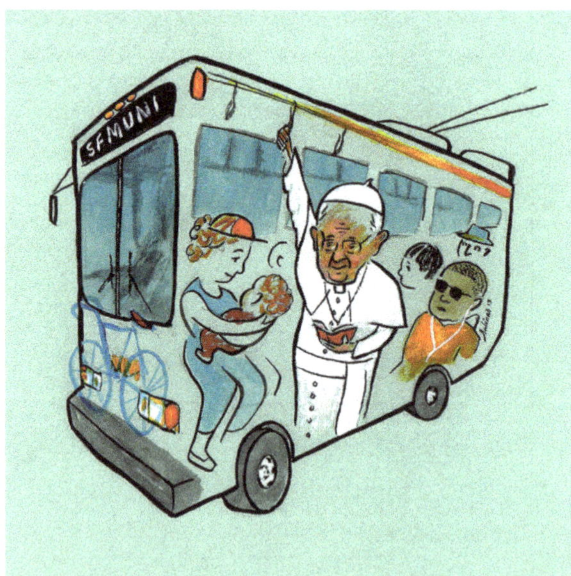

Christ Seed, 2013, Acrylic and ink on paper + digital, 10"h x 8"w
Peace, 2004, Acrylic on paper, 10"h x 8"w
Pope Francis on the Bus, 2013, Acrylic and ink on paper, 4"h x 4"w

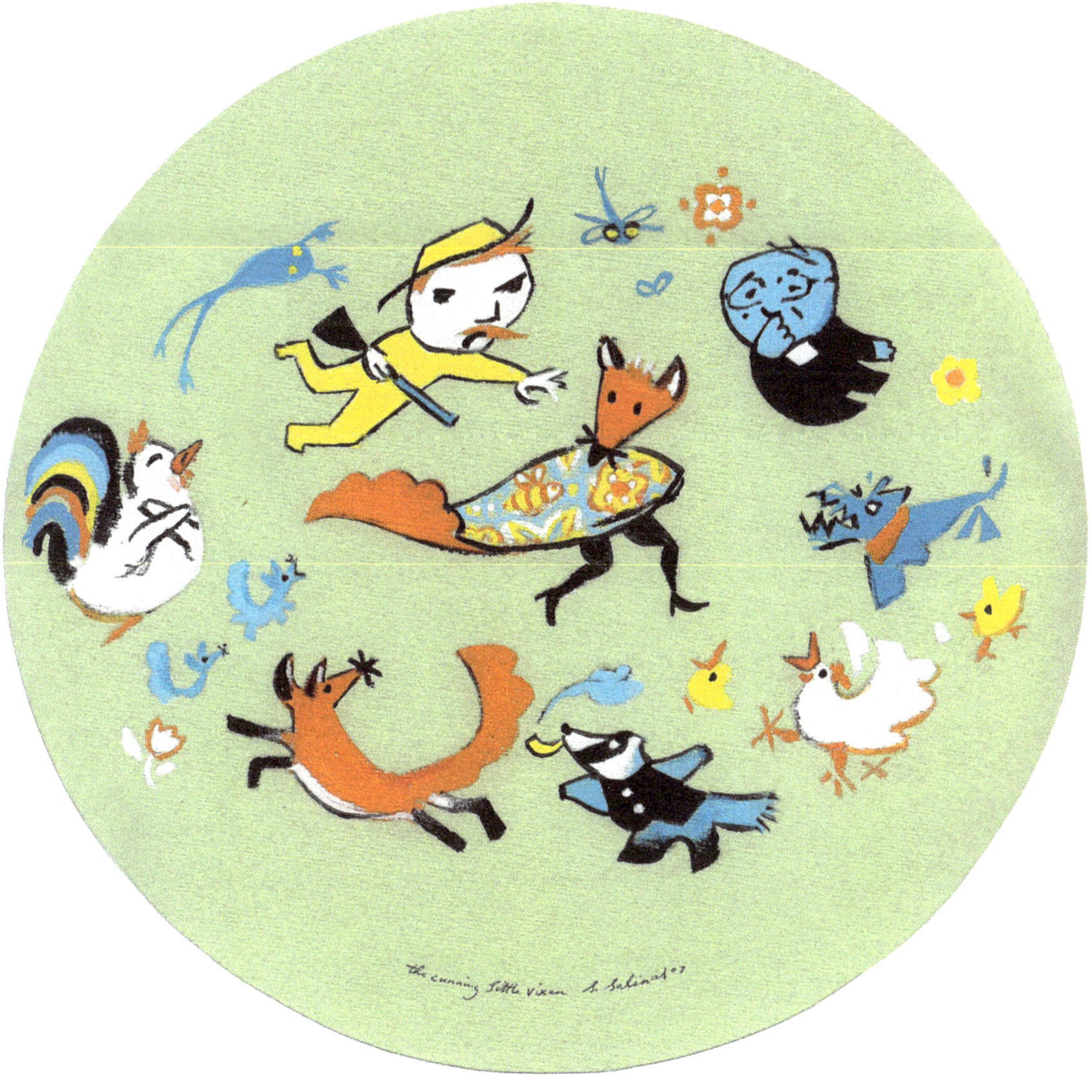

The Cunning Little Vixen, 2003
Acrylic on paper, 10"h x 10"w

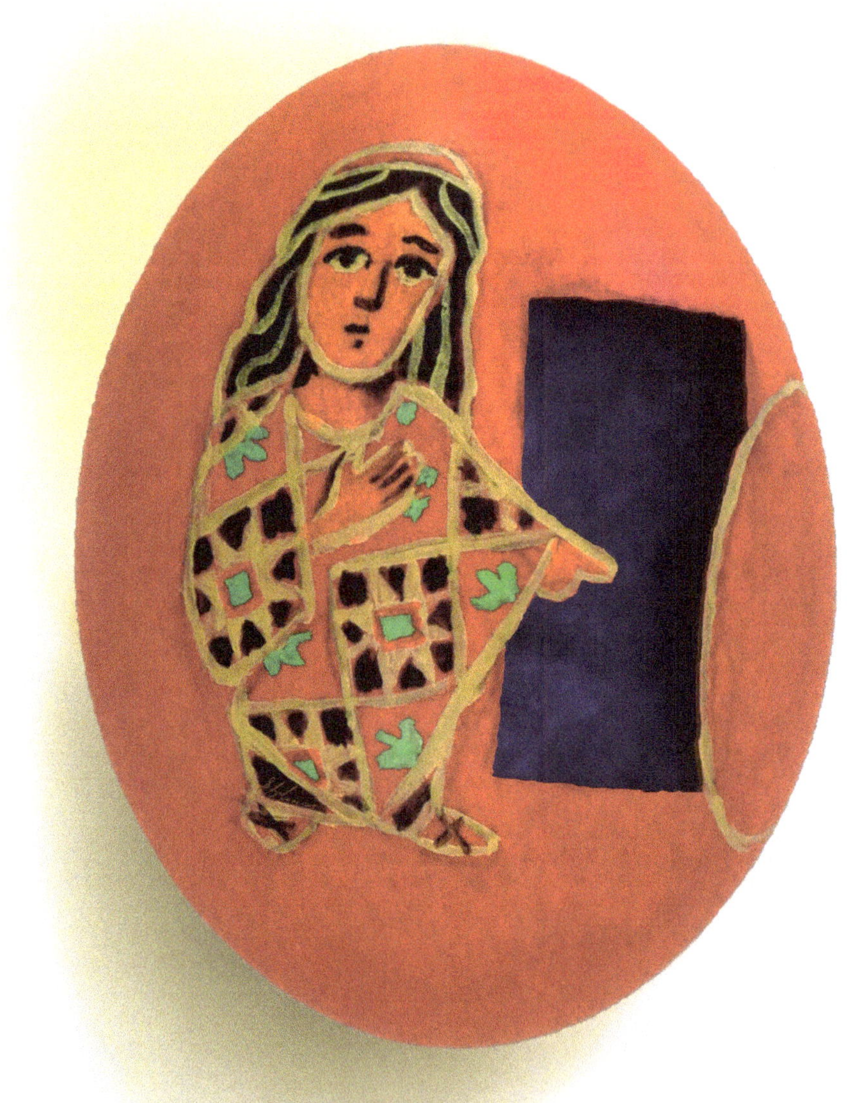

Mary Magdalene at the Tomb, 2010
Acrylic on eggshell + digital (final form as a print), 10”h x 8”w

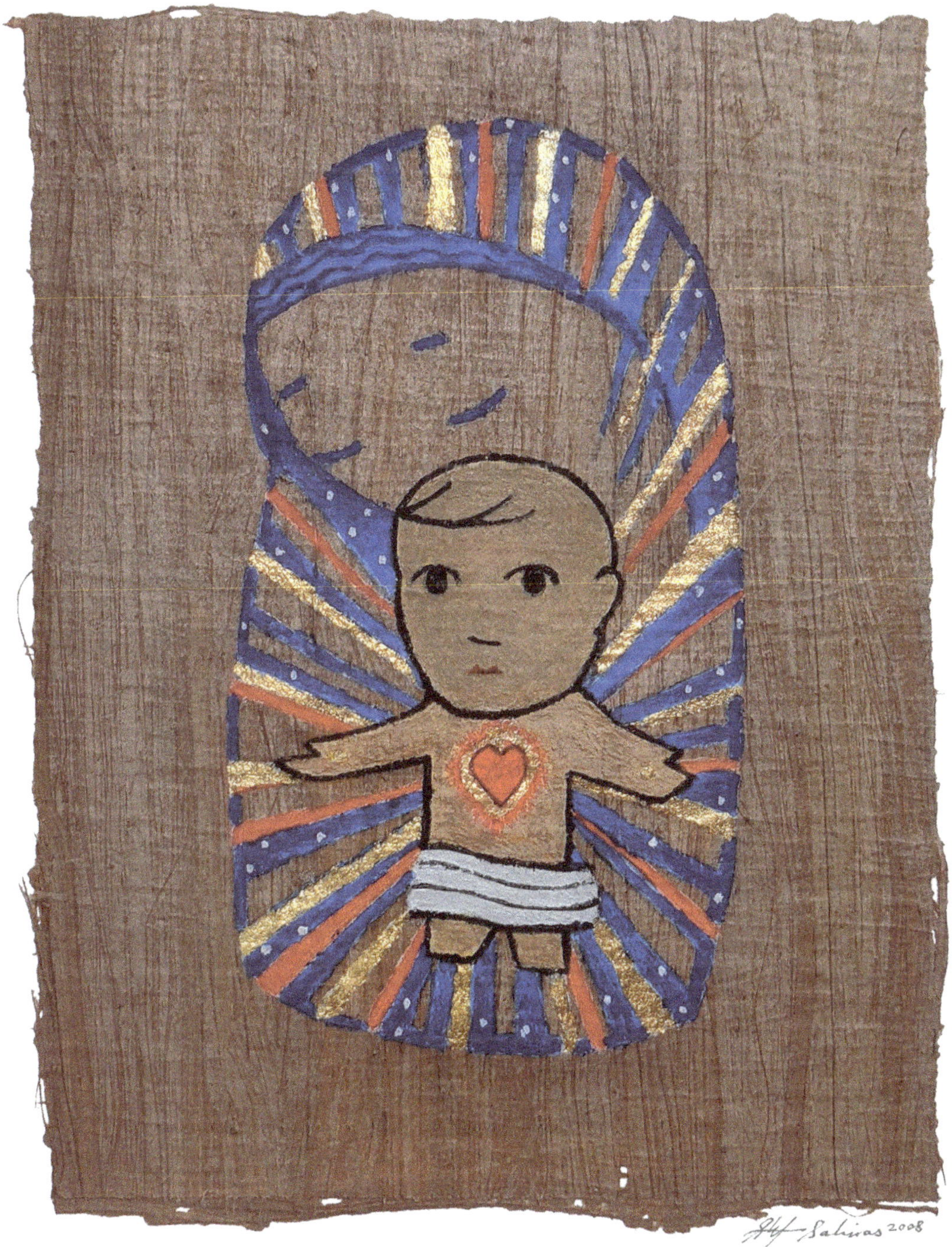

Christ Child, 2008
Acrylic and gold leaf on bark paper, 10"h x 8"w

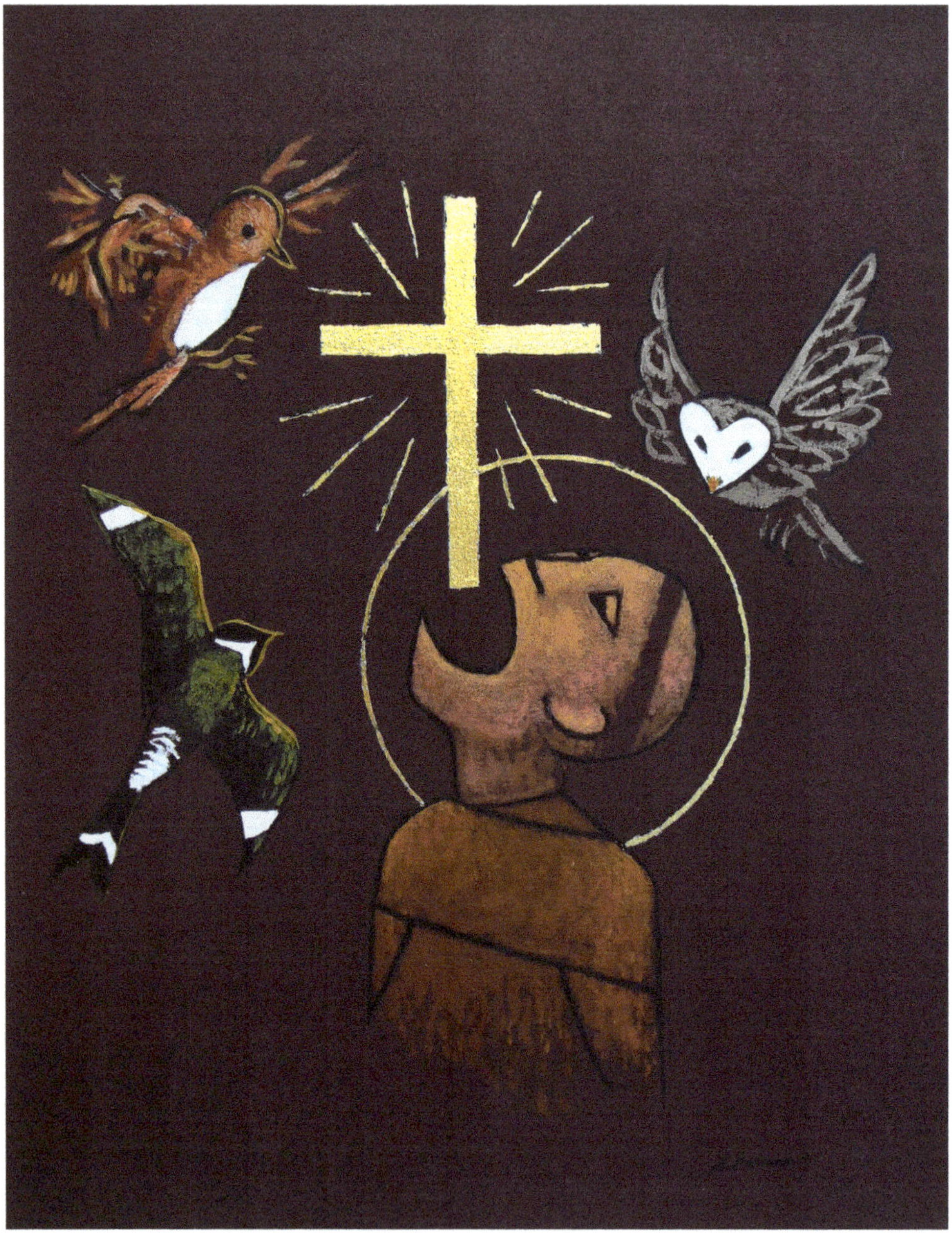

Sylvester's Vision of Saint Francis, 2014
Acrylic and gold leaf on paper, 10"h x 8"w

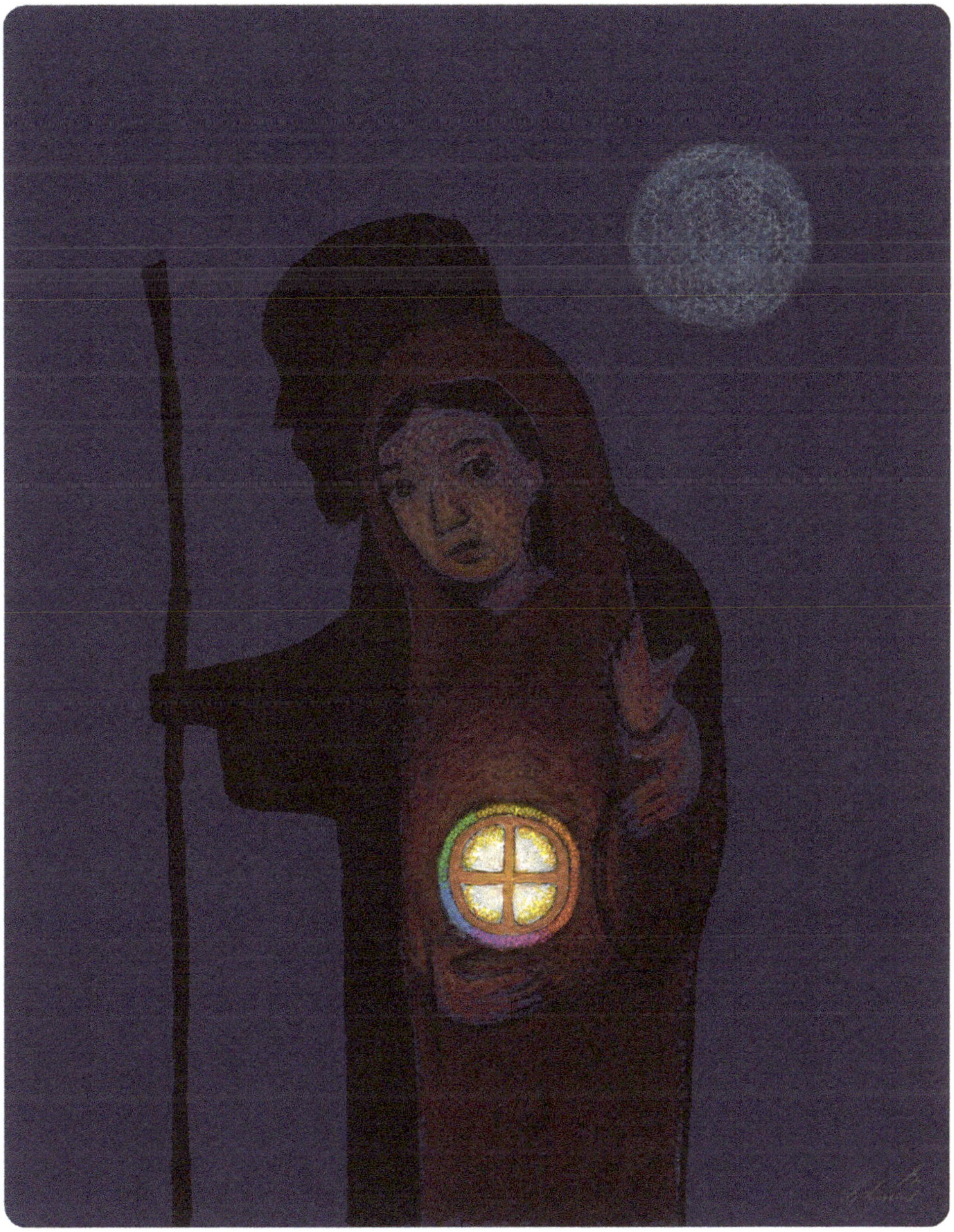

Mary and Joseph, 2014
Acrylic on paper, 10"h x 8"w

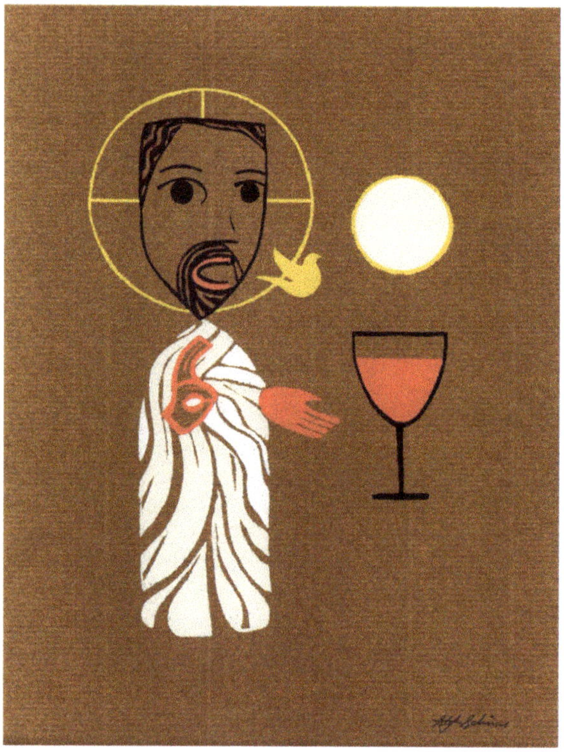

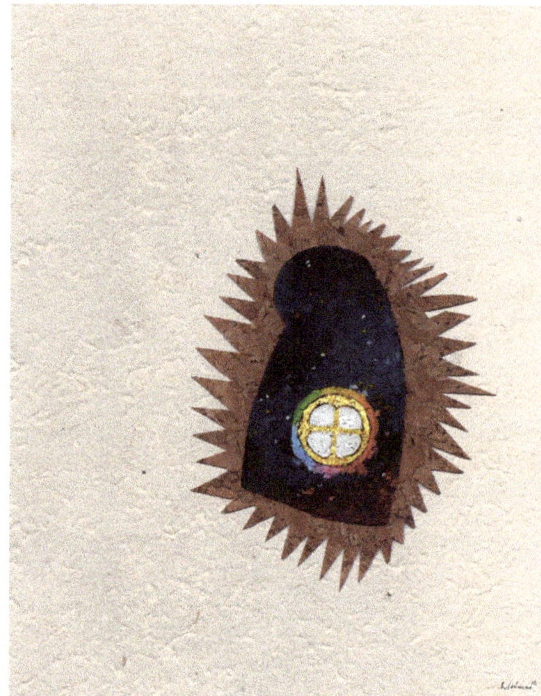

Communion, 2014, Acrylic and ink on paper + digital, 10"h x 8"w
The Madonna (Inner Cosmos), 2015, Acrylic and gold leaf on cork and paper, 10"h x 8"w

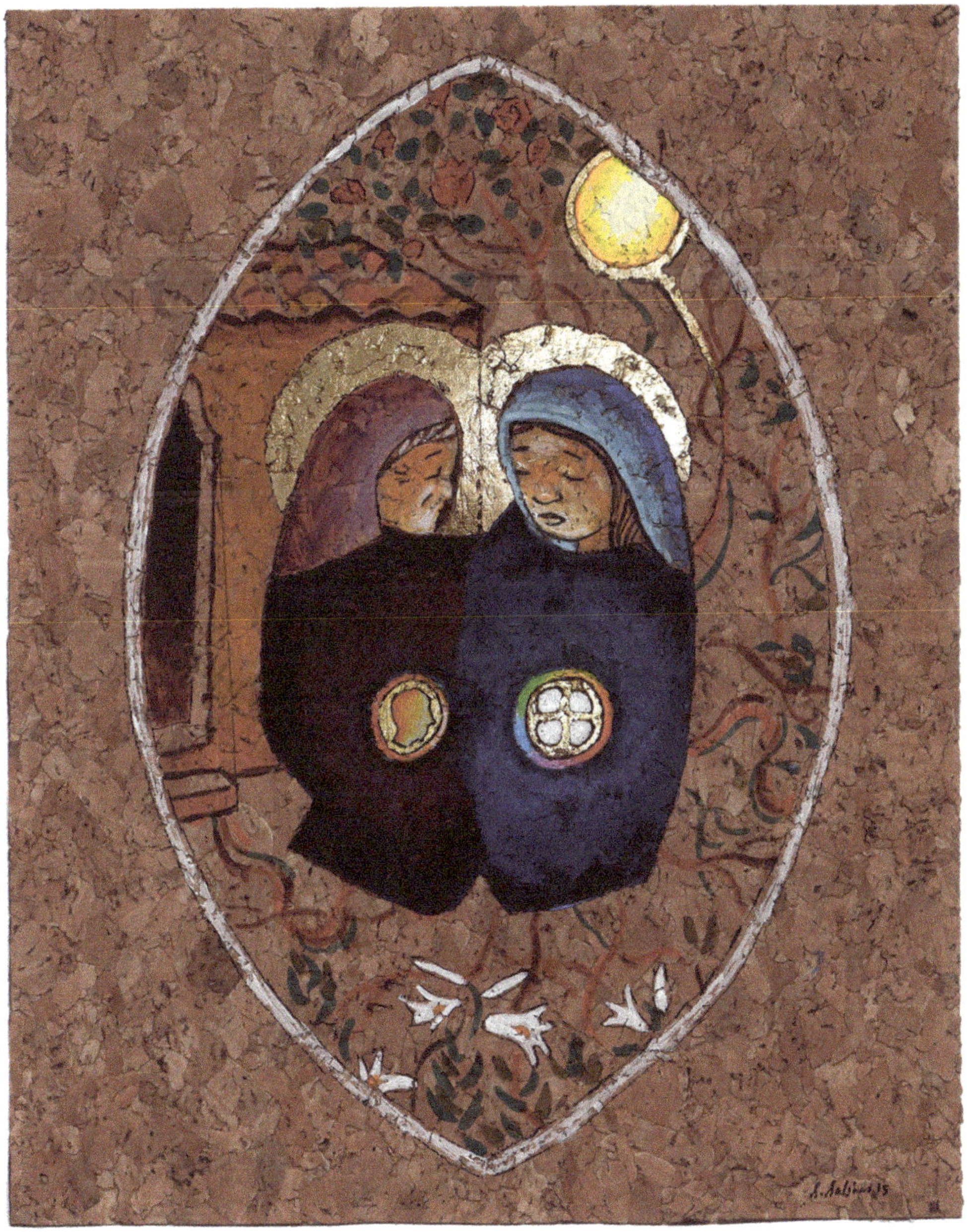

The Visitation (Inner Cosmos), 2015
Acrylic and gold leaf on cork, 10"h x 8"w

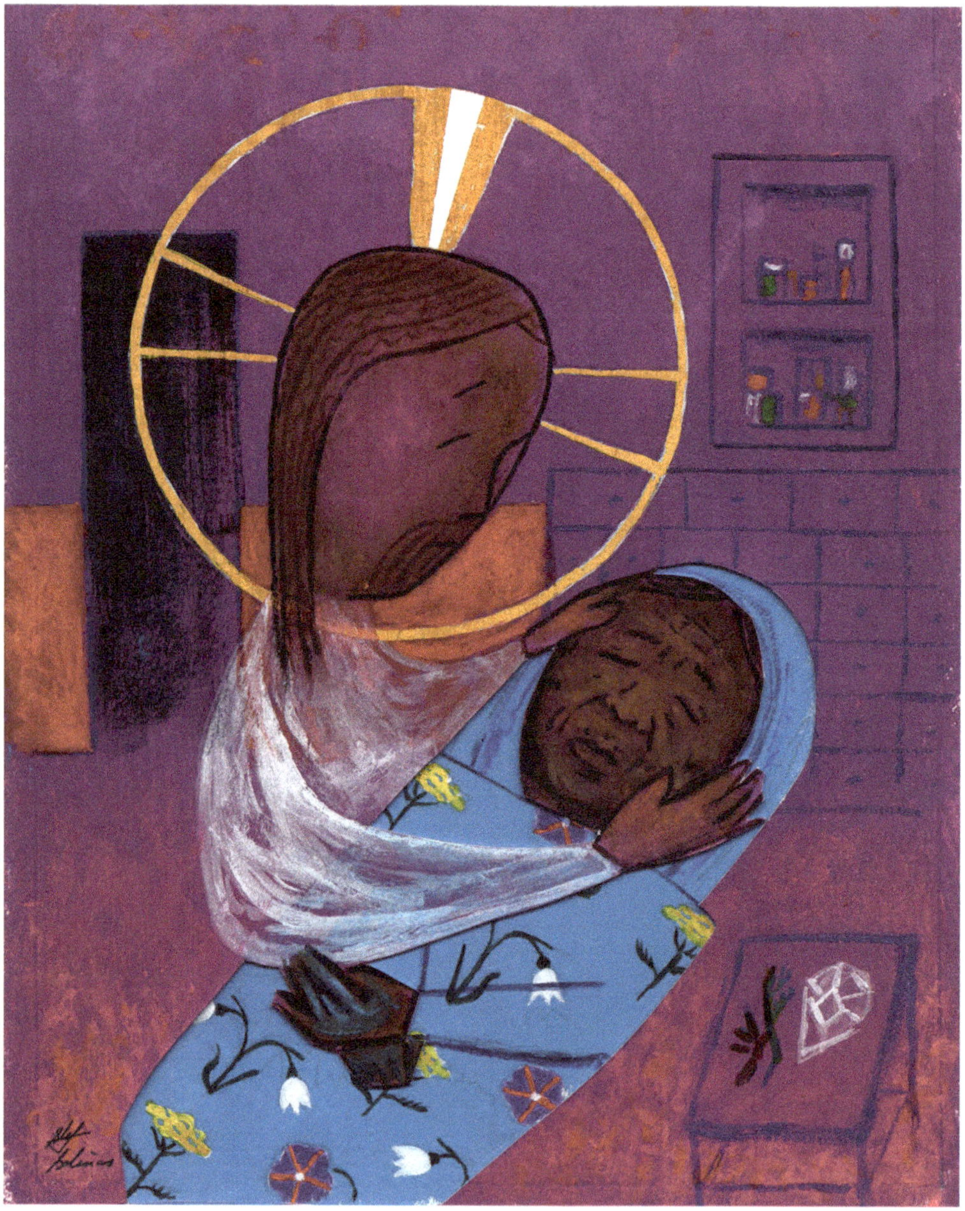

The Healer, 2013
Acrylic on paper, 10"h x 8"w

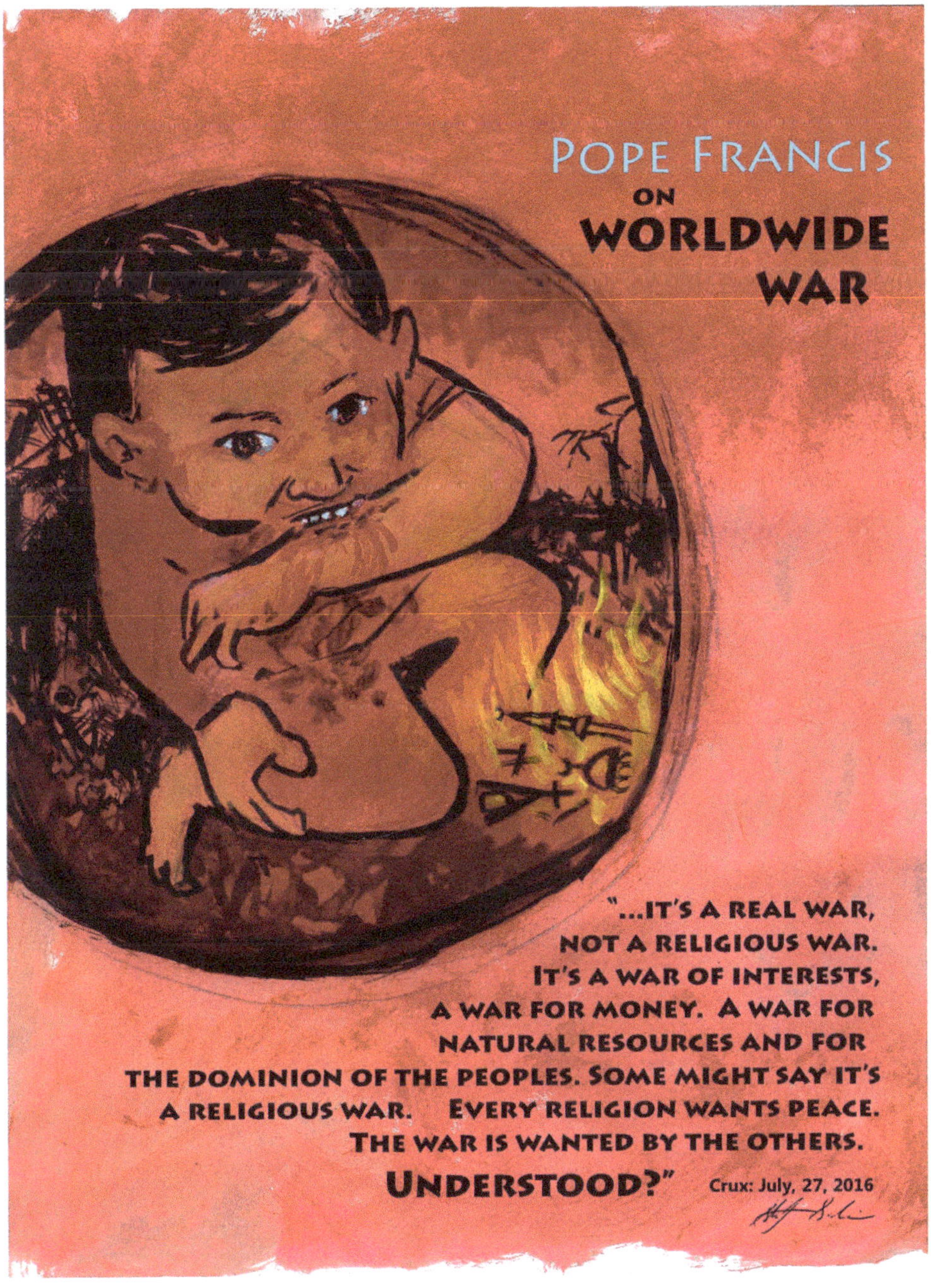

Pope Francis on Worldwide War, 2016
Acrylic on paper + digital, 11"h x 8.5"w

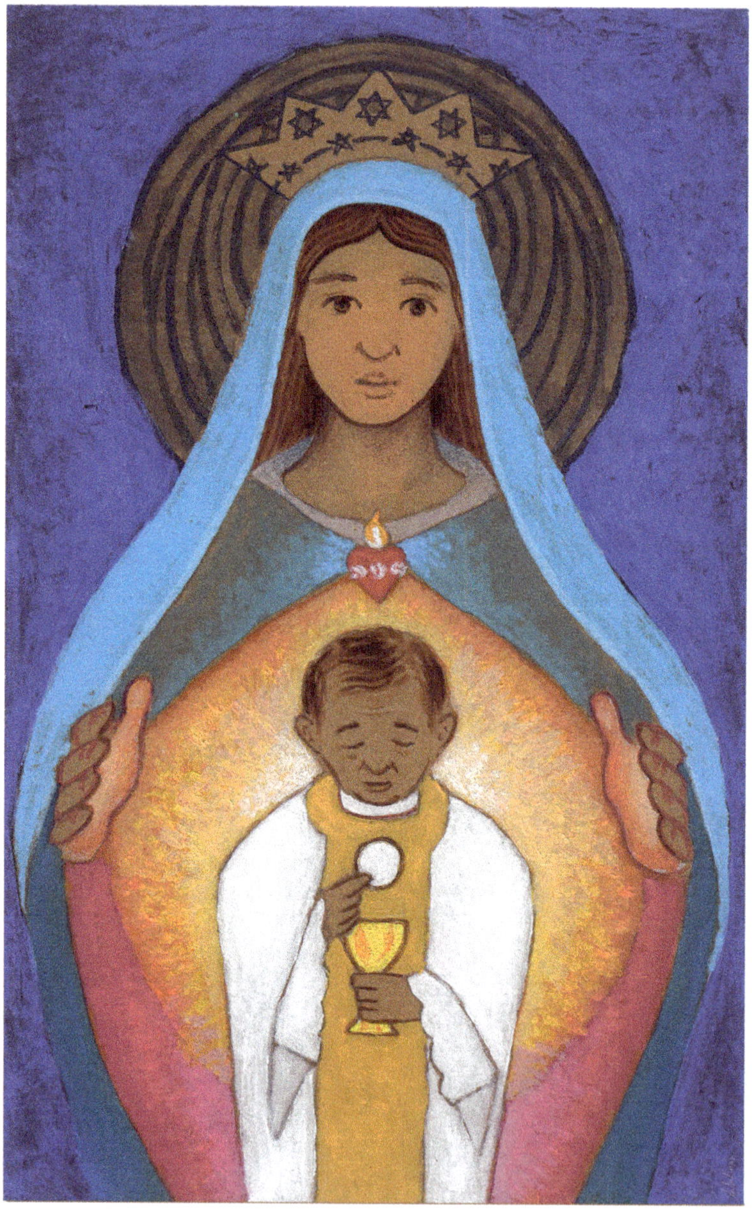

Our Lady of Clergy, 2017
Acrylic on paper, 10"h x 6"w

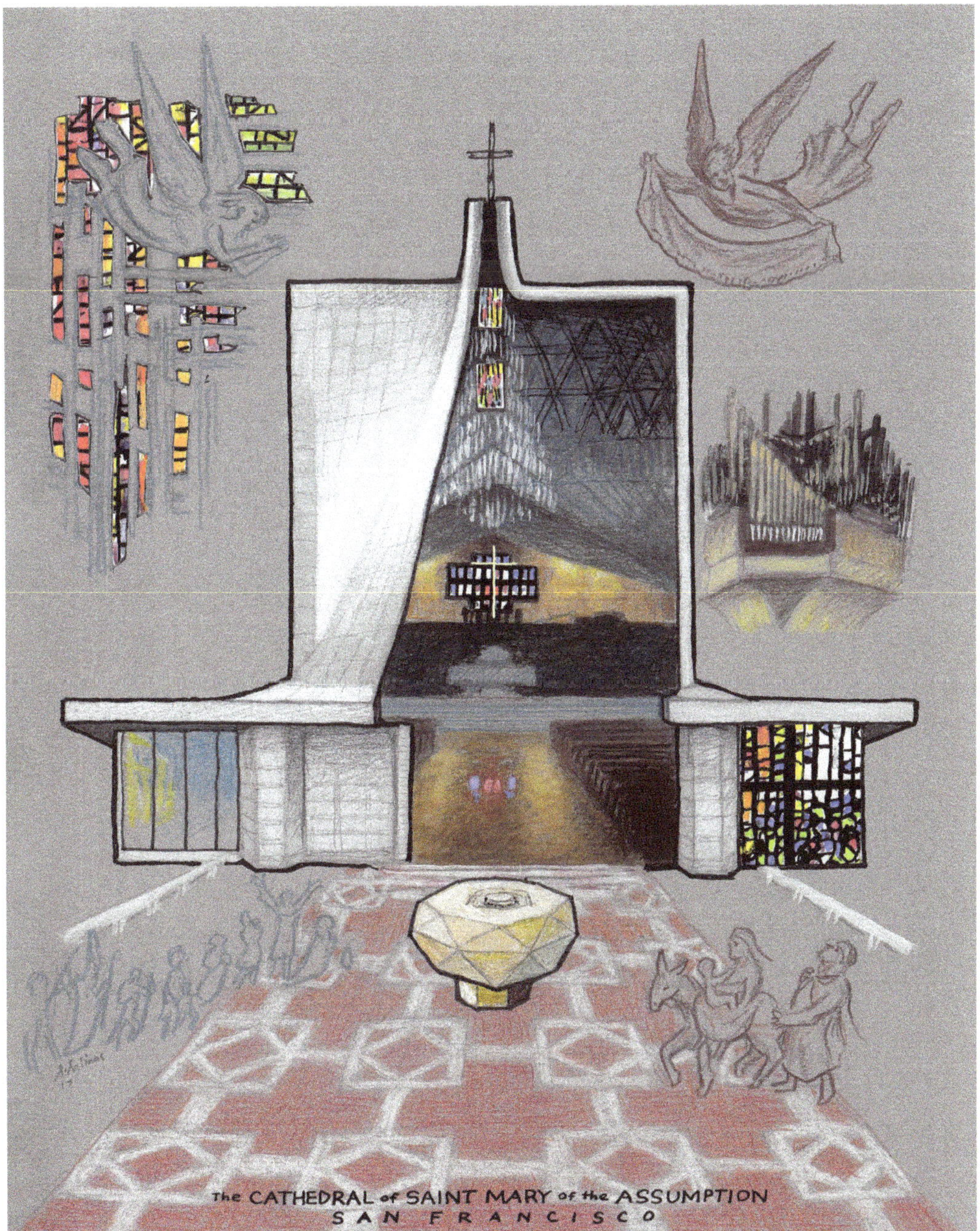

The Cathedral of Saint Mary of the Assumption, 2017
Acrylic, pencil and ink on paper, 10"h x 8"w

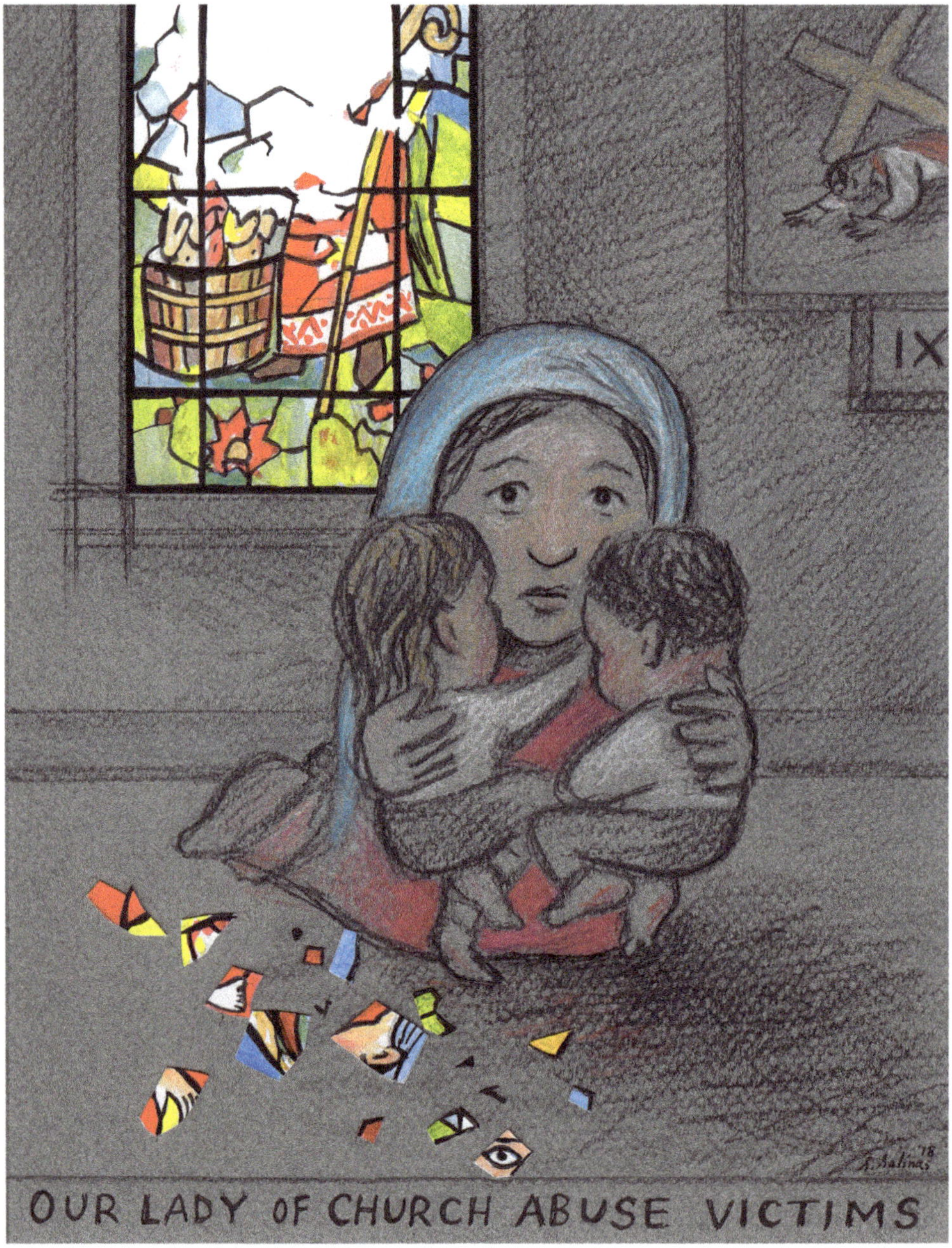

Our Lady of Church Abuse Victims, 2018
Acrylic, pencil and ink on paper, 10"h x 8"w

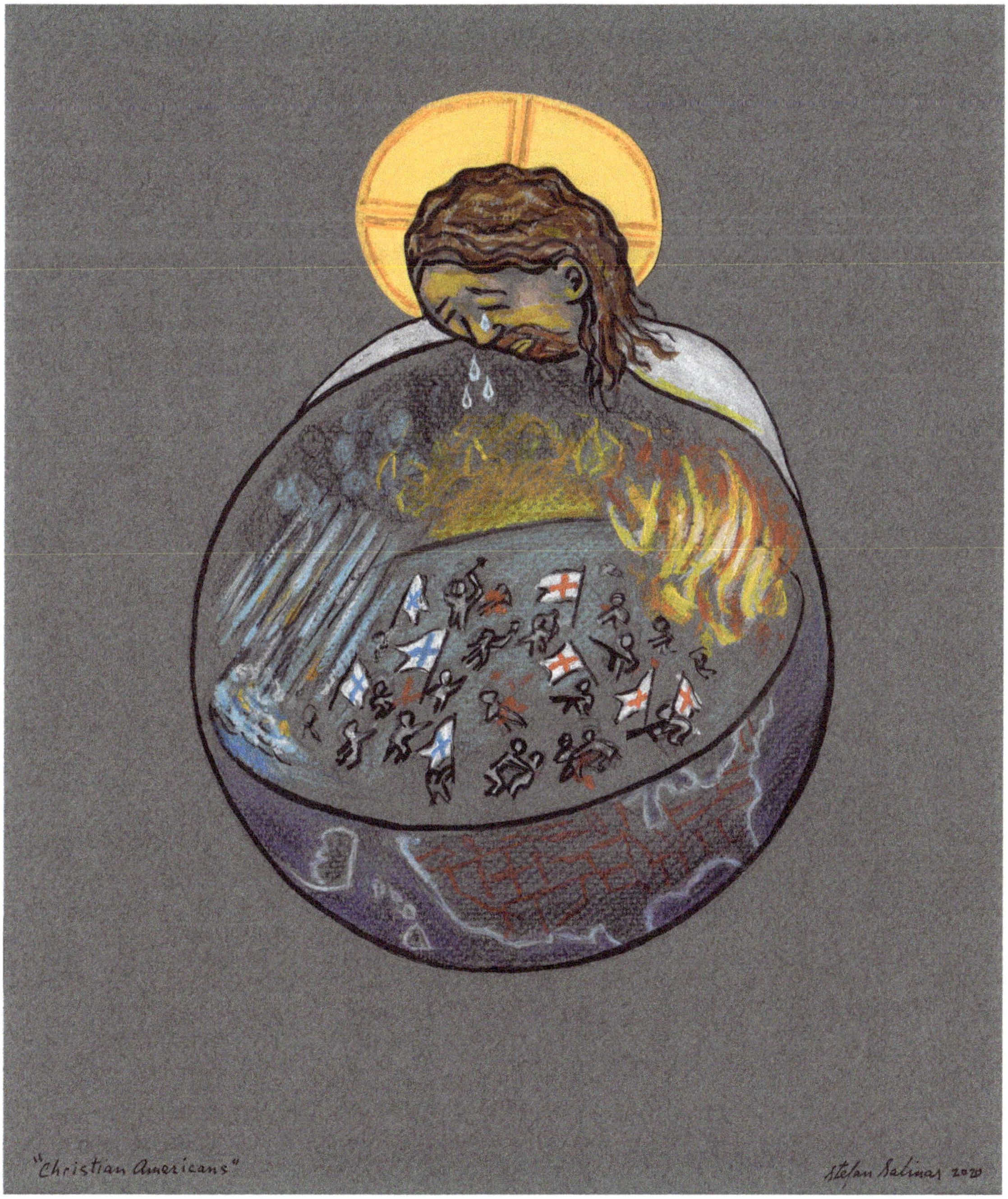

Christian Americans, 2020, Acrylic, pencil and ink on paper, 12"h x 9"w

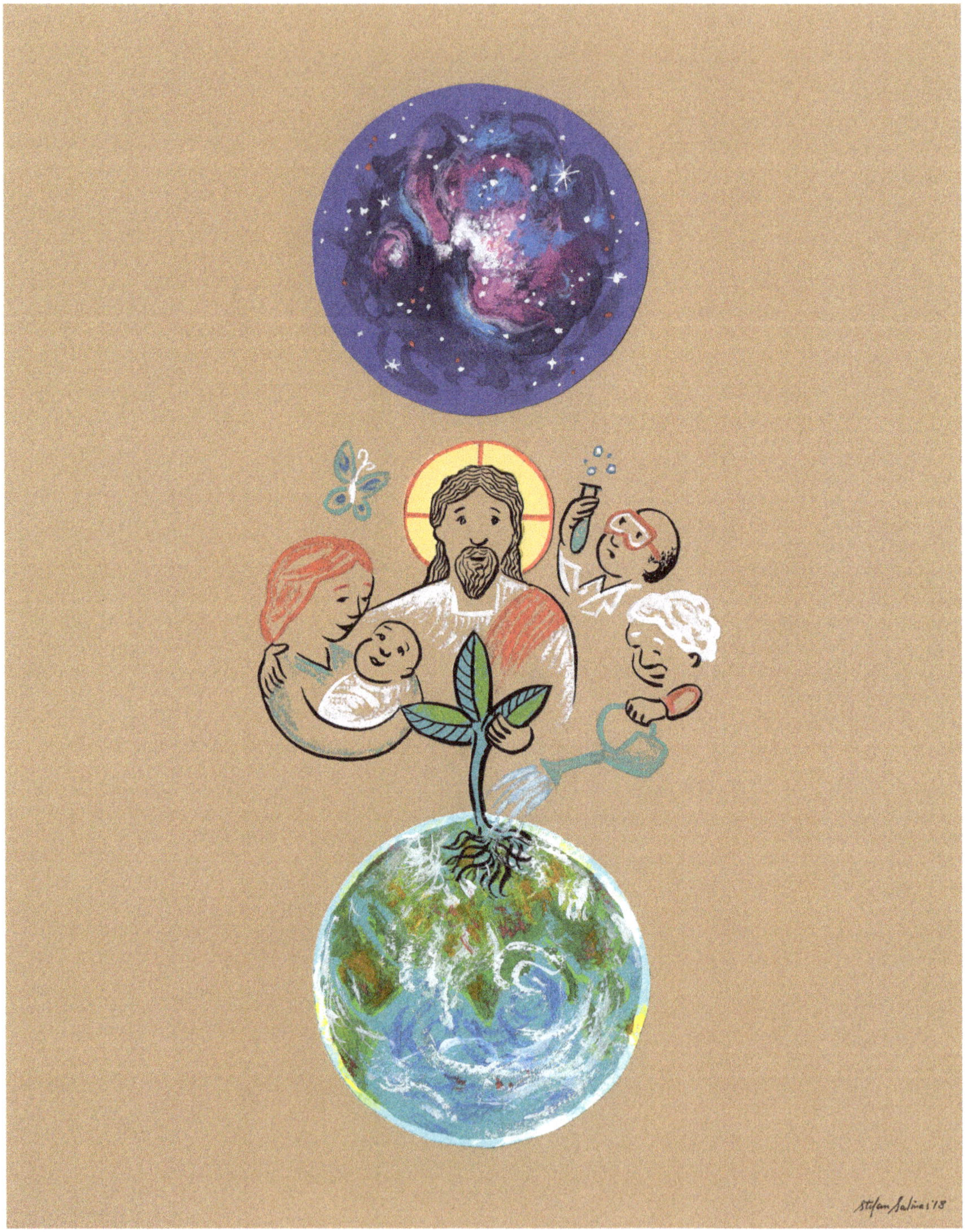

Care for God's Creation, 2018, Acrylic, pencil and ink on paper, 14"h x 10"w

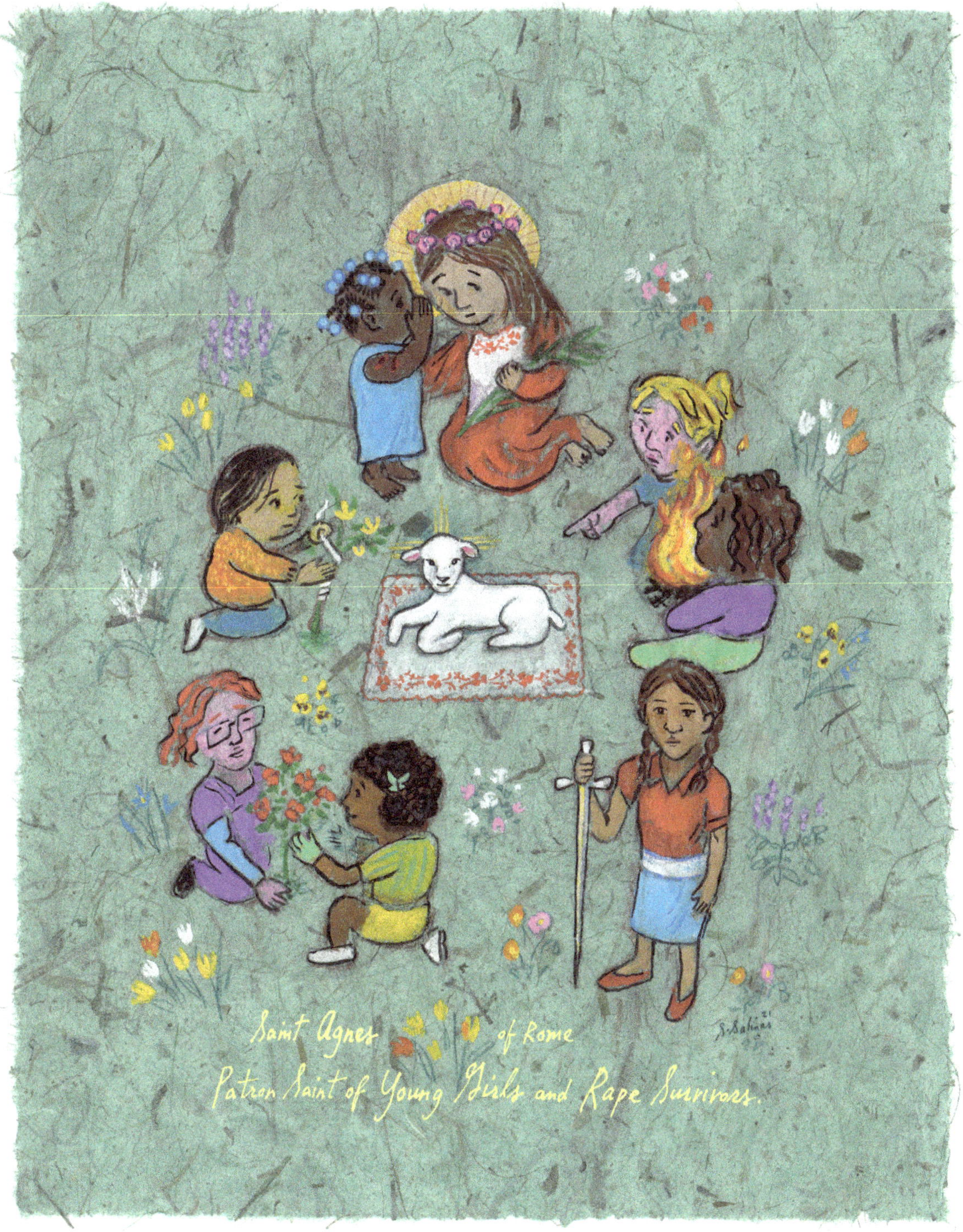

Saint Agnes of Rome, 2021, Acrylic, pencil and ink on paper, 14"h x 10"w

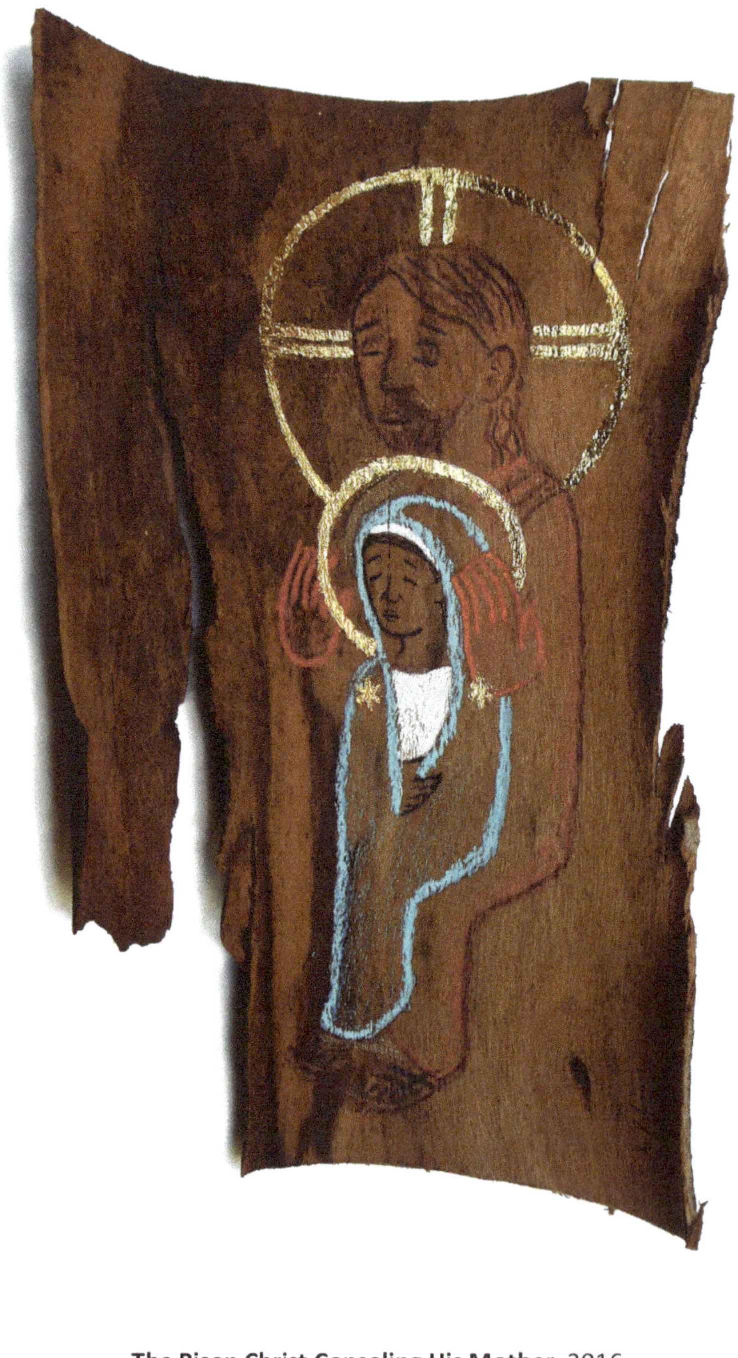

The Risen Christ Consoling His Mother, 2016
Acrylic, ink and gold leaf on eucalyptus bark (photographed for print), 10"h x 8"w

Liturgical and Public Art

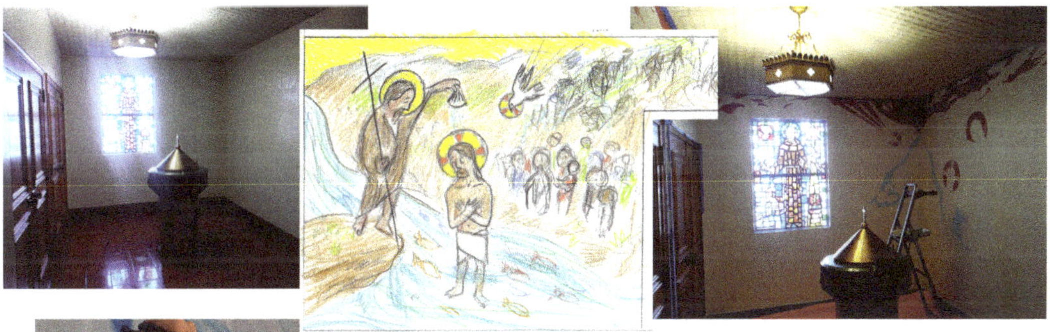

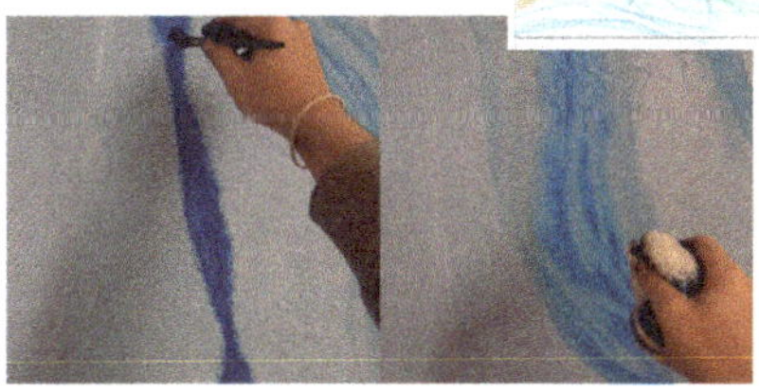

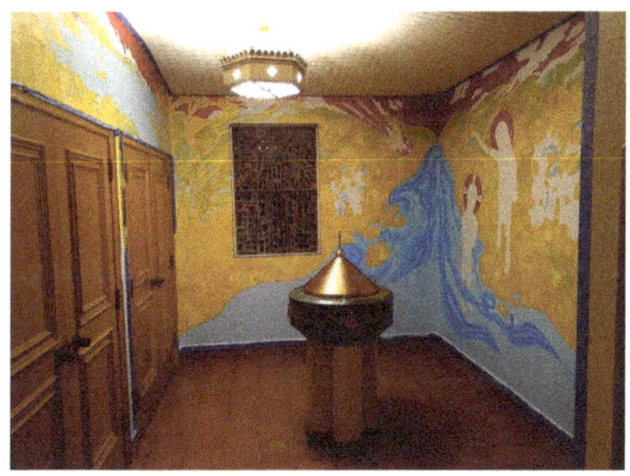

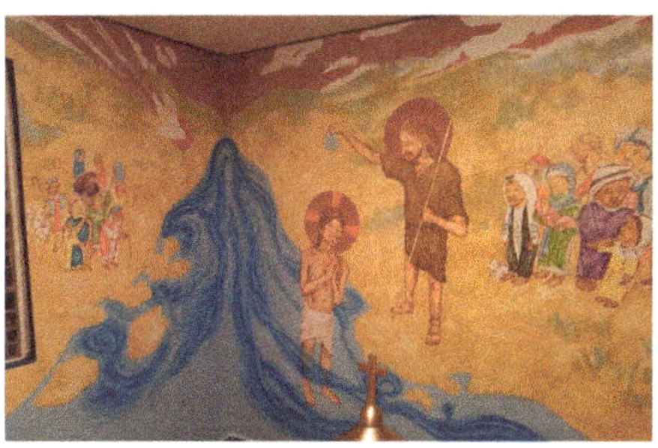

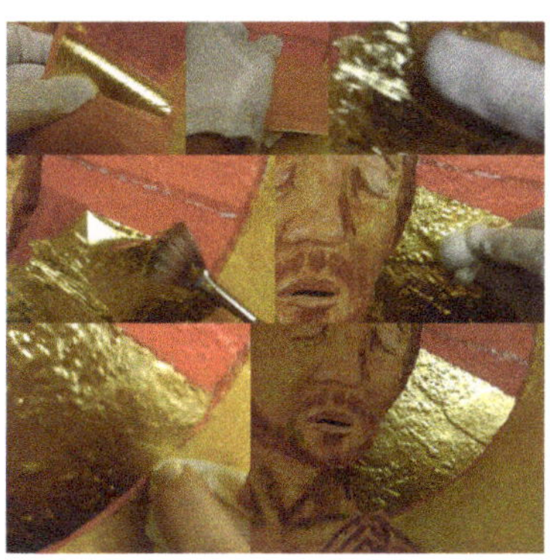

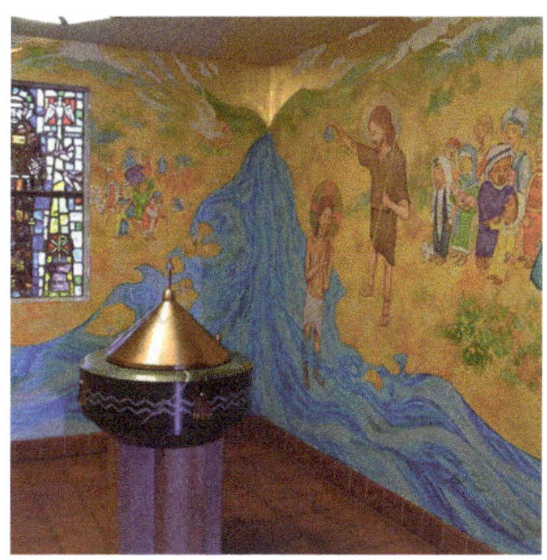

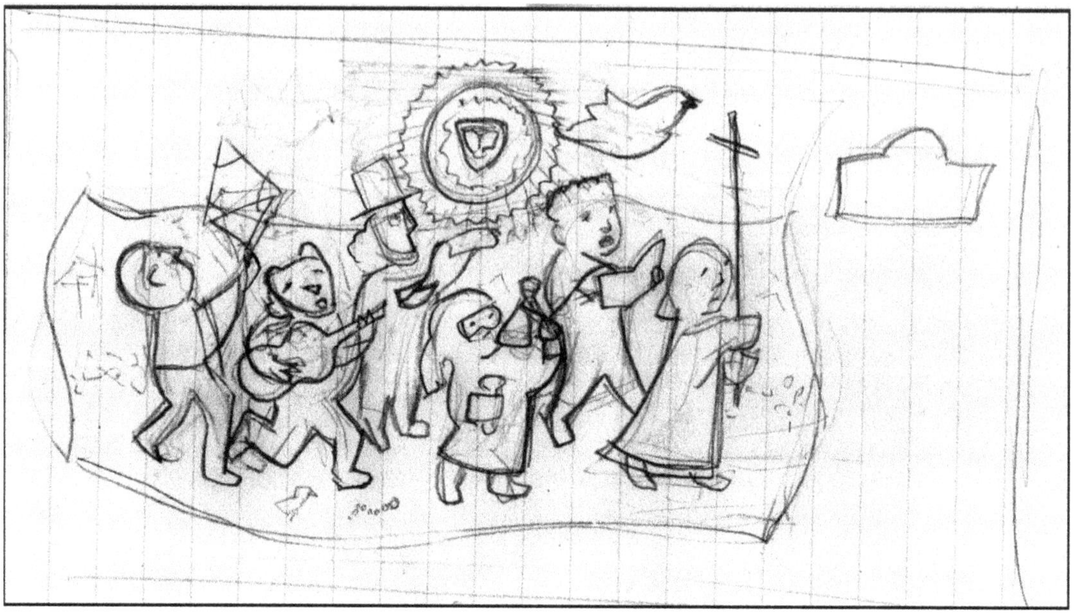

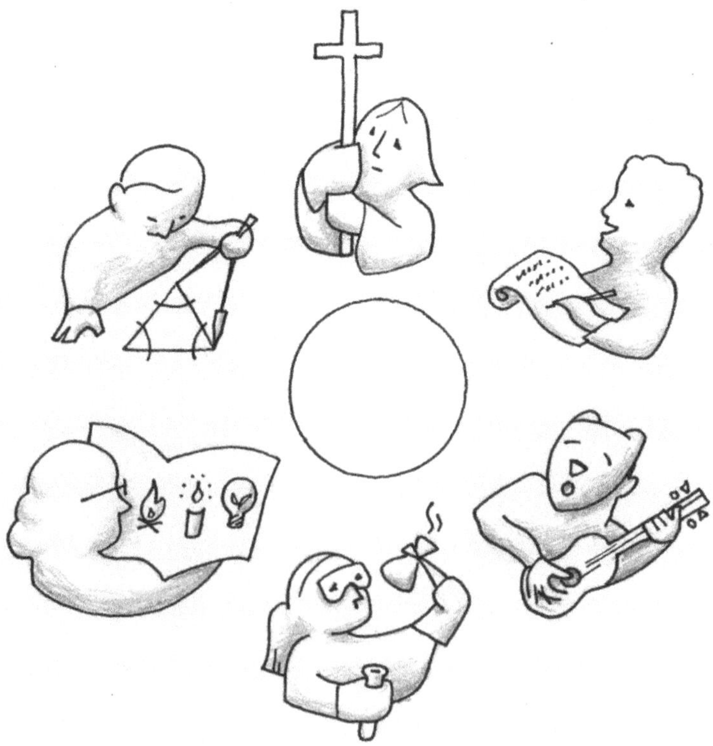

Since as early as I can remember, houses of worship transfixed my imagination. My parents raised us in the Modern Spiritualist religion. Their churches are fairly modest church-houses, but it was the Buddhist temples, Christian churches, and decorative mosques that really made my heart beat faster. We went to Europe when I was eleven to visit relatives and friends. The heavens opened up. Oh! The cathedrals!

In middle school, a Baptist friend I would spend weekends with let me join his family at their church for several Sunday services. I wonder if my parents ever knew. Being mischievous, he showed me how he found a way into the ceiling. One Saturday, we did climb up, walked in the roof, and even up into the steeple. Years later, while living in Binghamton, New York, for a summer, I spent many days visiting churches, several of them Orthodox Ukrainian, Greek, and Russian. At the time, most of the churches there kept their doors unlocked. On occasion, a sexton or pastor would be around and give me a tour. Once a contractor led me into and atop a church's bell tower. Little did I know, fifteen years later, I would convert to Christianity, and three years after that, create my first work of art for a church. I had designed outdoor banners and posters for a Unitarian Universalist church (I was a Unitarian for a while), but those were proclamations, not instruments to help one pray.

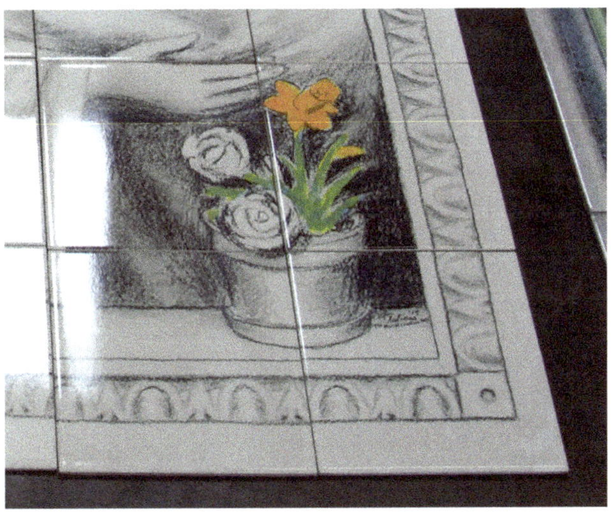

Tiles for **The Visitation**, 2015

What a marriage of art and architecture, mosaics, murals, colored glass, gold leaf, coming alive with incense, organ music, choral voices, and processions of parishioners! A man-made structure of wood, brick, and stone, meant to point us to the unseen, ethereal divine. It's the highest form of visual art, in my opinion. Producing it asks the artist to center himself and allow the Holy Spirit to enter within, ignite the heart, and maneuver the hand. Some craftsmen spent most of their lives creating the great cathedrals and temples. While visiting Barcelona, Japanese sculptor Etsuro Sotoo was so moved by Gaudi's Sagrada Familia, he has dedicated the rest of as many of his years left as necessary to help complete it. He even converted to Catholicism in the process!

Although my heart is with Catholic art, I am open and willing to work in temples of other denominations and faiths. It's all up to where the Lord leads me.

The Holy Spirit Icon, Church of the Visitacion

2014, Oil and gold leaf on wood, San Francisco, CA
Commissioned by Rev. Thuan V. Hoang

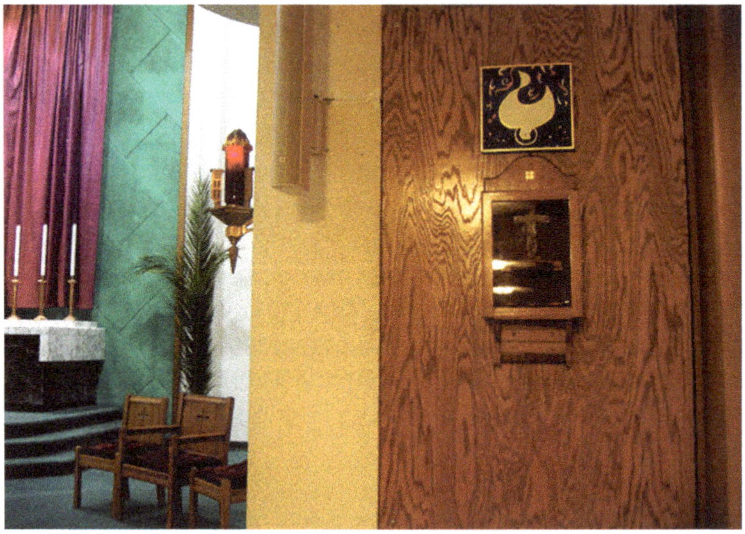

The pastor, whom I had volunteered alongside for years, commission me to create an icon of the Holy Spirit for his church. It felt like a natural leap from my children's book on churches, published earlier that year.

The Holy Spirit is depicted here as a fierce graphic enigma; a shape suggesting a dove or a treble clef, or some foreign symbol employed by the archangels? An abstract force, beyond our comprehension, from the Heavens; from outer space. A comet? A UFO? A great white phantom from the Greater Unseen?

The dove is a bright white that pierces through the darkness, which echoes Christ emerging from the darkness in the painting of Divine Mercy, to the right of the ambo and icon.

The accompanying flames? Lively and playful, like fireworks or paper streamers falling on a parade. This is a celebration! And the color tiles below, is this confetti? The stained glass windows feature some of San Francisco's buildings, so here we have a quiet Visitacion neighborhood night scene.

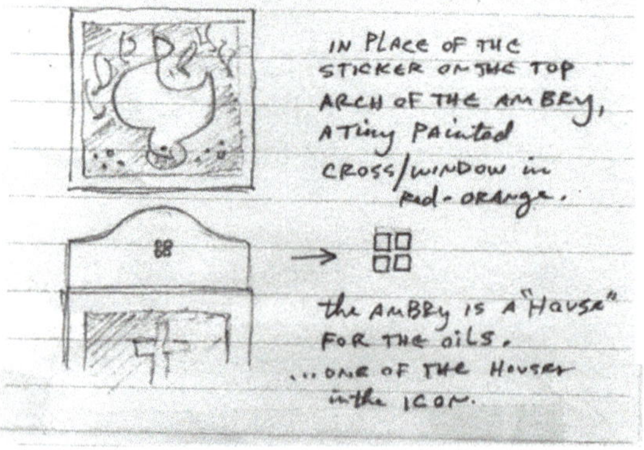

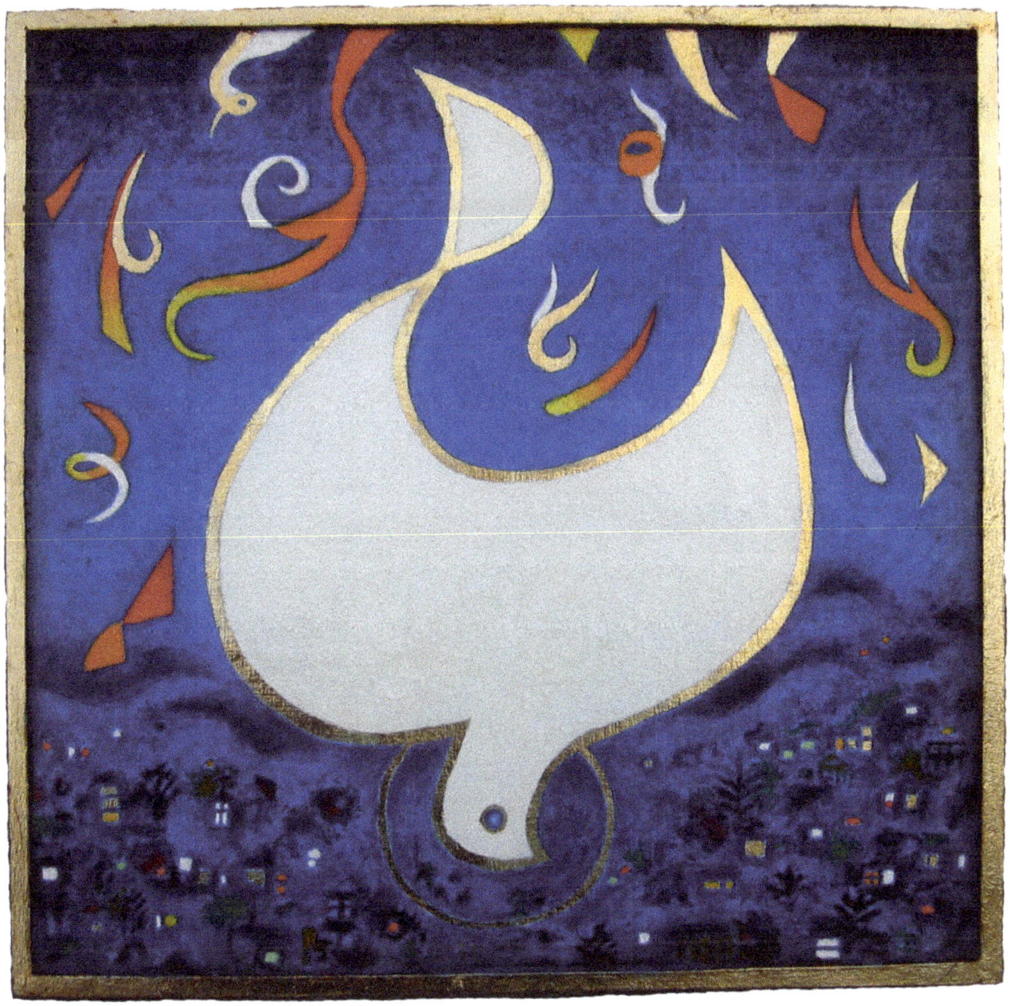

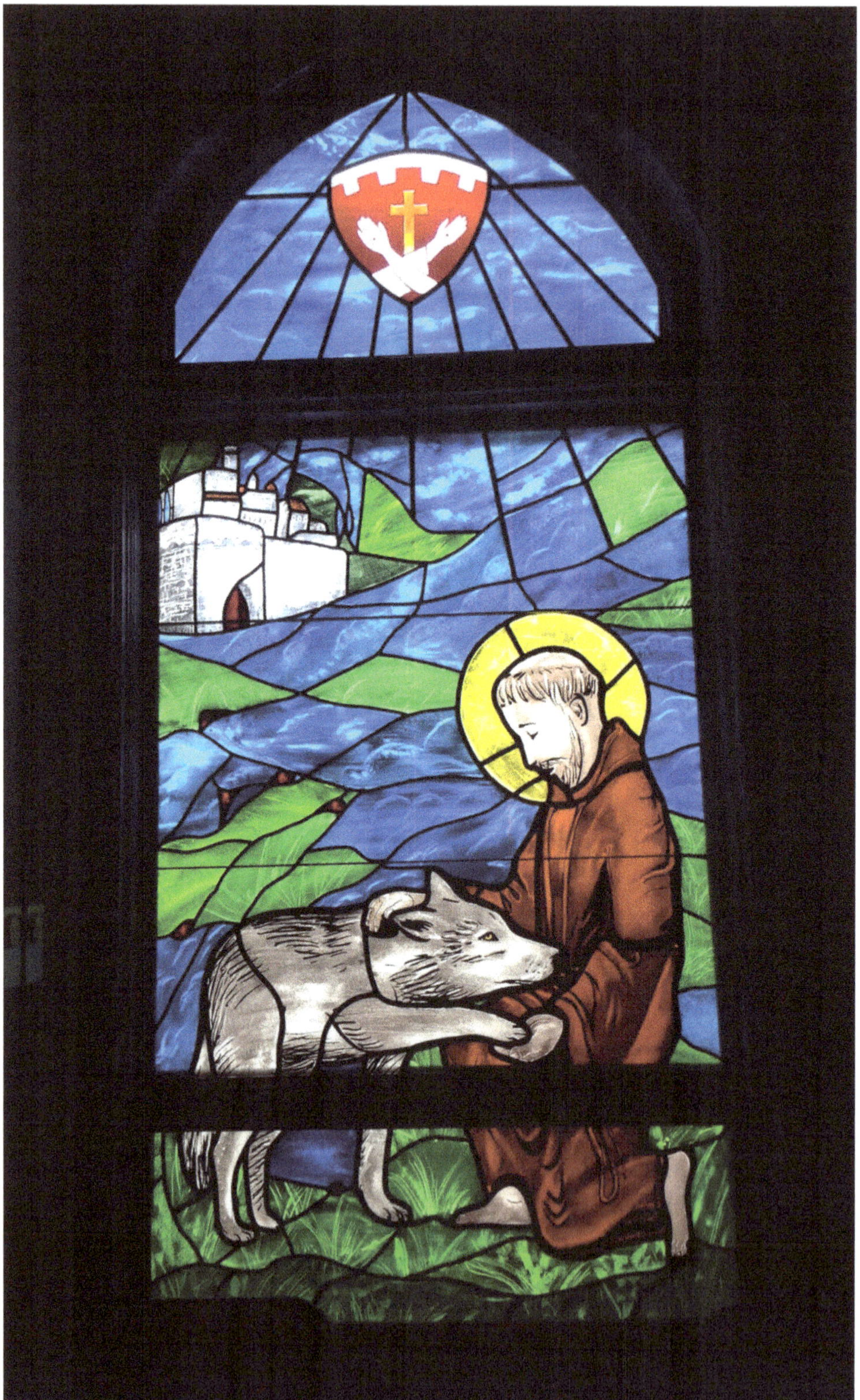

St. Francis and the Wolf of Gubbio
Stained Glass Window, St. Philip the Apostle Chapel

2015, Stained glass, San Francisco, CA
Made by Hogan Studios, commissioned by Rev. Tony LaTorre

The pastor at the time, Rev. Tony LaTorre, approached me with a commission to design a window in the chapel to replace the colorful contact paper that was currently up. This room was formerly the Bridal Room. A window of Mary's Ascension dates from the 1950s, and one of Christ's Divine Mercy was gifted to the parish in the 1980s.

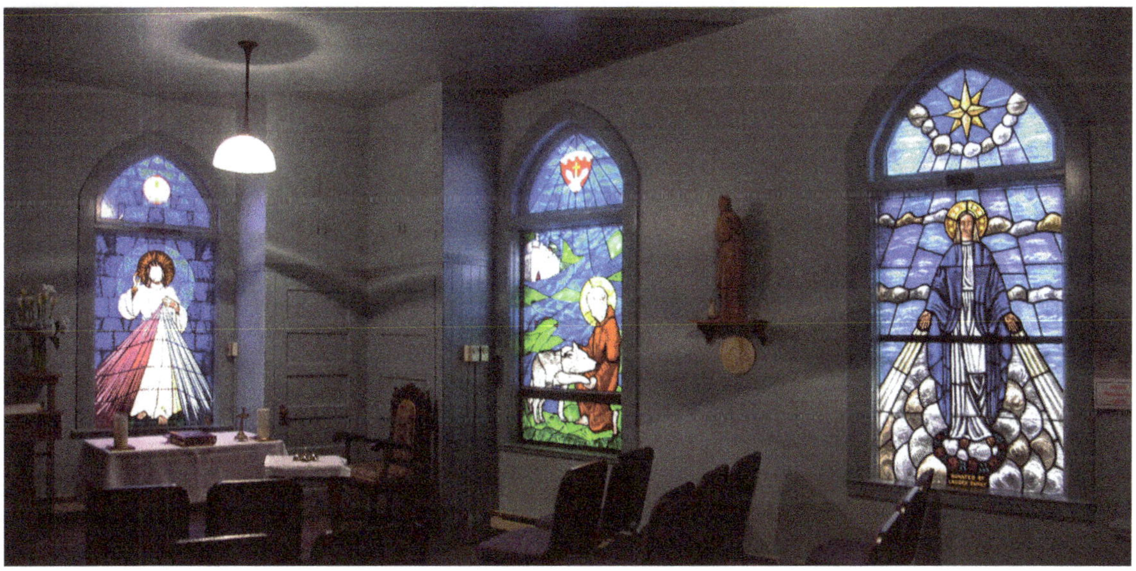

In conceptualizing the style in which this window would be rendered, I began with paying attention to the way in which the existing windows in the room were realized. Both existing windows are done in a "Naïve" style, a simplified representational approach. The Madonna brought to my mind Primitivism, the Nabis and Symbolist painters of the late nineteenth century, and Post-Impressionists like Paul Gauguin and Maurice Denis. I also looked at sources such as Giotto, Fra Angelico, and other medieval painters.

The rendering of Umbria is based on actual buildings. A wall surrounded the town at the time of the story. The buildings are almost all white, with a red door, to quote the stark red and white shield above (taken from the San Francisco Archdiocese's coat of arms).

Red poppies are sparsely peppered about. They are present in Umbria and are a common symbol for those who have died in war (WWI). This red is also quoted in the shield (as Christ's suffering) and in the closed door (that which bars the "others" out). Francis is here to make peace between enemies.

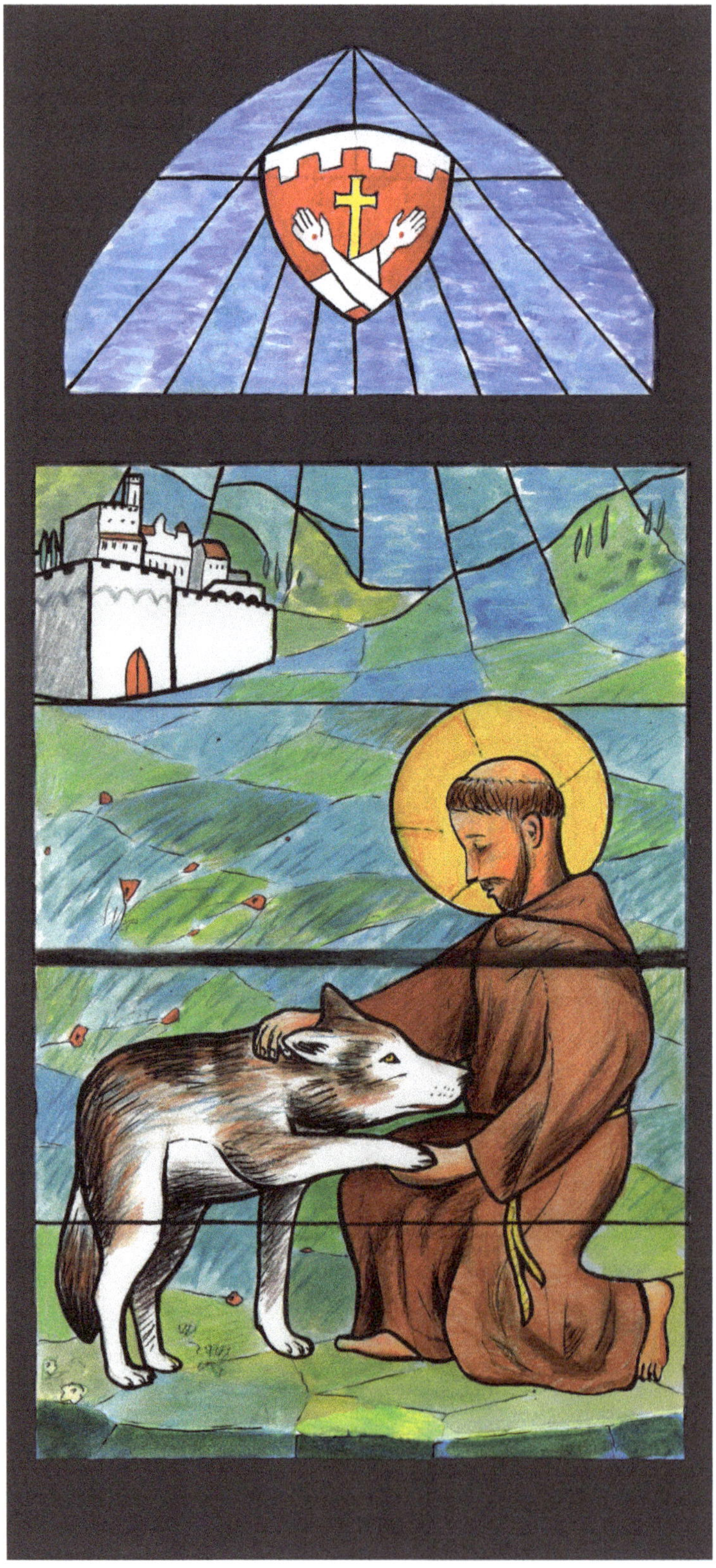

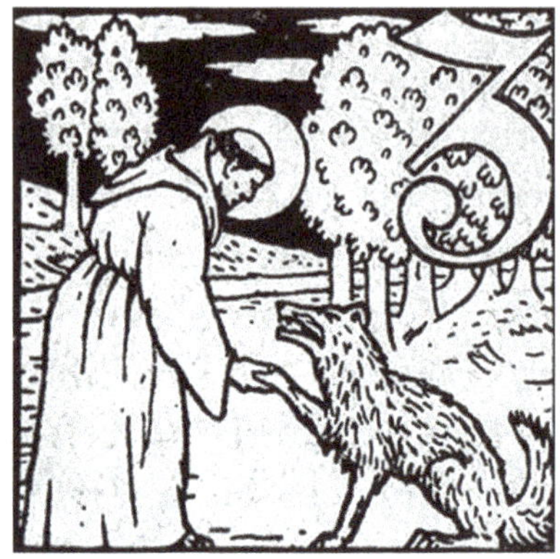

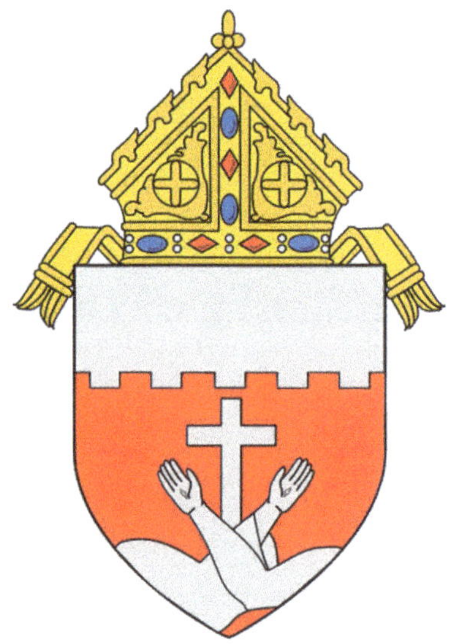

Archdiocese of San Francisco
Coat of Arms

This being the only stained glass window I have designed thus far, I relied on the team at Hogan Studios to adjust the lead lines where necessary.
This was an honor to co-create.
I am most grateful to Fr. Tony for this and the other commissions at this church and St. Stephens.

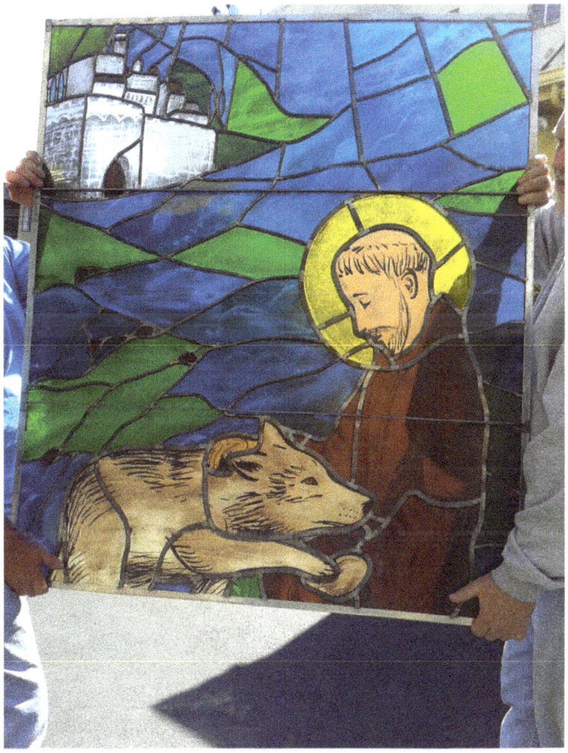

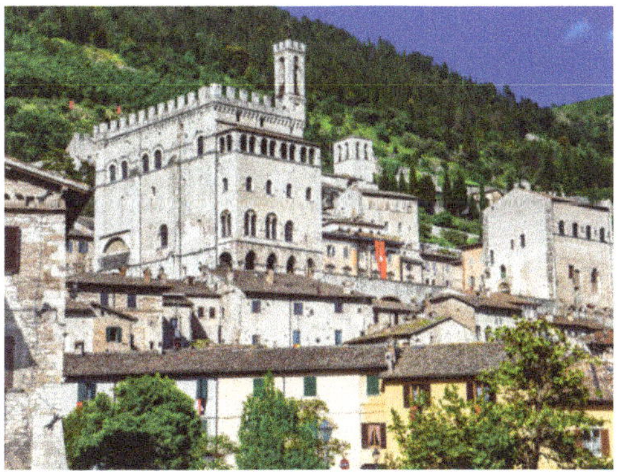

Gubbio, Italy

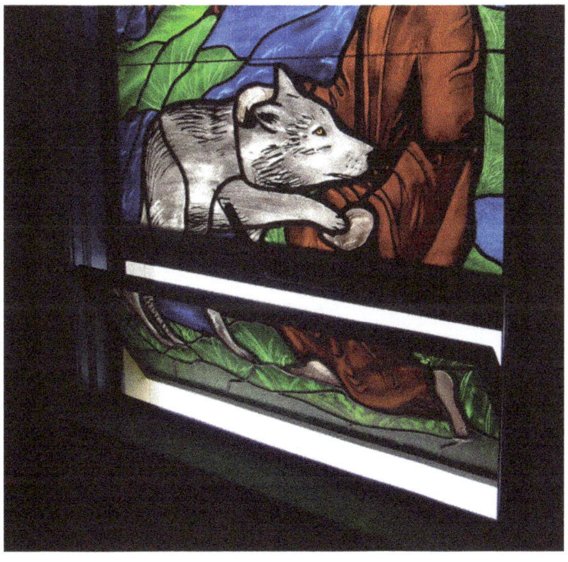

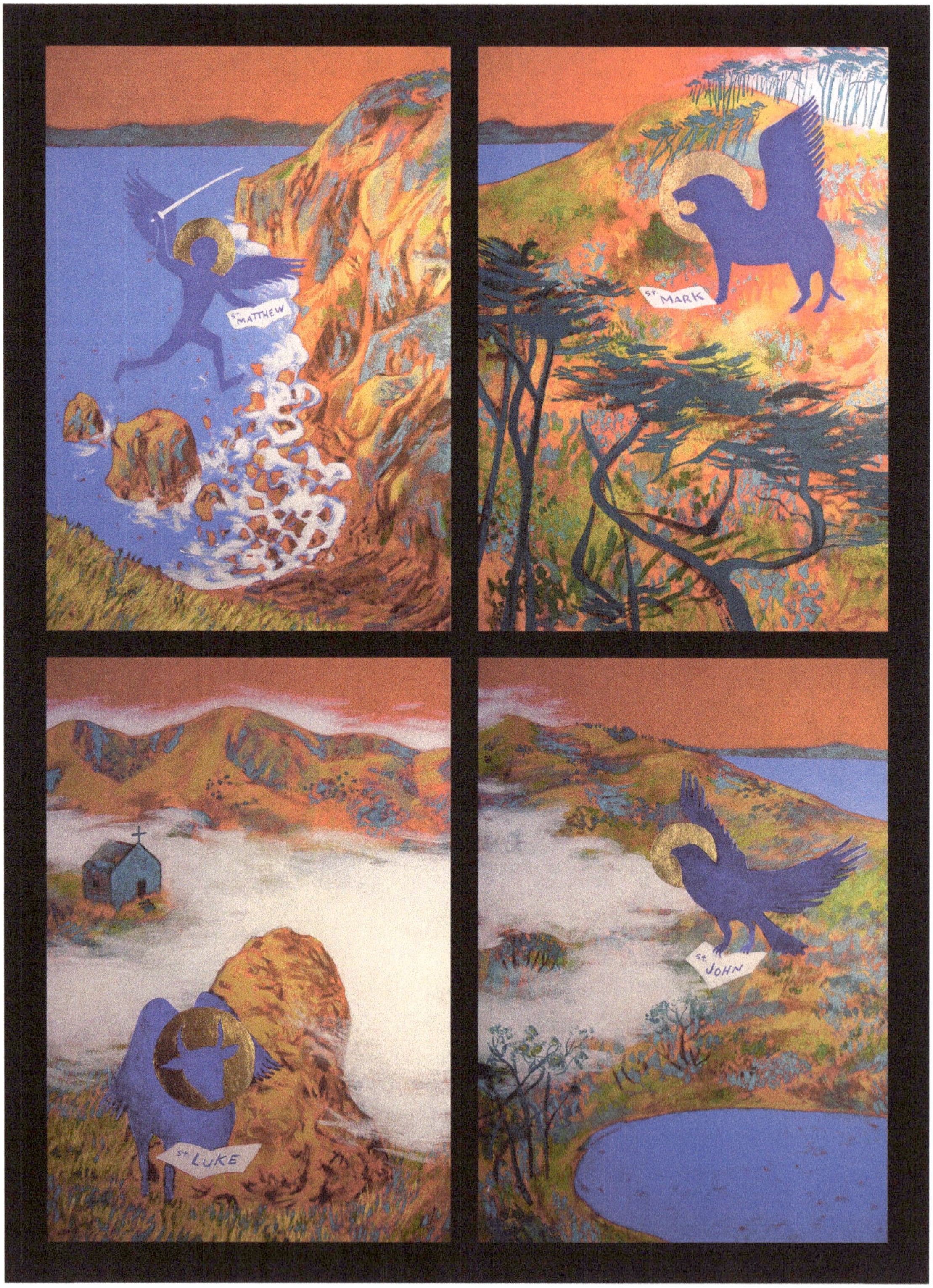
ST MATTHEW
ST MARK
ST LUKE
ST JOHN

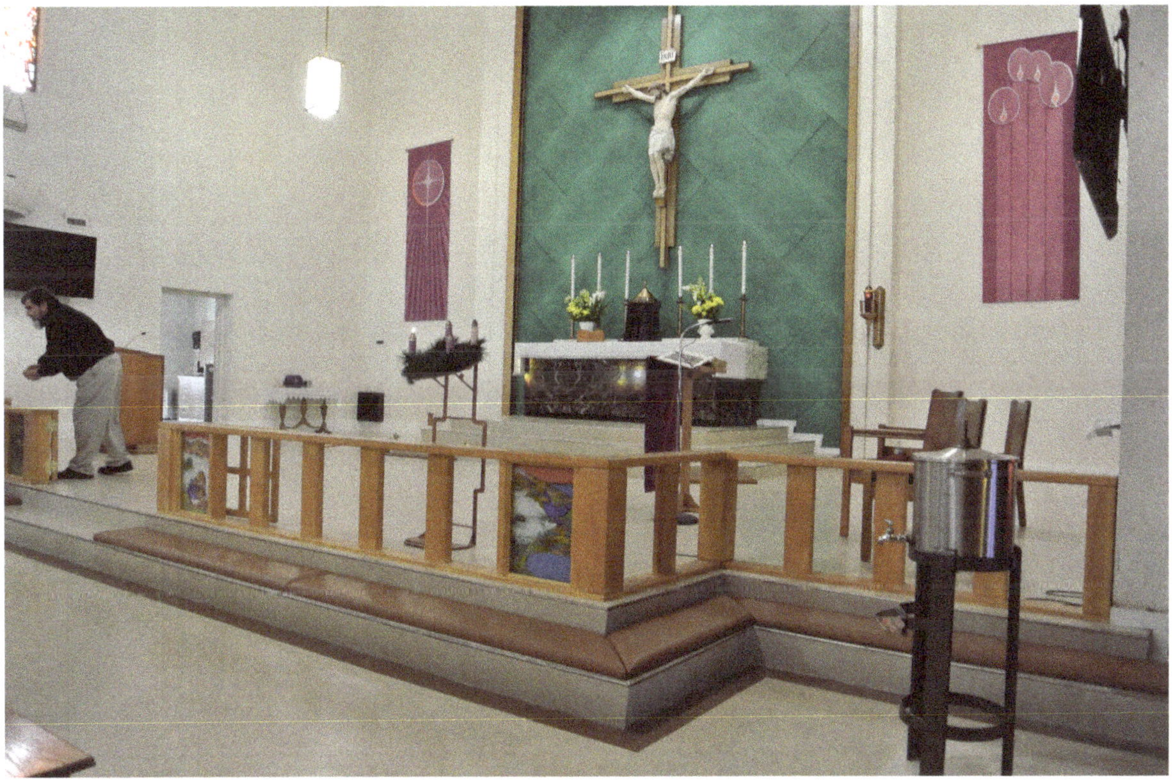

The Four Evangelists Altar Rails, Church of The Visitacion

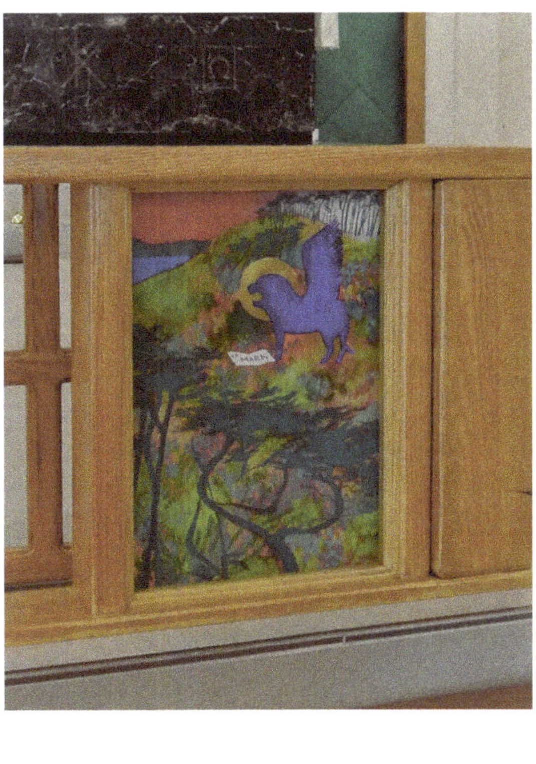

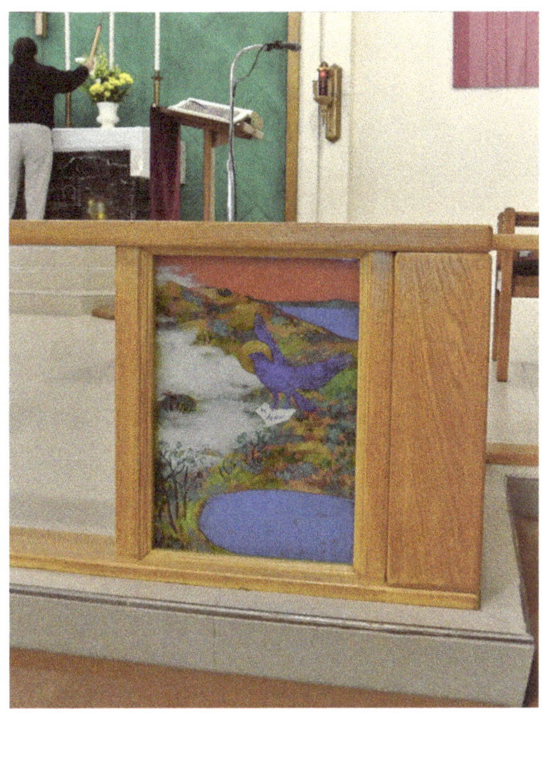

2014, Railing: oak, Paintings: acrylic and gold leaf on linen, San Francisco, CA
Design: Stefan Salinas and Toan Tieu, Paintings: Stefan Salinas
Carpentry and installation: Toan Tieu, with assistance from Tuan and Minh
Commissioned by Rev. Thuan V. Hoang and the Mothers Club of Church of the Visitation

In order to frame the sacred space, the pastor, Rev. Thuan Hoang, asked that I design an altar rail, and for it to include four panels featuring the Gospel writers: Luke, Matthew, Mark, and John. This was a daunting task, as aside from sculpture classes in school, I have never created a serious work of art or architectural structure in the third dimension. He wanted them in oak, in a style like the other wood furnishings: simple, mid-century modern. I dug into the research, and the carpenter who helped construct it, Toan Tieu, made a few critical measurement adjustments and added trim to the gates. The paintings are acrylic and gold leaf on linen, stretched over poplar panels. To protect them, as they are so low to the ground, thick, bullet-proof glass was installed in front of each.

The bold-colored stained glass windows feature San Franciscan architectural landmarks and bridges, something I have yet to see in another Catholic church's windows. They are in the chunk rock 1960s style, with vibrant blue skies. Coincidentally, Hogan Studios, which constructed the St. Francis window I designed, made these windows, as well as the windows in St. Stephen's Church, where a few more of my commissions are.

Early on, I knew I wanted to depict the Evangelists by their assigned symbols, but where to set the figures visually? One walk along the natural, rocky shore of Land's End gave me the inspiration. If the windows feature notable local architecture, the panels will portray the Bay Area's flora and fauna!

We enter from the Pacific Ocean to Land's End, then travel to Visitacion Valley, and finally to San Bruno Mountain, where we exit to the Bay at Brisbane (a nod to Our Lady of Guadalupe this parish's mission church).

The Holy Spirit in the icon over the holy oils is a white dove in silhouette as if it is a porthole from our realm to the light of the heavens, so these "messages" brought to us via the four Gospel writers similarly pierce through the curtain of the visible world. Silhouettes of deep blue symbolically stand for the Great Mystery; the Cosmos, God above and beyond our perception and understanding.

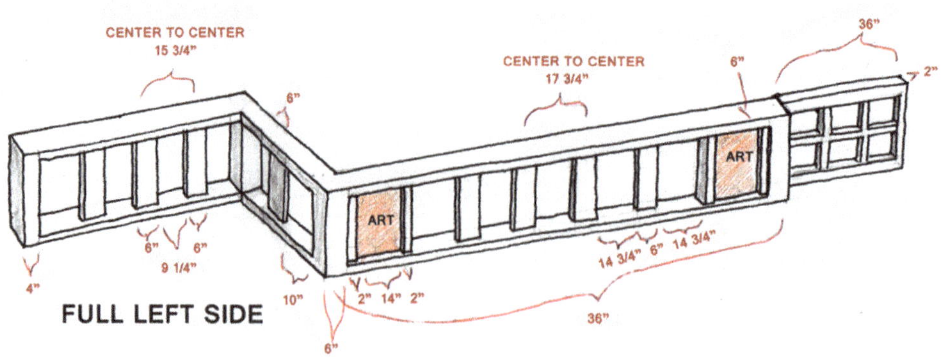

The Holy Spirit electrifies and invigorates the environment, and so I referenced technicolor techniques of the post-Impressionists and Fauvist painters.

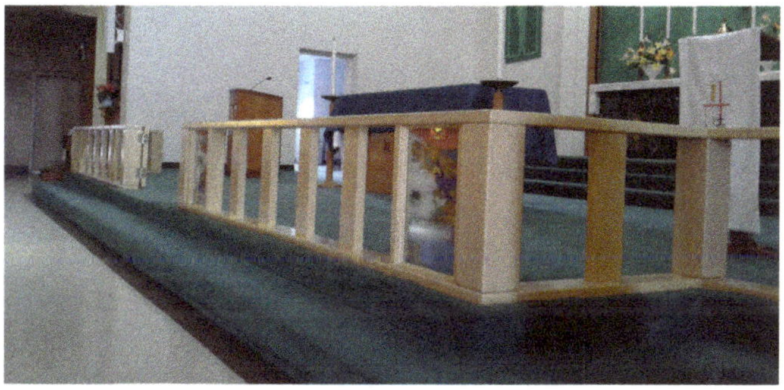

The skies in traditional iconography are usually gold but are occasionally red when referencing the resurrection (the cornerstone of our faith) and Pentecost (the birth of the Church). In icons, red can also be a substitute for the sun; gold. Water, long the symbol of spirituality and baptism, is a bright blue, alluding to Mary. I reserved the gold leaf for the halos.

And I did not forget about our San Franciscan fog. White, like the vestments on high holy days. It covers portions of the setting – a screen between this world and the Greater Unknown? The Great Veil had lifted...

In 1777, a party of Spanish soldiers and Franciscan friars traveling north to the Presidio in San Francisco became lost in a heavy fog and determined to camp overnight. They awoke the next morning to find a beautiful valley beneath their gaze. They named their discovery Visitacion Valley, *as the date was July 2, the Feast day of the Visitacion. According to lore, before continuing their journey, the priests offered a mass, using a large rock as their altar.*

- Visitacion Valley History Project 2005

The sole man-made structure depicted in the paintings is the original Visitacion church building, and on that same panel is that rock-turned-altar in the foreground.

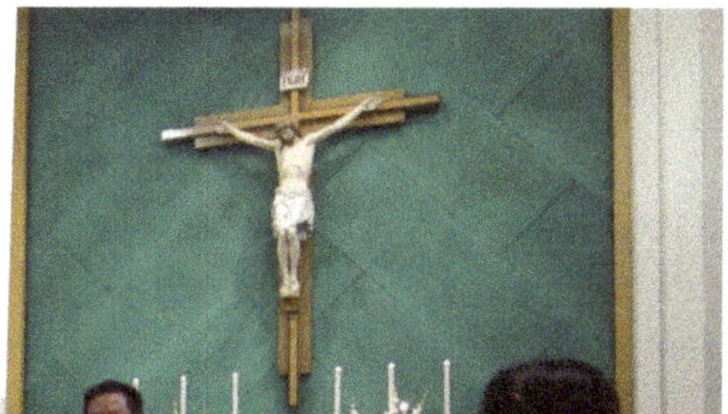

This was a challenging, enriching, and rewarding experience. It was an honor to collaborate with Fr. Thuan in elevating the spiritual environment within which parishioners pray and worship.

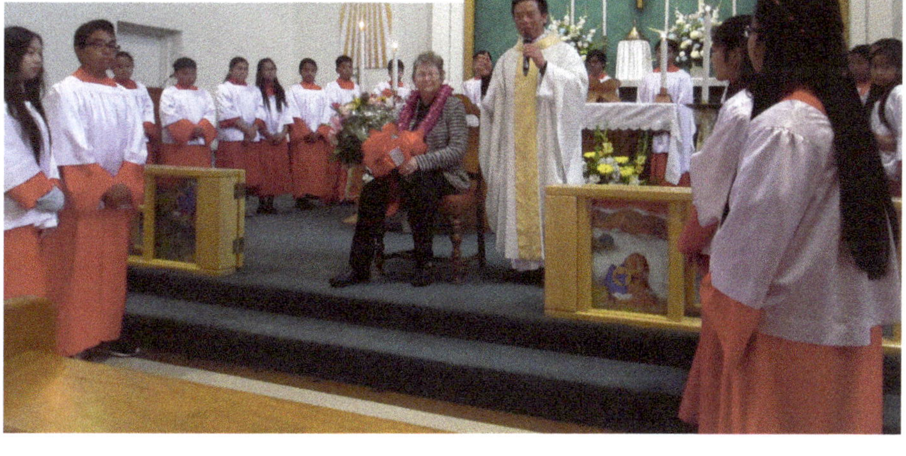

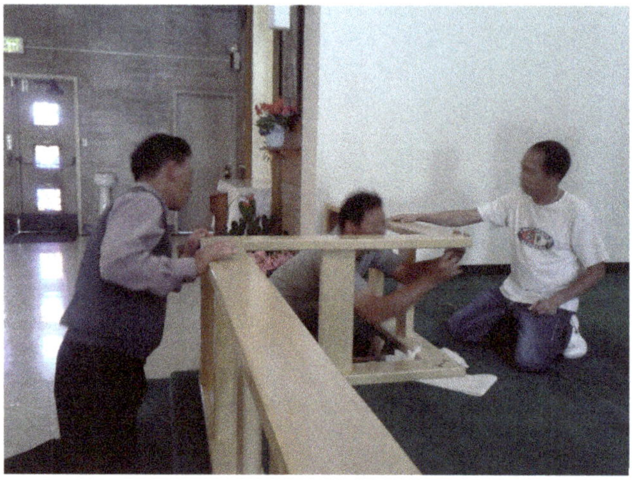

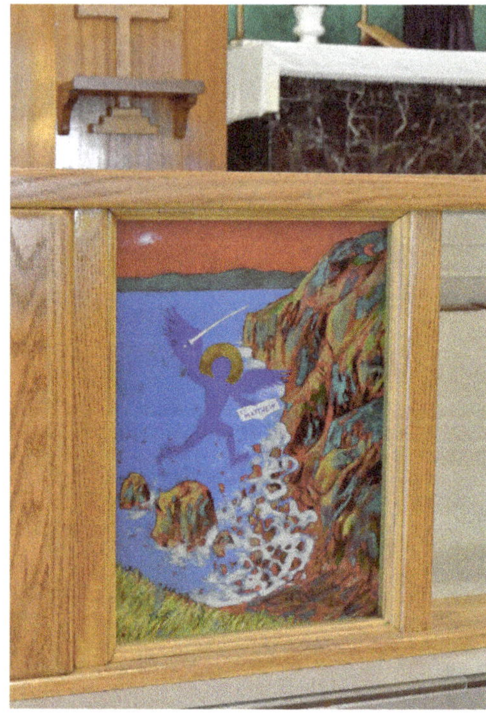

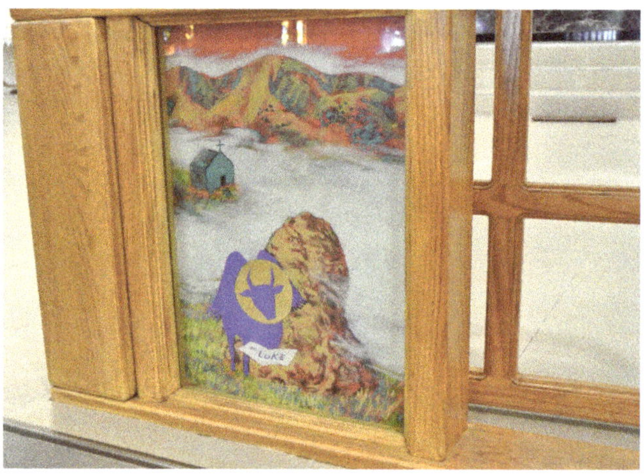
LUKE

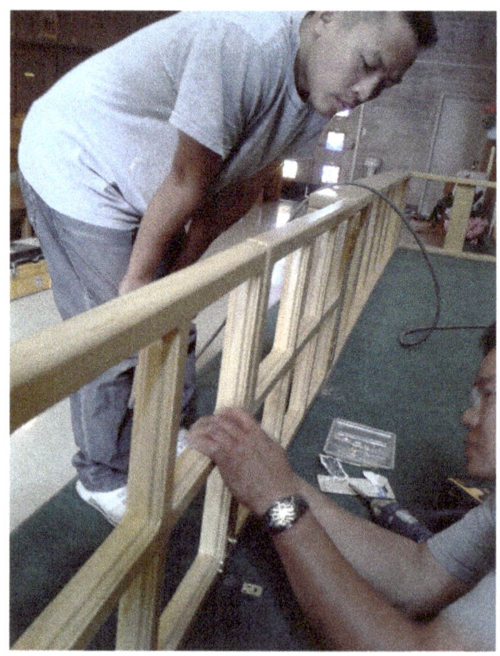

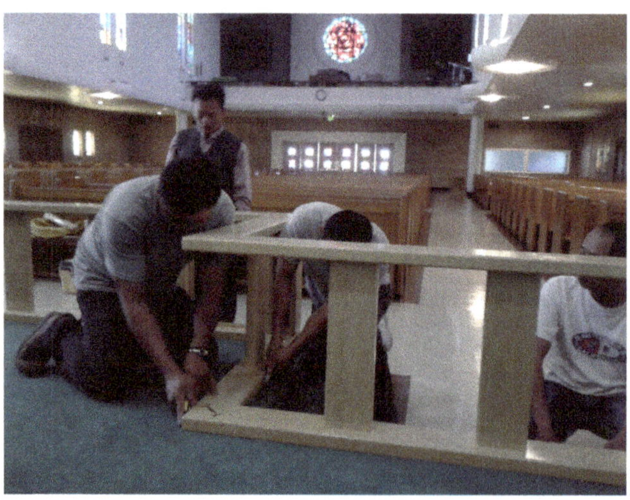

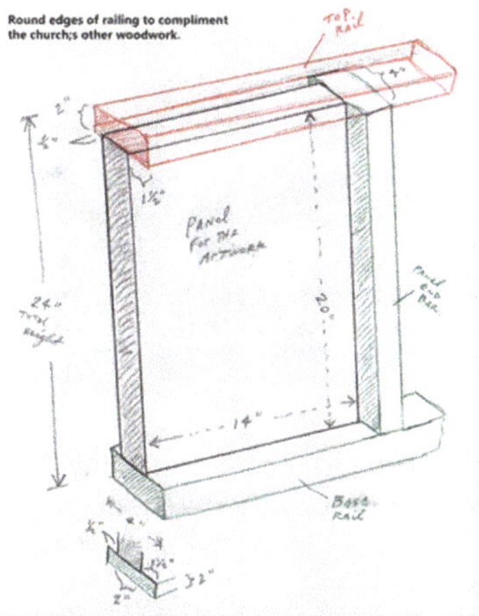

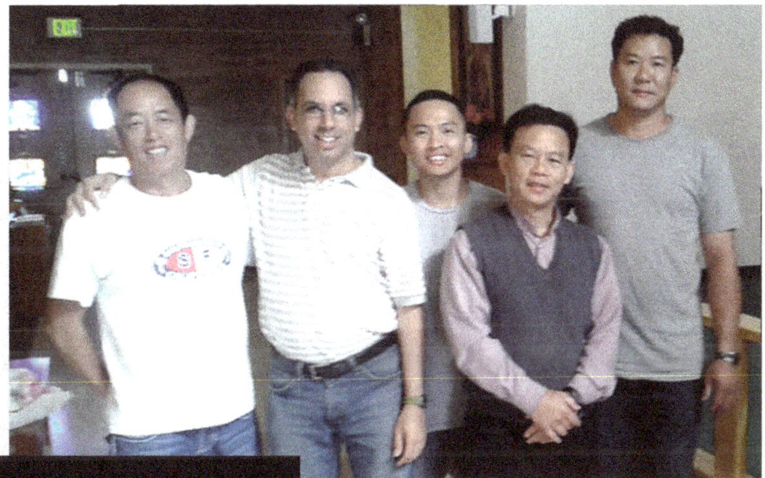

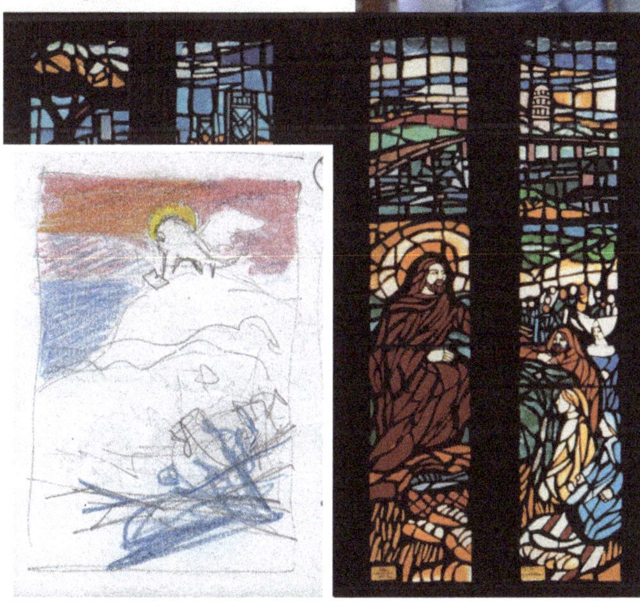

The stained glass windows, which feature San Franciscan architectural landmarks.

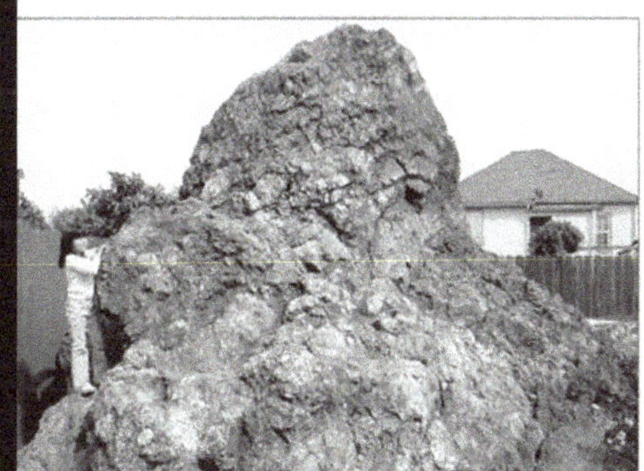

(Courtesy Russel Morine.)

The large rock European settlers used as an altar.

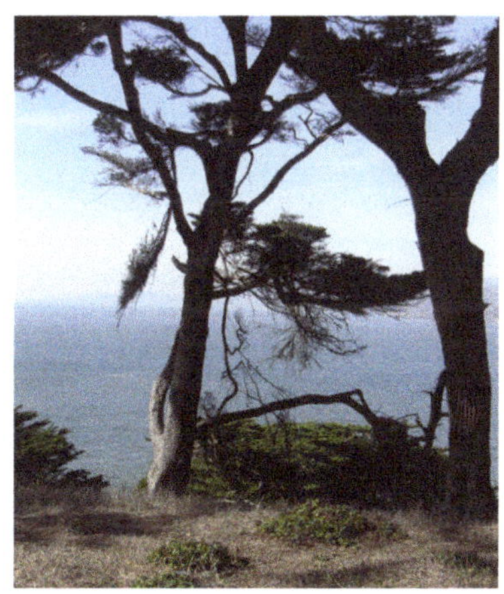

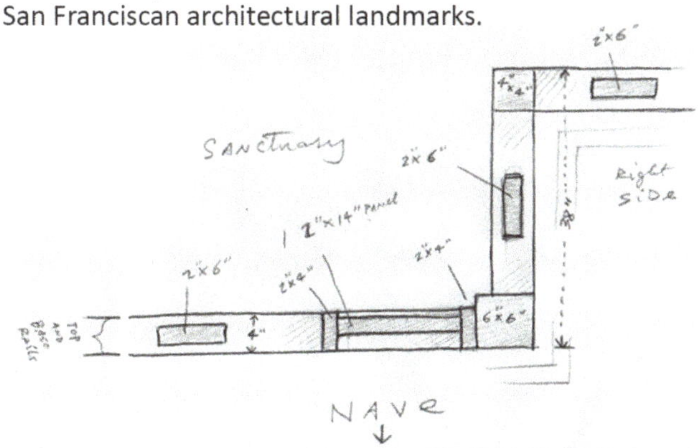

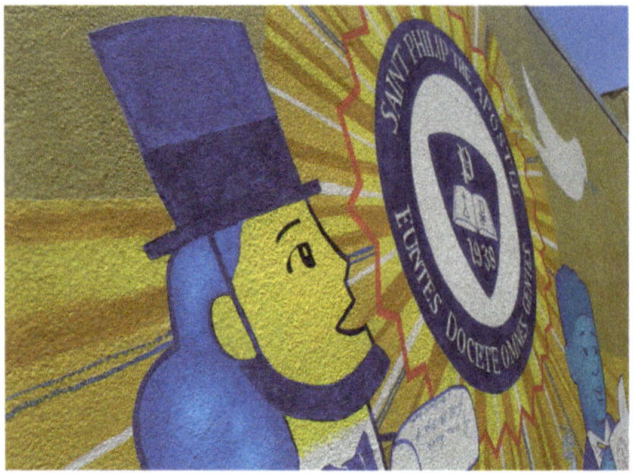
SAINT PHILIP THE APOSTLE
1938
EUNTES DOCETE OMNES GENTES

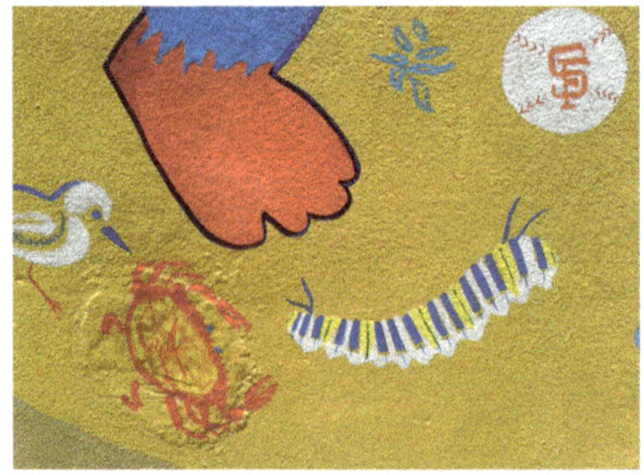

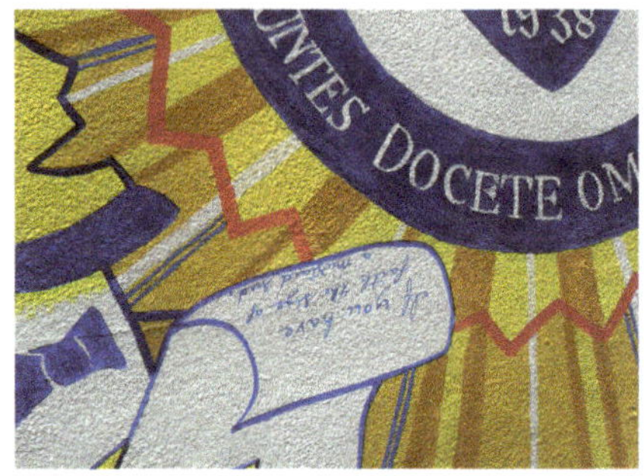
EUNTES DOCETE

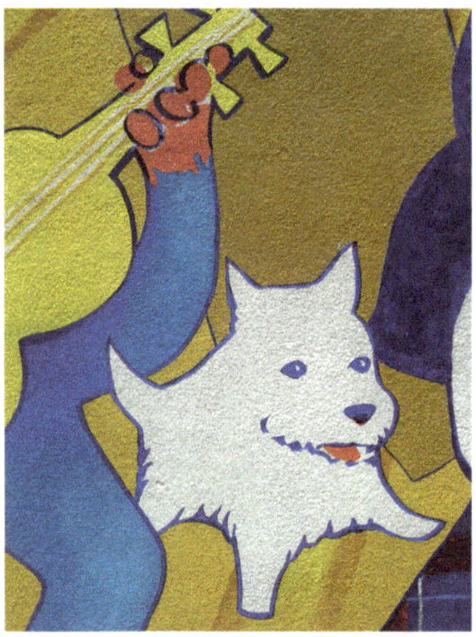

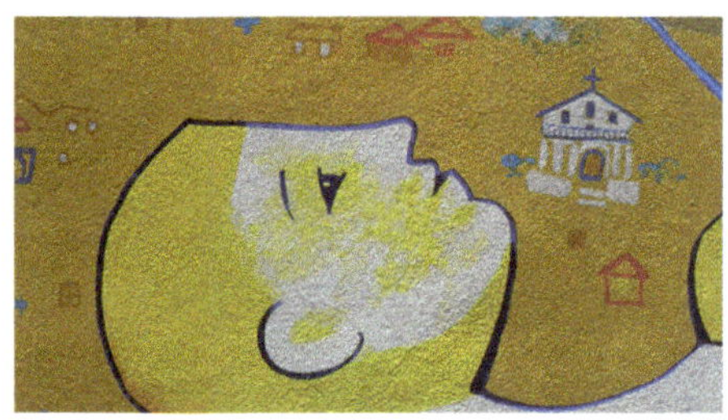

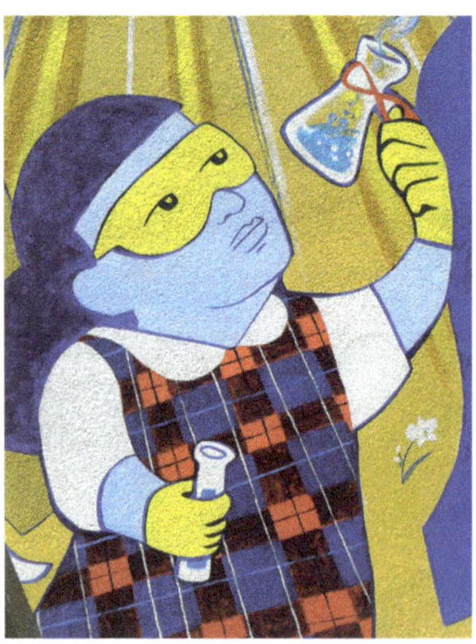

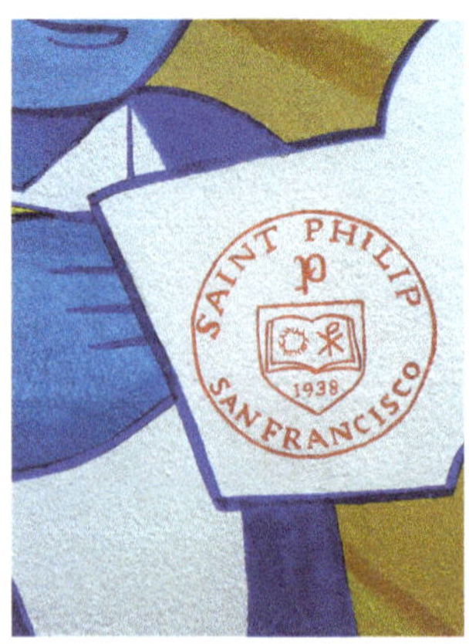
SAINT PHILIP
1938
SAN FRANCISCO

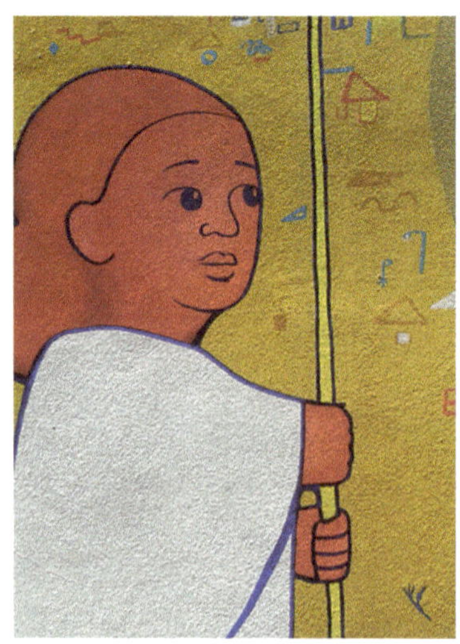

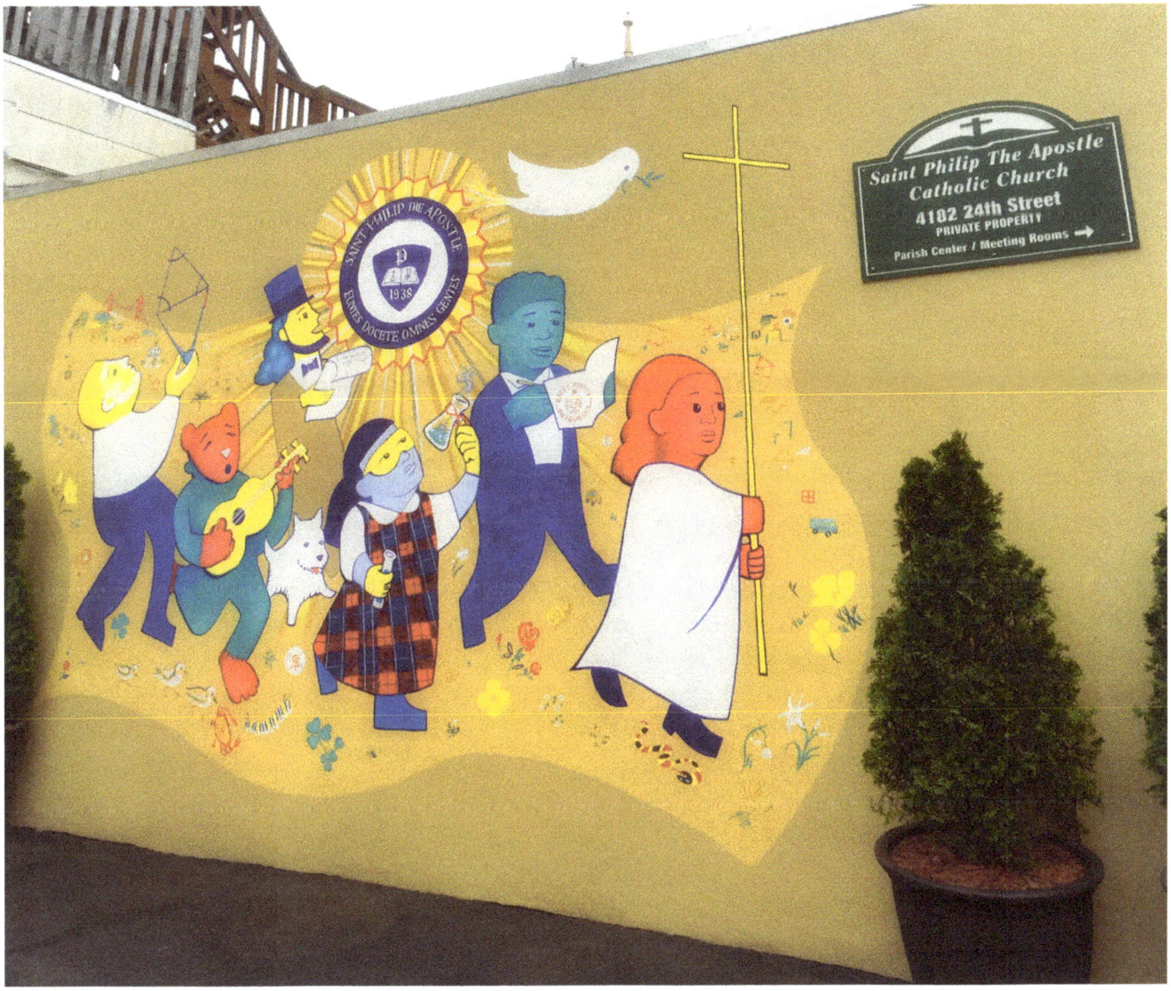

St. Philip the Apostle School Mural

2015, Acrylic mural paint,
San Francisco, CA
Paints from Precita Eyes
Commissioned by Rev. Tony LaTorre

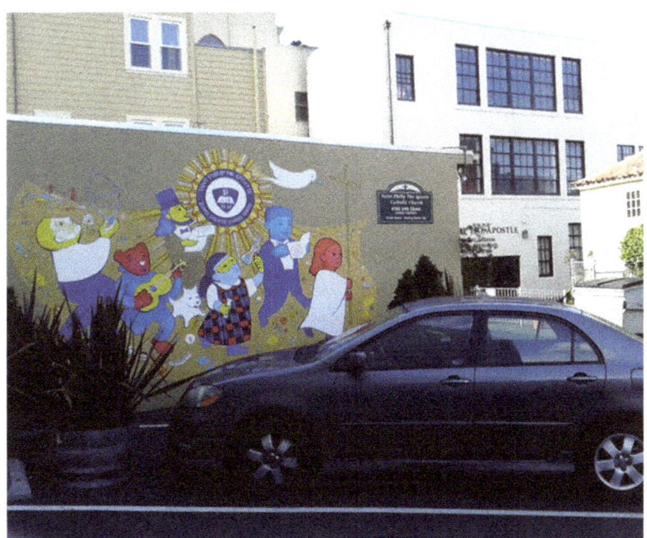

The schools disciplines and arts are all represented by children in a procession.

Faith instruction leads, followed by literature, science, history, the arts (the mask is a face of a bruin -

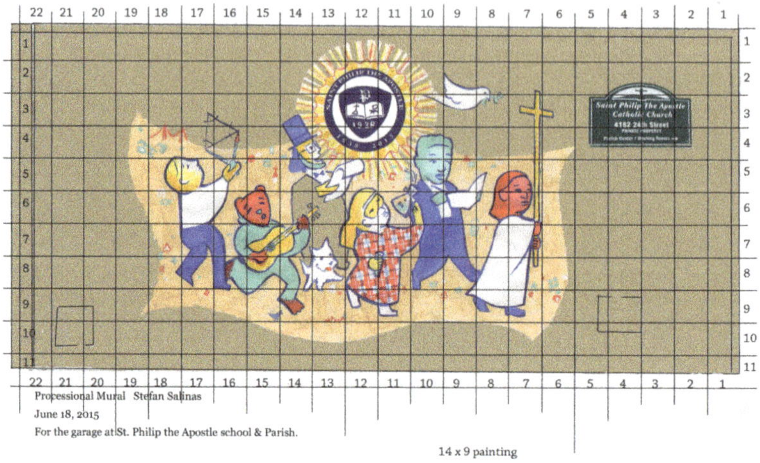

an English folk term for *brown bear* - the school's mascot) and mathematics. The girl carrying the cross is stepping over a snake, a visual reference to images of the Virgin Mary stepping on the serpent. Other flora, fauna and architecture is local. A crab with the initials *SLT* in cursive on it represents Fr. Tony's relative's seafood restaurant, Sabella and LaTorre, down at Fisherman's Wharf. Somehow, his dog Tennessee leapt into the mural.

The scripture on the document the student dressed as Lincoln is from the Gospel of Matthew, when Jesus said to his skeptical apostles,

"Amen, I say to you, if you have faith the size of a mustard seed, you will say to this mountain, 'Move from here to there,' and it will move. Nothing will be impossible for you."

– Matthew 17:20

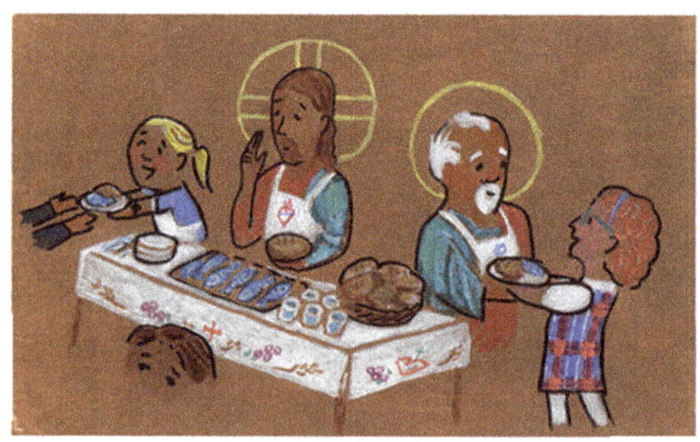

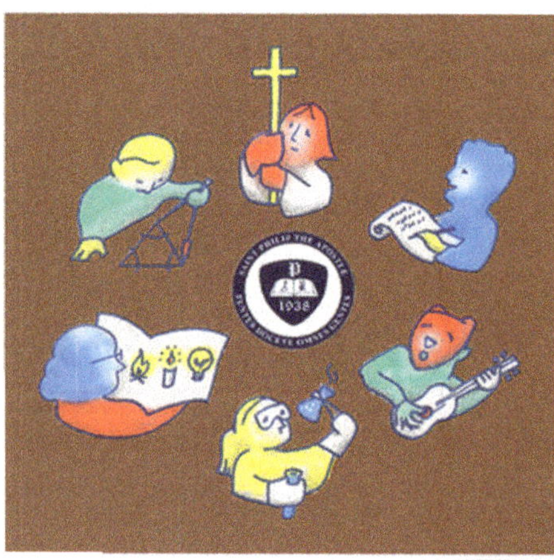

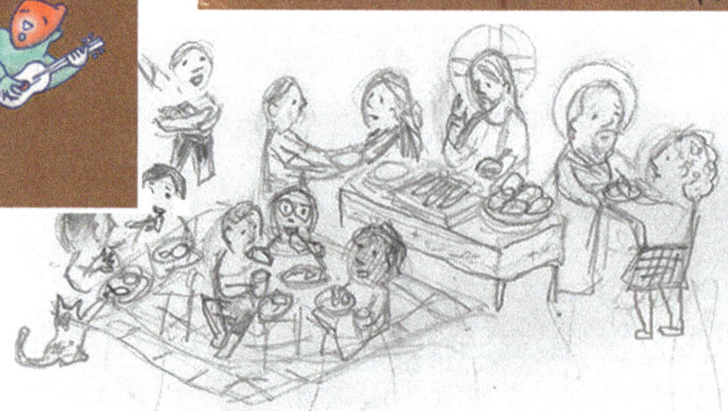

The Visitation Tile Mural
Church of the Visitacion

2015, Ceramic tile and cement, San Francisco, CA
Tile creation: Tile Mural Creative Arts, Tile installation: Jesus Lara
Wall construction & design: Jesus Lara, Miguel Campos & Stefan Salinas
Commissioned by Rev. Thuan V. Hoang and the Mothers Club of Church of the Visitacion

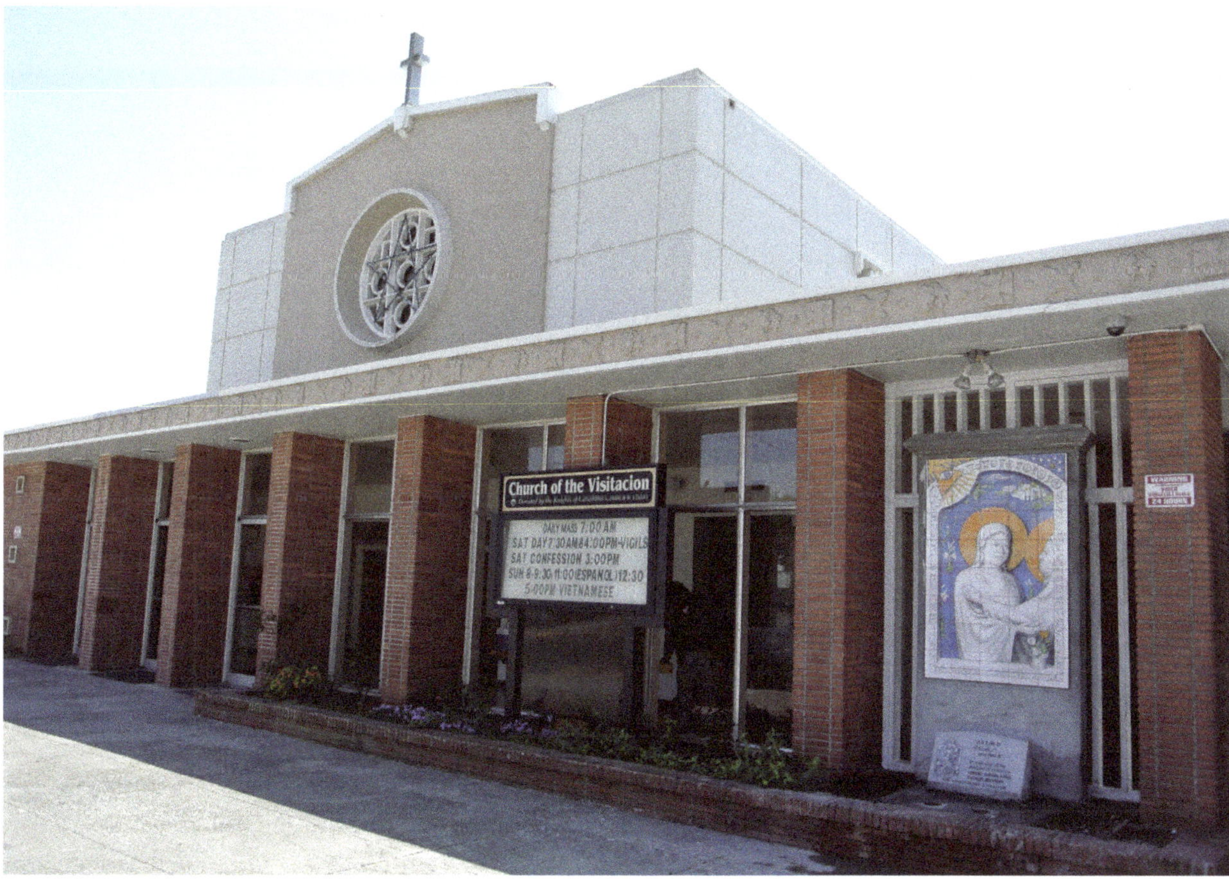

Luke 1:39-45 Mary Visits Elizabeth

At that time Mary got ready and hurried to a town in the hill country of Judea, where she entered Zechariah's home and greeted Elizabeth. When Elizabeth heard Mary's greeting, the baby leaped in her womb, and Elizabeth was filled with the Holy Spirit. In a loud voice she exclaimed:

"Blessed are you among women, and blessed is the child you will bear! But why am I so favored, that the mother of my Lord should come to me? As soon as the sound of your greeting reached my ears, the baby in my womb leaped for joy. Blessed is she who has believed that the Lord would fulfill his promises to her!"

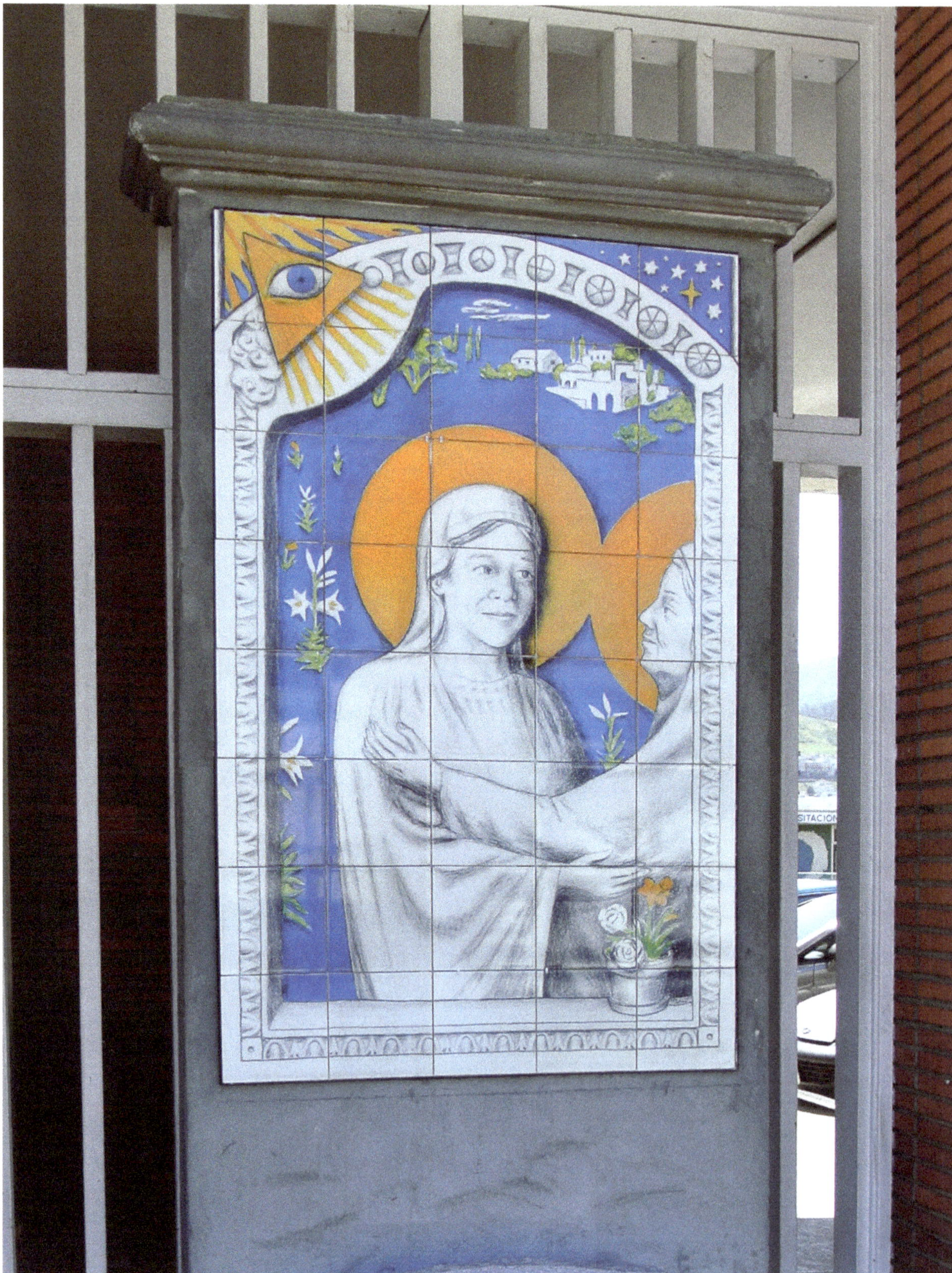

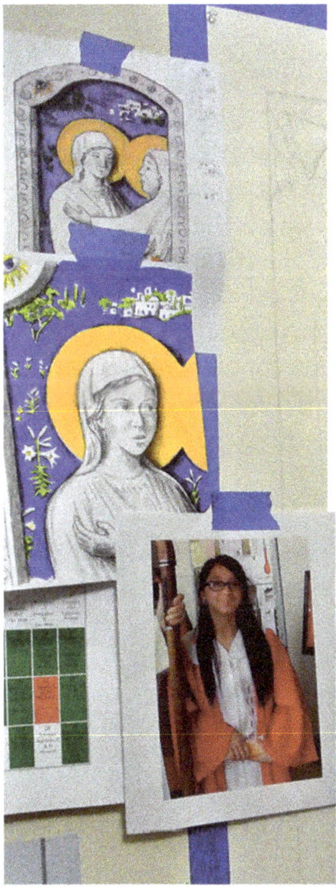

Here we have a printed tile mural proposal to accompany a very modern church structure. What ceramic and pottery adornments outside church buildings have we to look to for inspiration?

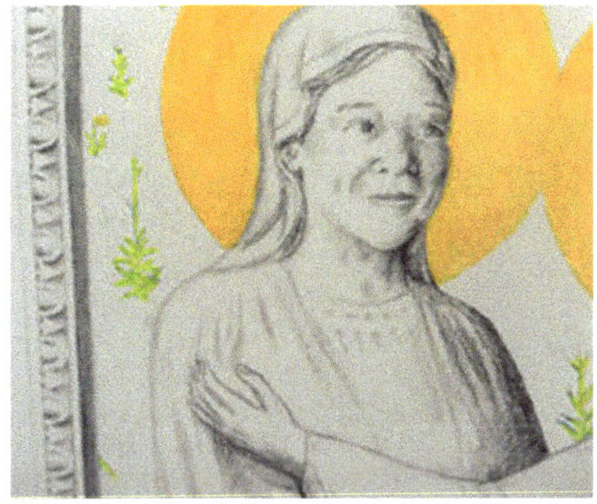

Very striking examples can be found in Italy and date from the fifteenth century: for instance, the glazed terracotta works of Luca della Robbia. With the gentle, classically posed figures and compositions, glazed in palettes usually limited to two to five colors, the tableaus sit well with tradition and yet are bold and easy to read from a distance. I felt that referencing clayware for porcelain tile work was apropos.

Charcoal and acrylic on paper, scanned, then sent to the tile manufacturer.

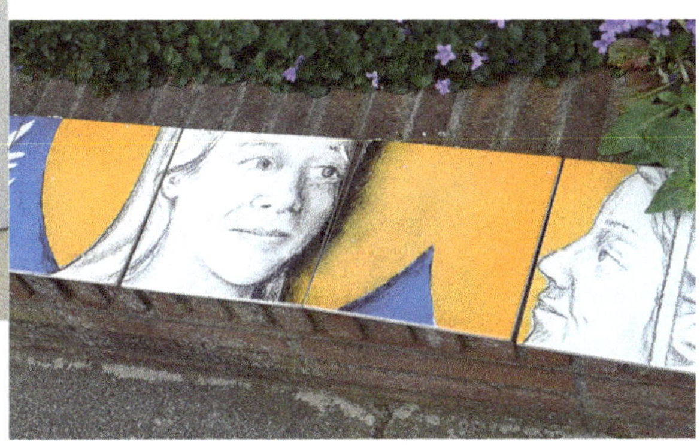

Plus, employing the European technique of trompe l'oeil and having the pop art movement of the 1960s somewhere in my mind (since the church that stands today was erected in the 1950s, with windows made within the next few decades), it all came together.

And now for the rest of the elements.

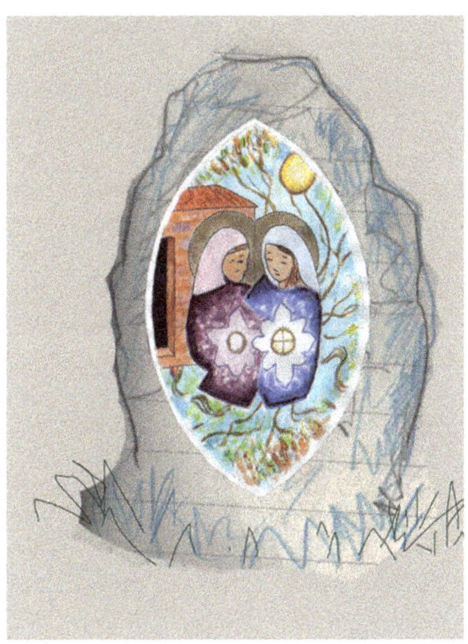

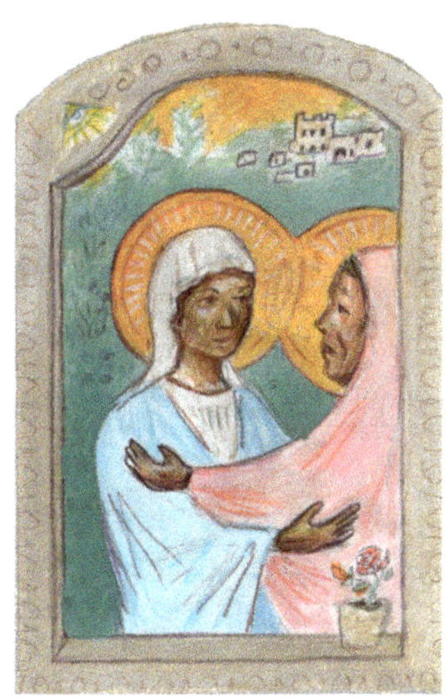

God the Father is represented by the *Eye of God* at the upper left corner, shining down upon Mary (the Eye-within-Trinity symbol predates the Freemasons, as it is in paintings and churches dating back to the early sixteenth century). The sun is backing the triangle, as there are many

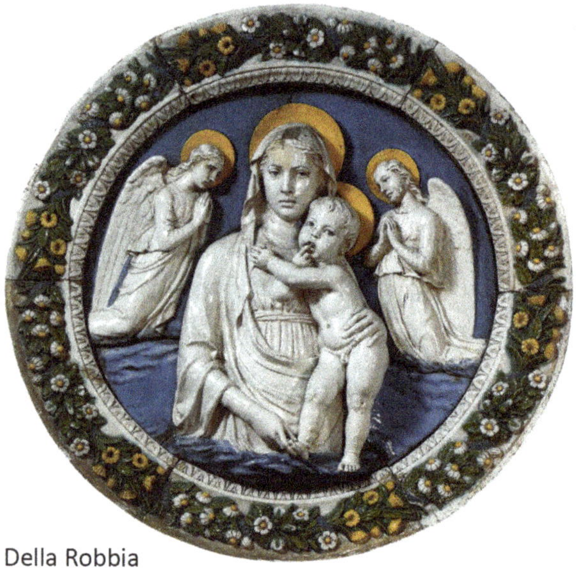

Della Robbia
ceramic example

references to Christ, God, and the Holy Spirit as being sun-like. To the right is the starry sky, with the Star of Bethlehem shining brightly. Across the top, starting from the corner of the Eye of God (have you heard the saying "when you were just a twinkle in your father's eye"?) are seven spheres, relating to the seven days of creation. Each is divided into more sections, and the sphere's increase in size, alluding to a human zygote developing and traveling through the fallopian tube. White roses stand for Mary's purity. In early Christian art, the Angel Gabriel offers pure white lilies to the Virgin Mary, and this symbolizes that she will be the mother of Jesus.

Purity; hope; life; Easter. Daffodils signify eternal life, the resurrection. The egg and dart motif (in the frame) is a pattern that has been in use from ancient Greek times, through the Renaissance, and to the present day. It is a design celebrating life and death, the life cycle.

The porcelain tiles were created by Tile Mural Creative Arts in Calabasas, CA. They have been kiln-fired at 1,800 degrees, able to withstand the elements for decades to come.

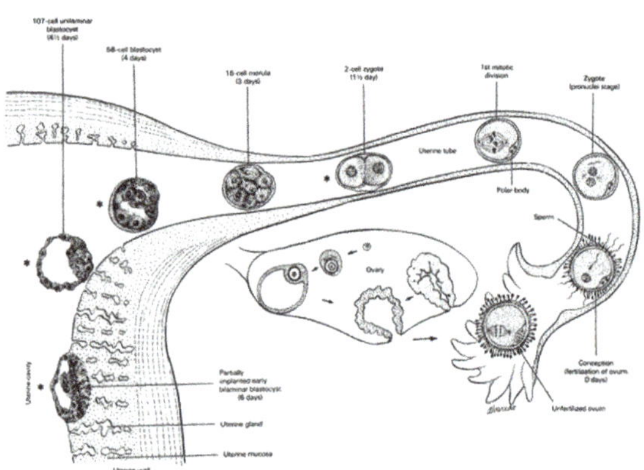

A zygote traveling through the fallopian tube.

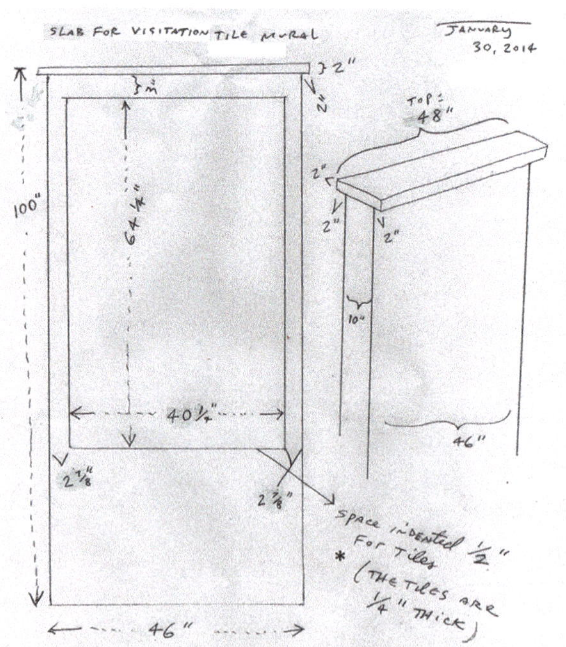

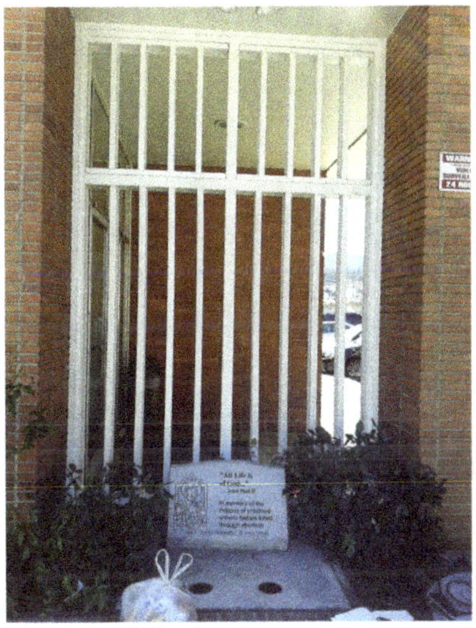

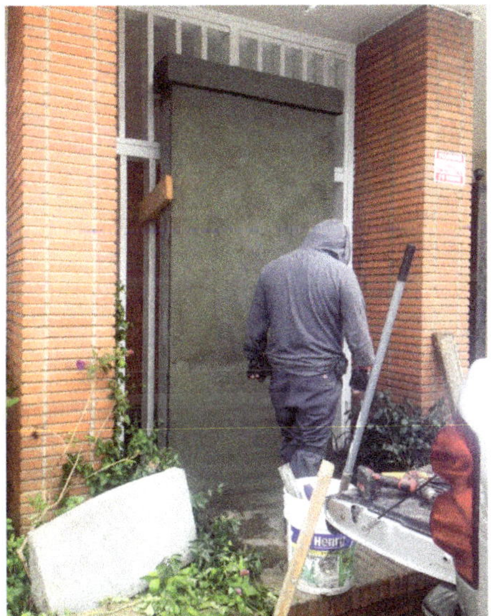

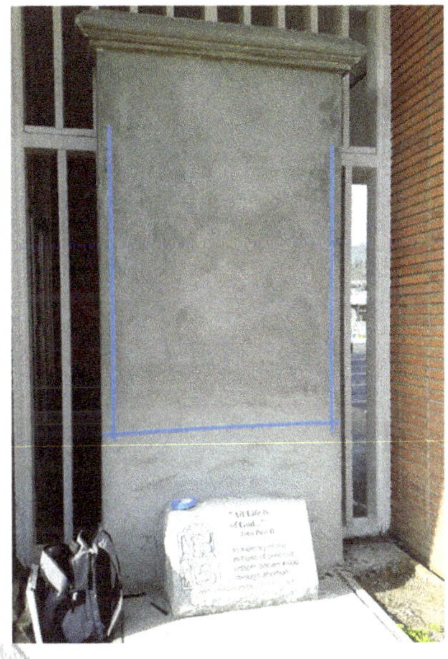

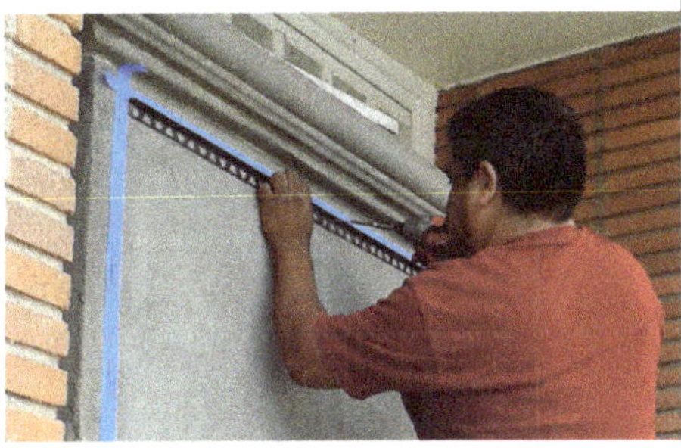

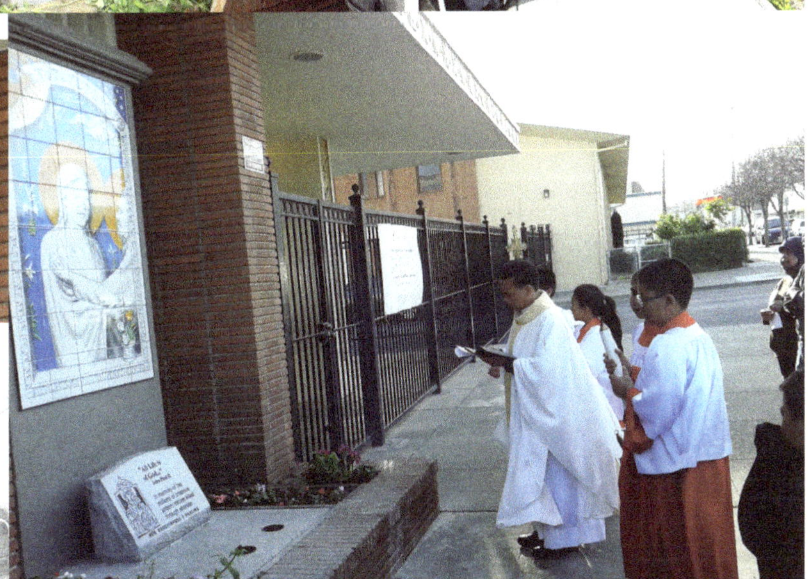

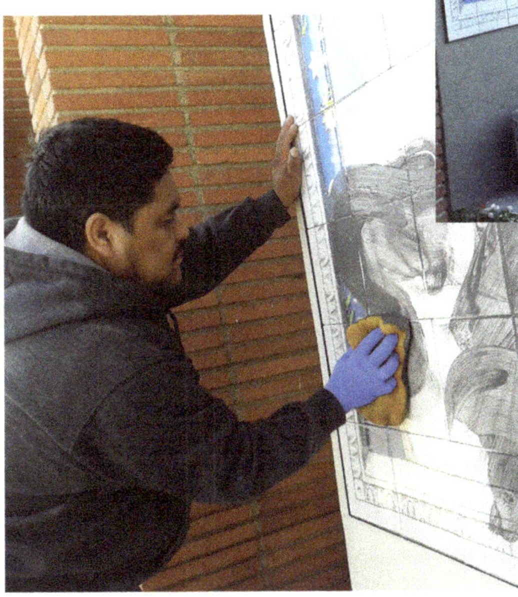

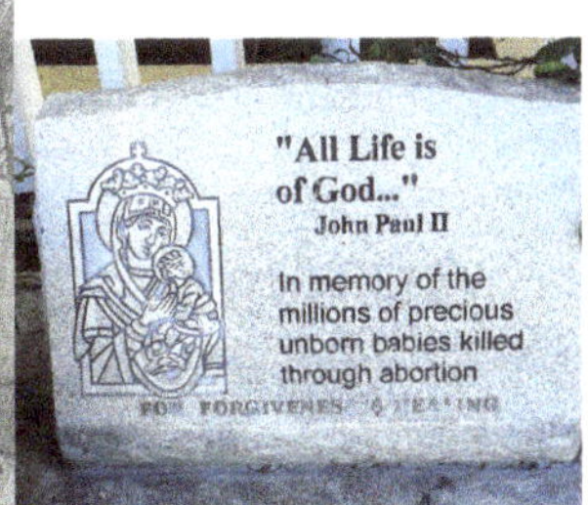
"All Life is of God..."
John Paul II
In memory of the millions of precious unborn babies killed through abortion

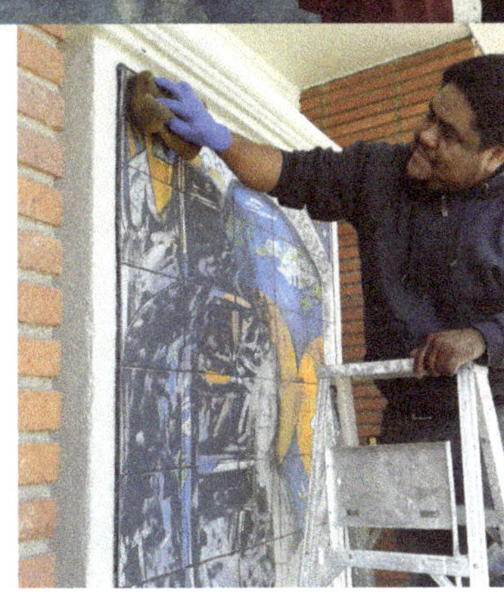

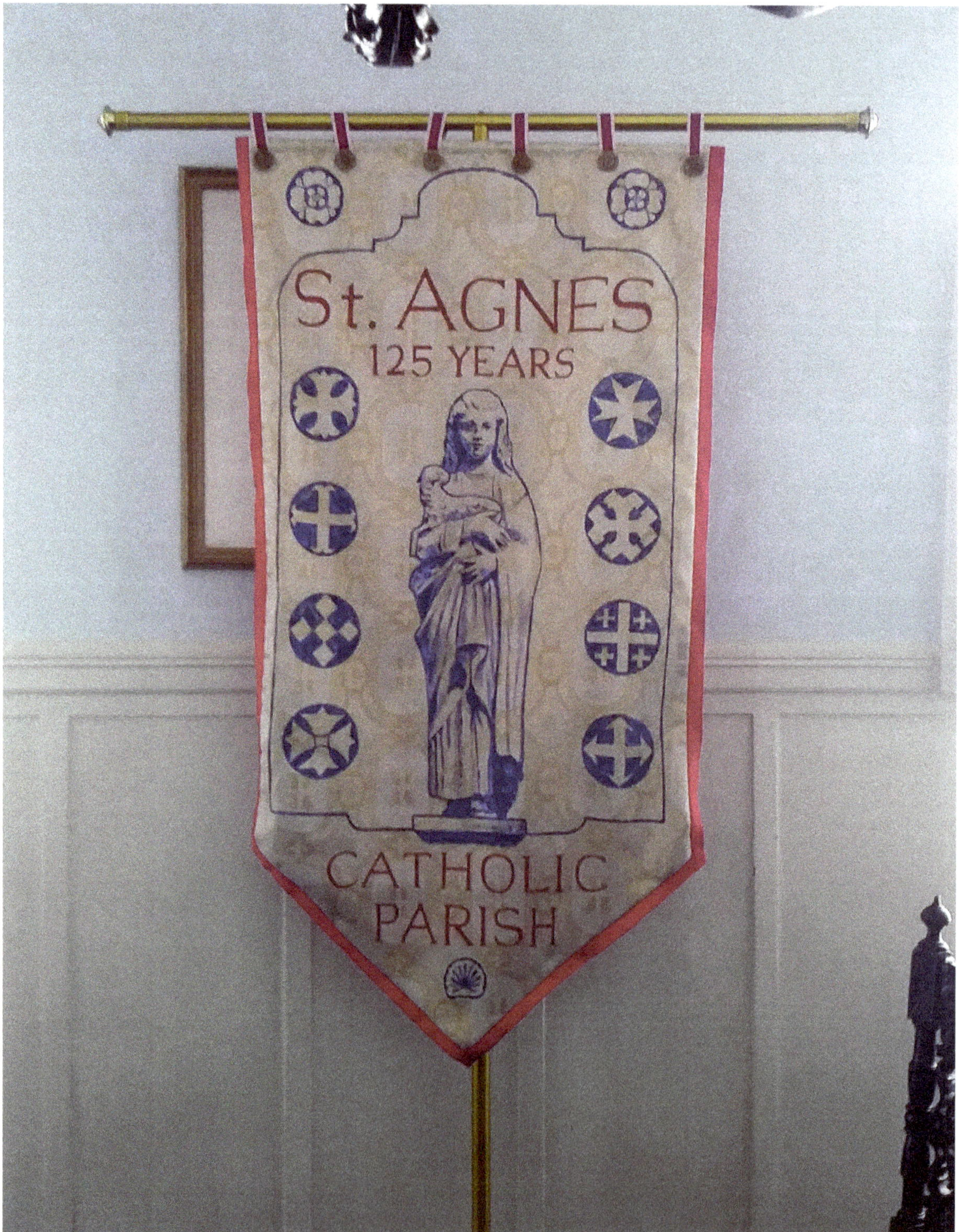
St. AGNES
125 YEARS
CATHOLIC
PARISH

St. Agnes' 125th Anniversary Processional Banner, St. Agnes Catholic Parish

2018, Acrylic on fabric, San Francisco, CA
Tailors: Quong Sing Shop & Stefan Salinas
Commissioned by Christine Morris and the parish
Project leader: Christine Morris

Christina Morris, a staff member at St. Agnes parish, saw a display of mine at the main library for my book *A Muslim Family's Chair for the Pope* and contacted me for a project. You never know what one work of art will lead to. They were preparing for celebrating the parish's 125th anniversary, and a processional banner was in order.

I have created painted banners and cloth backdrops in the past. Most of them were for political protests and backdrops for non-profit benefits. This, however, was the first fabric liturgical art for me. The tailors at Quong Sing Shop cut and stitched the main body together, and I fashioned hanging loops. The depiction of St. Agnes holding the Lamb of God is one I took from a statue on the church's original entrance façade. The geometric cross variations were from designs on the choir loft wall. Fuchsia trim and backing were inspired by the dusty pink ceiling.

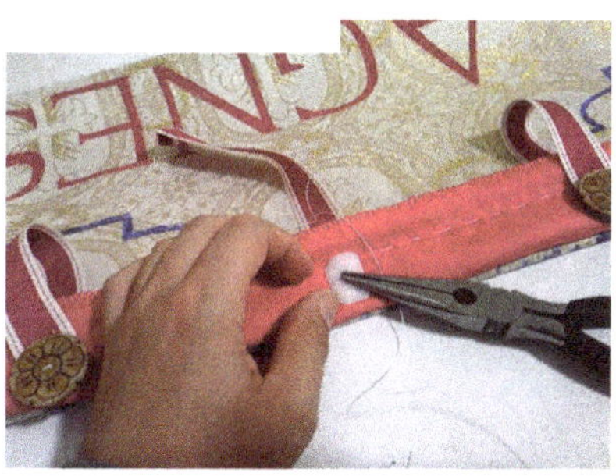

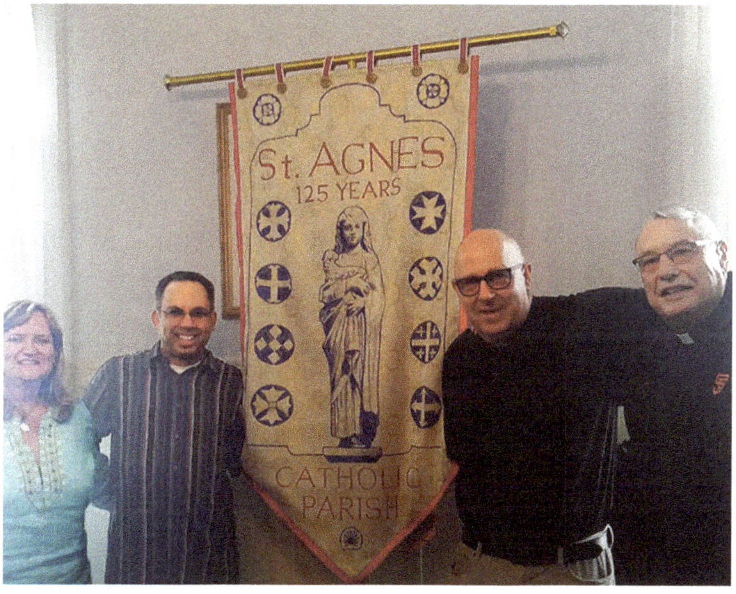

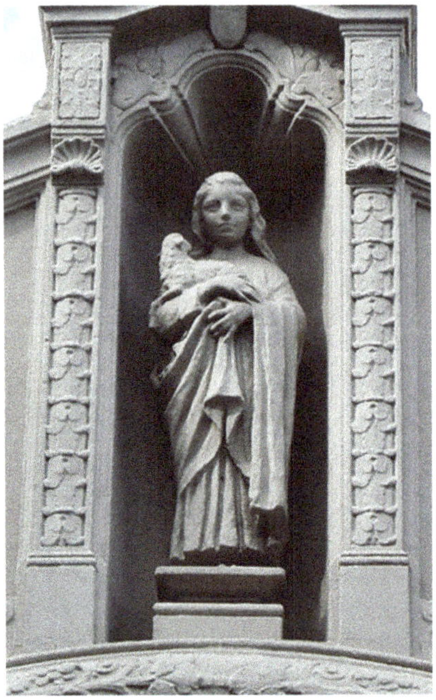

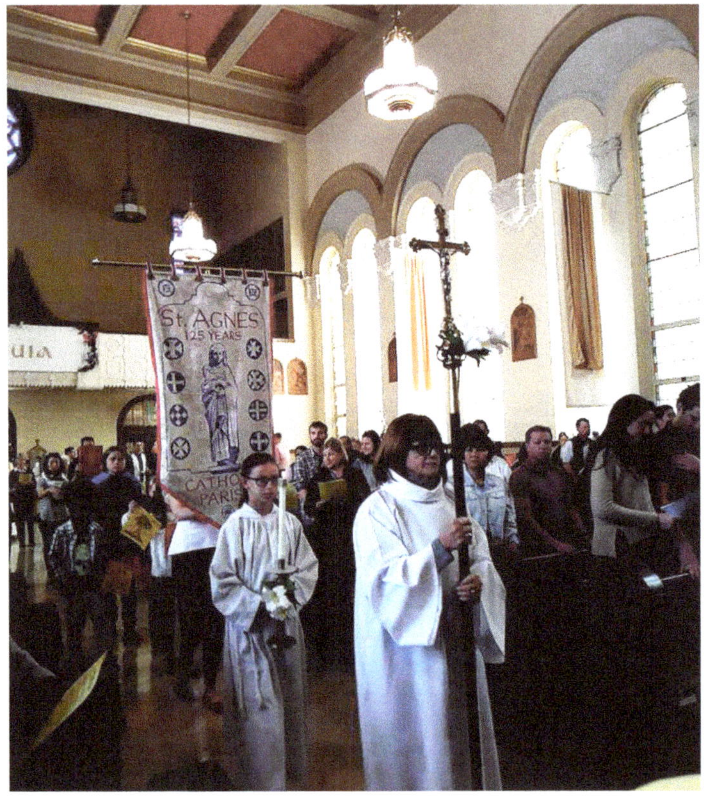
St. AGNES
125 YEARS

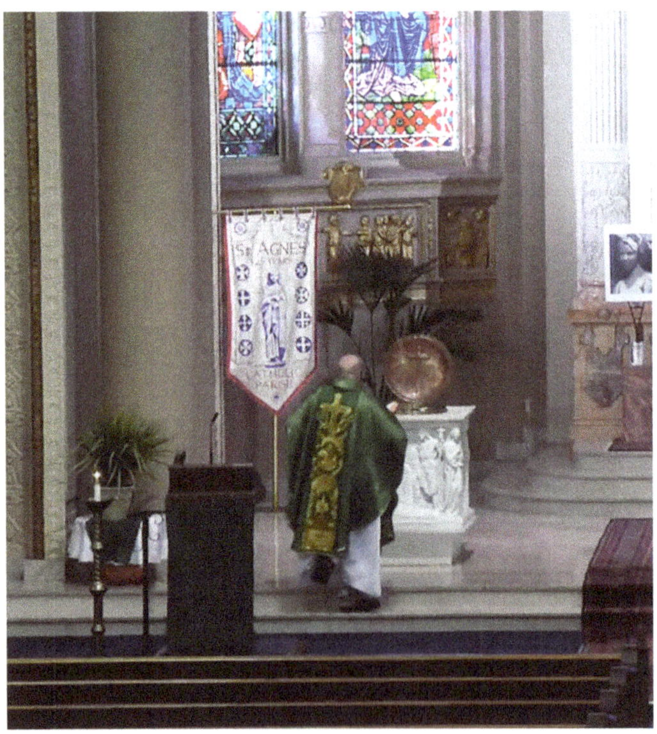

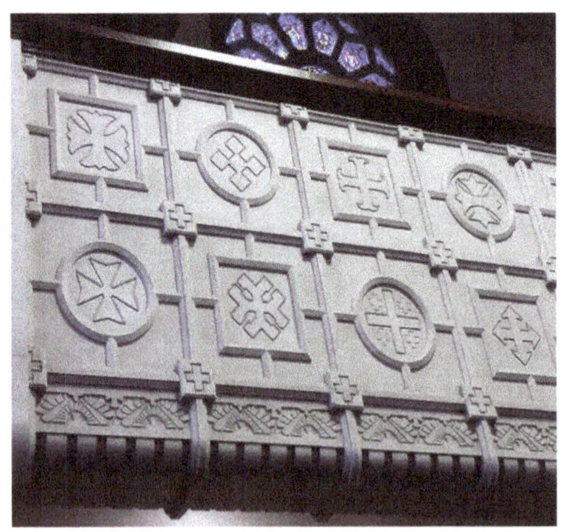

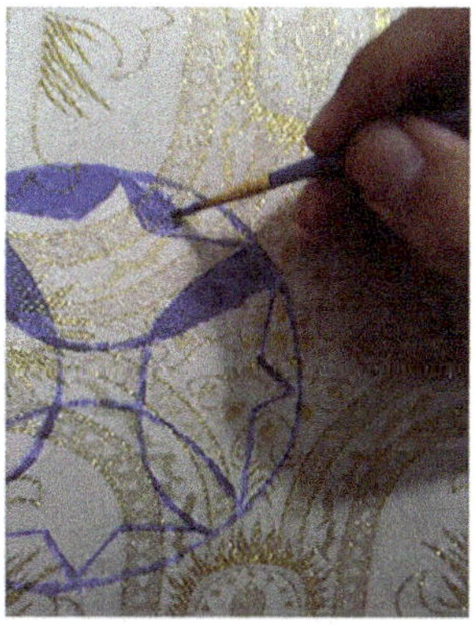

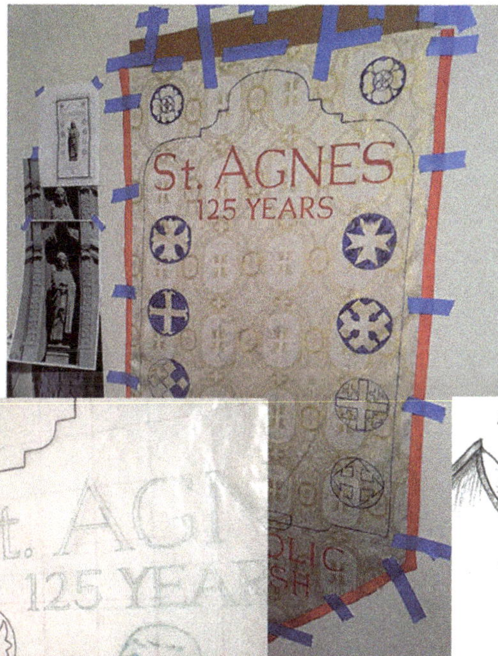

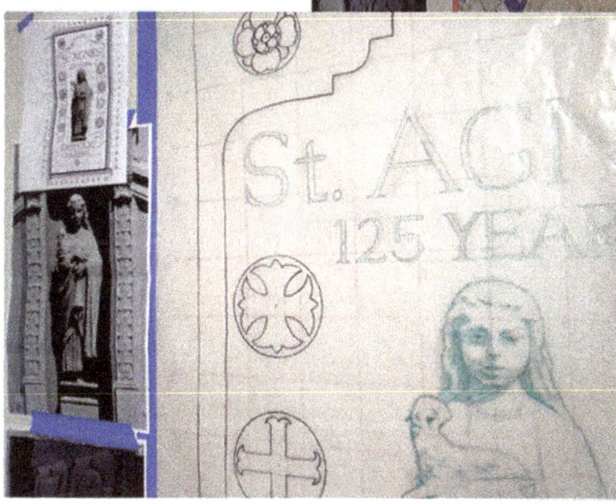

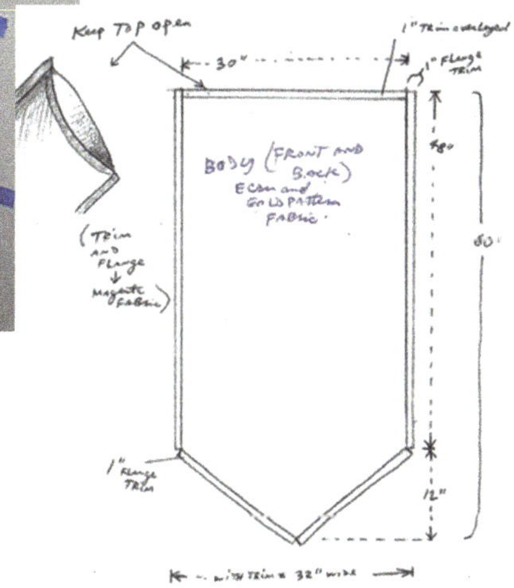

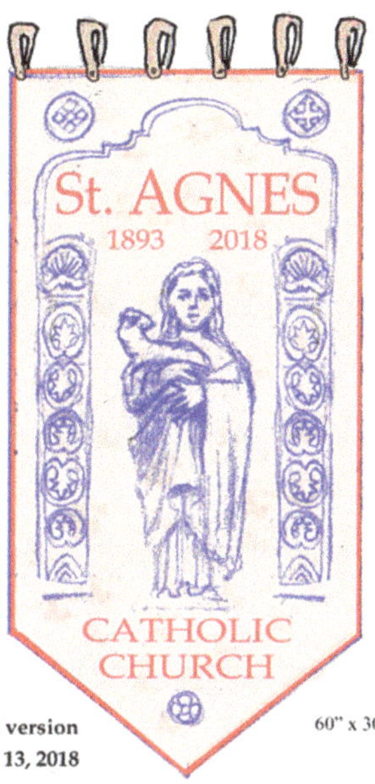

2nd version
Feb 13, 2018

60" x 30"

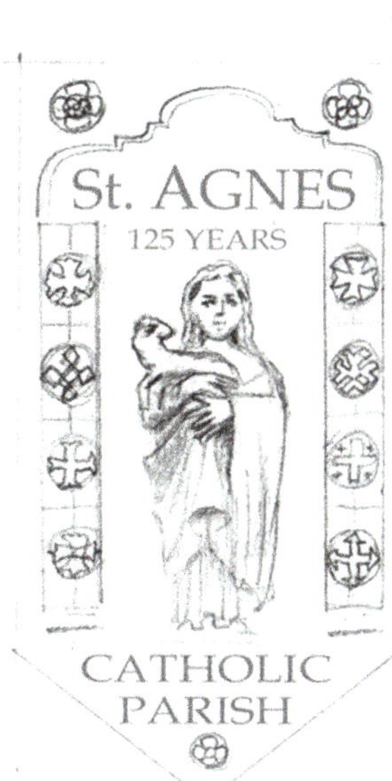

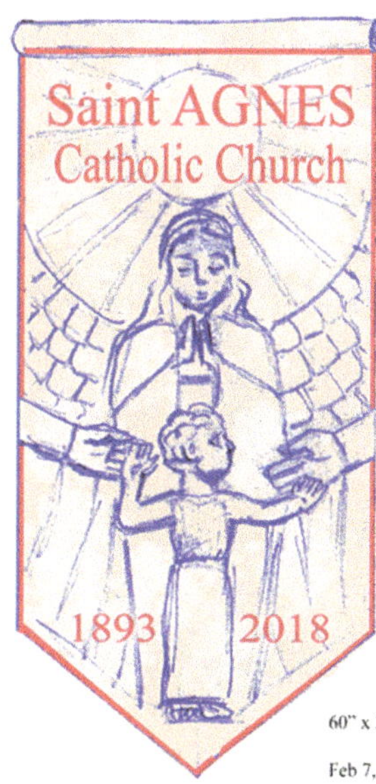

60" x 30"

Feb 7, 2018

St. Agnes Quasquicentennial Processional Banner Sketch

Peace Earth Mandala
World Peace Vigil
Ignatian Spiritual Life Center

2016, Acrylic on board
San Francisco, CA

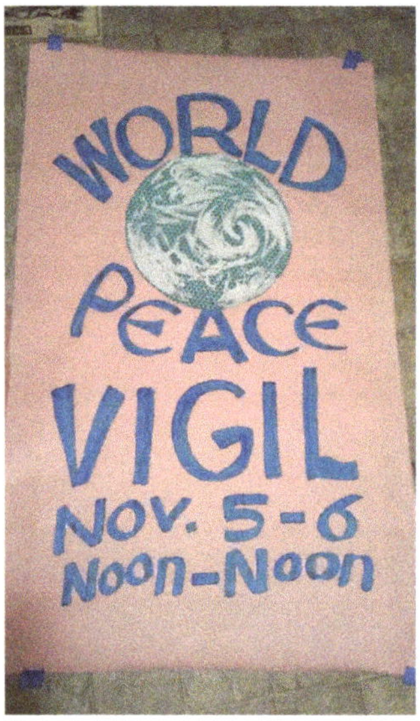

The center is connected with St. Agnes Parish. I was invited to help present to the congregation a prayer flag project, for all to paint their own flag. They were then hung on the property. Prayer flags can be found in various spiritual traditions, from Ireland to Japan to India. Alongside this was a peace vigil, which this mandala was made for. The parish is welcoming and inclusive to all, and is nestled within the East-meets-West cultural Haight District. Tibetan and Indian paintings, along with European gothic geometric patterns, informed the design.

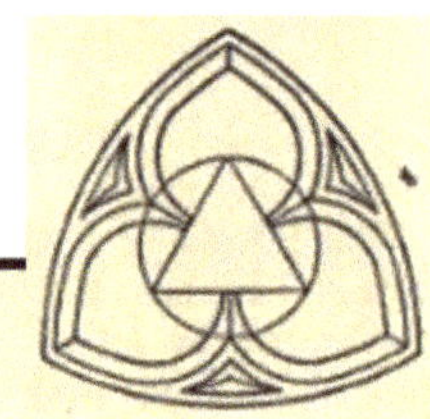

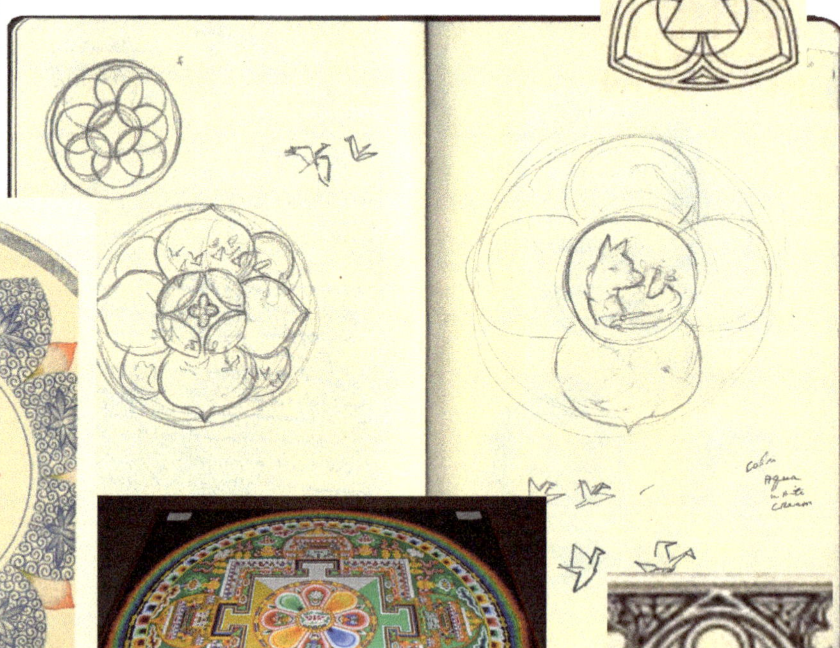

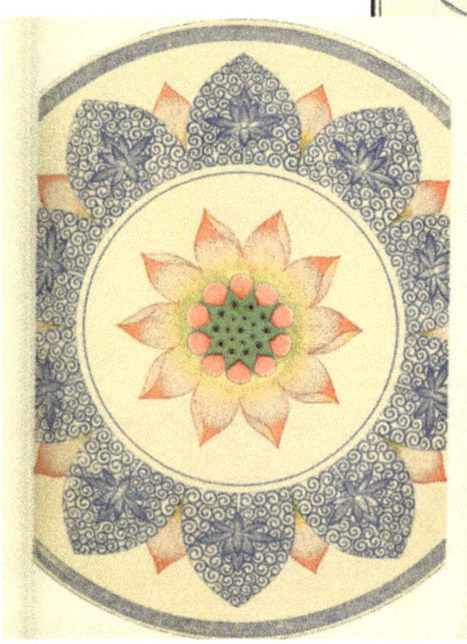

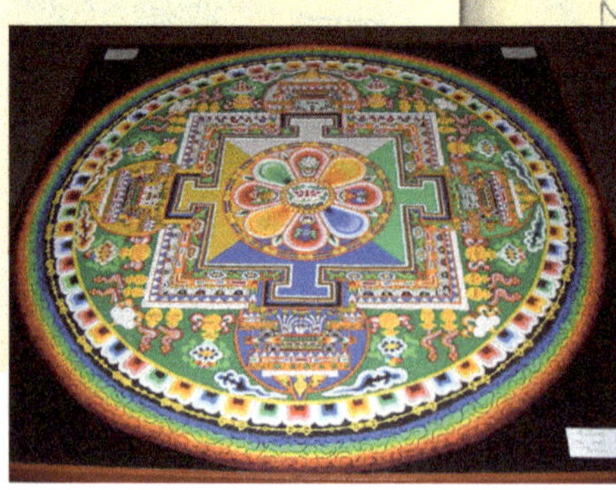

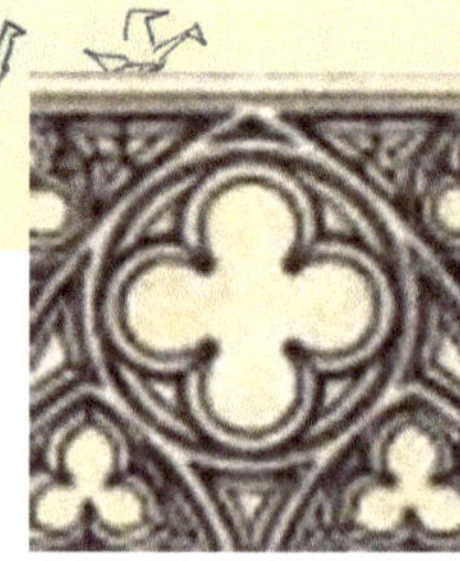

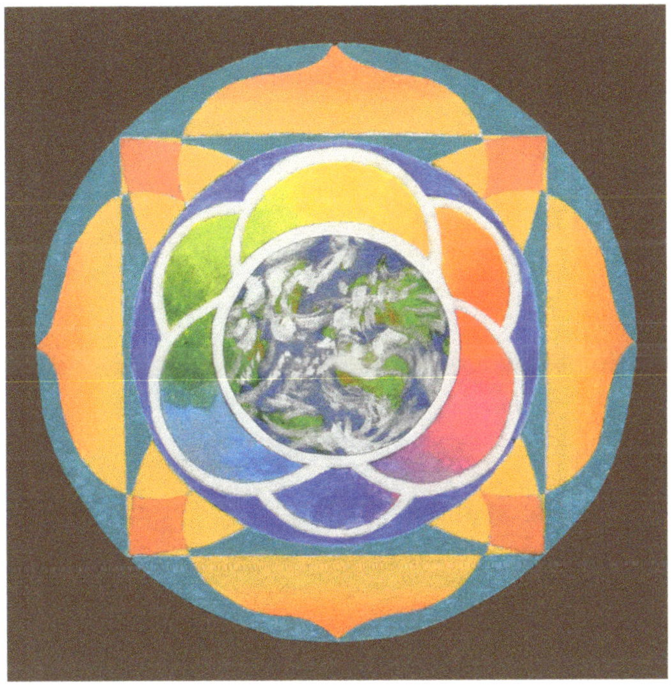

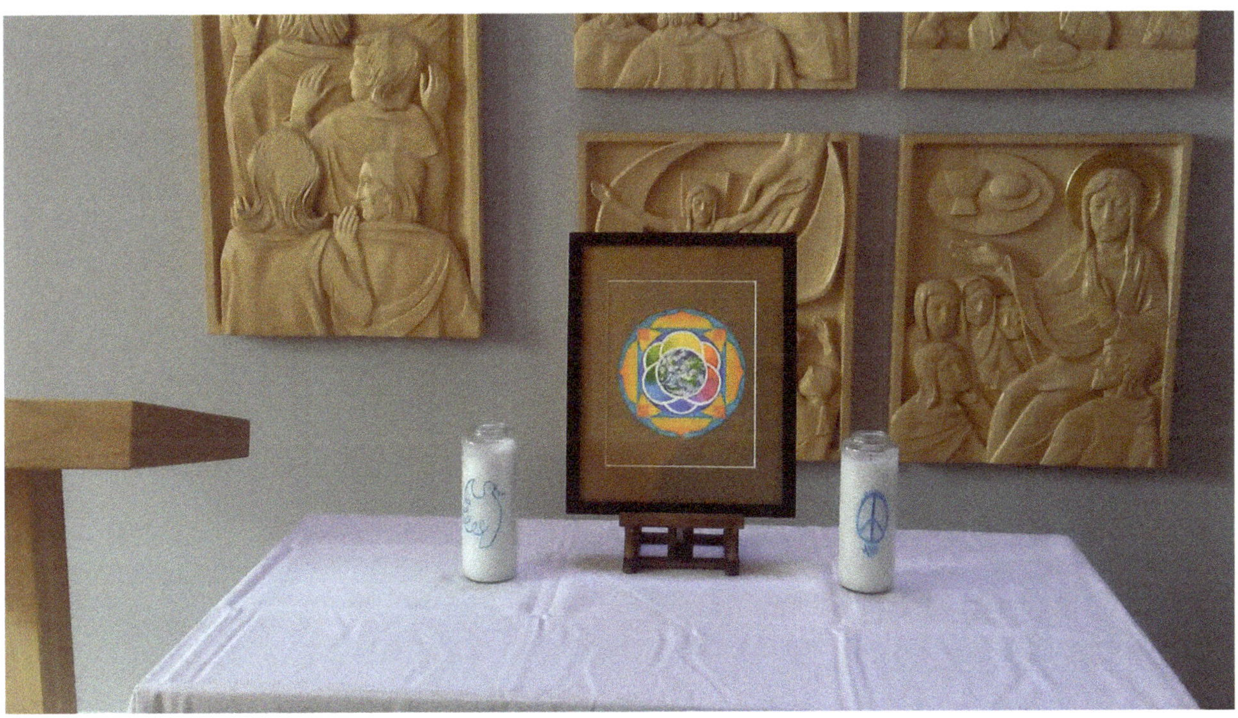

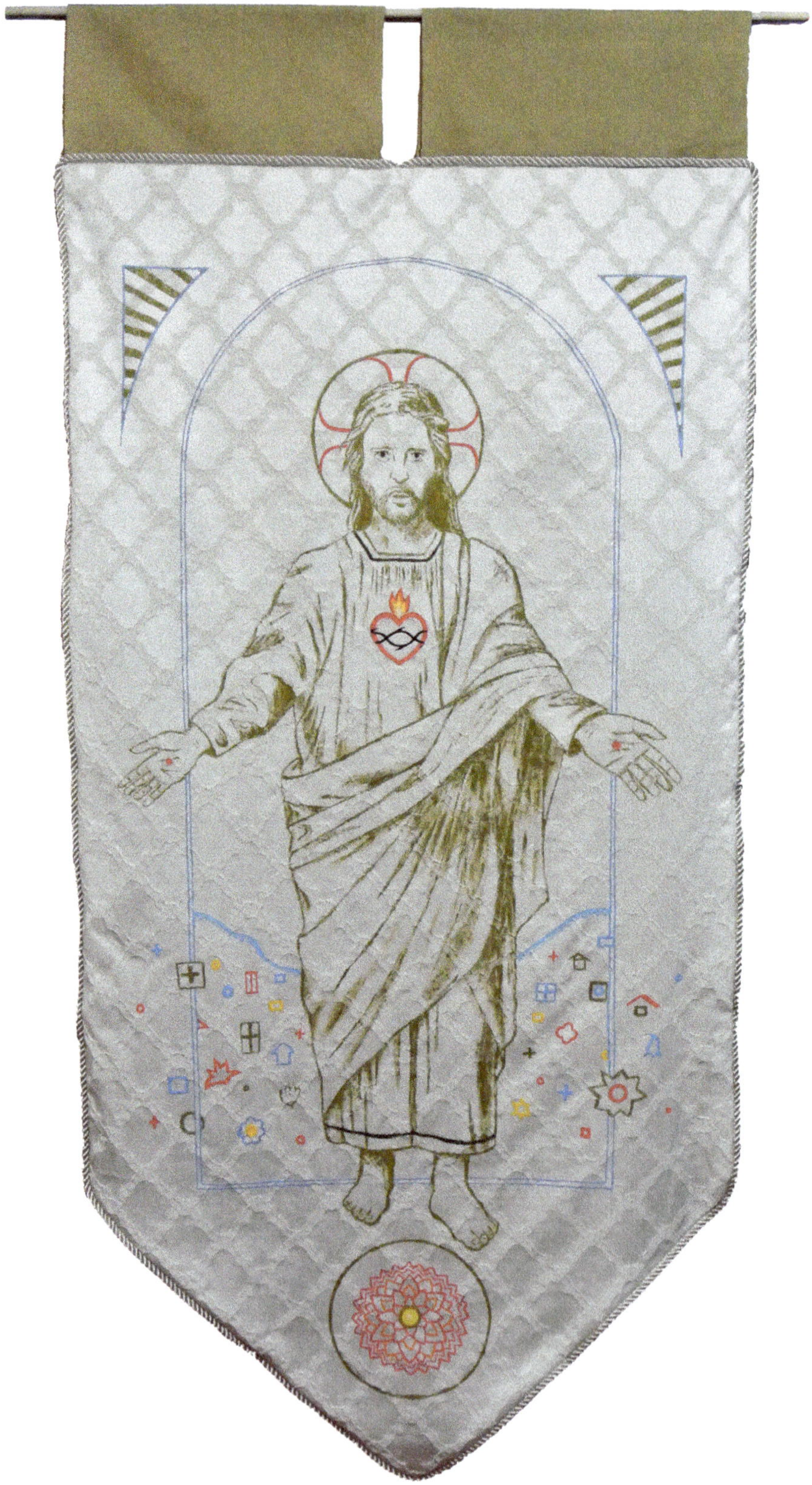

Most Holy Redeemer Processional Banner
Most Holy Redeemer Parish

2018, Acrylic on fabric, San Francisco, CA
Sewn by Liz TerboLizard / SF Seamstress, commissioned by William Mathews

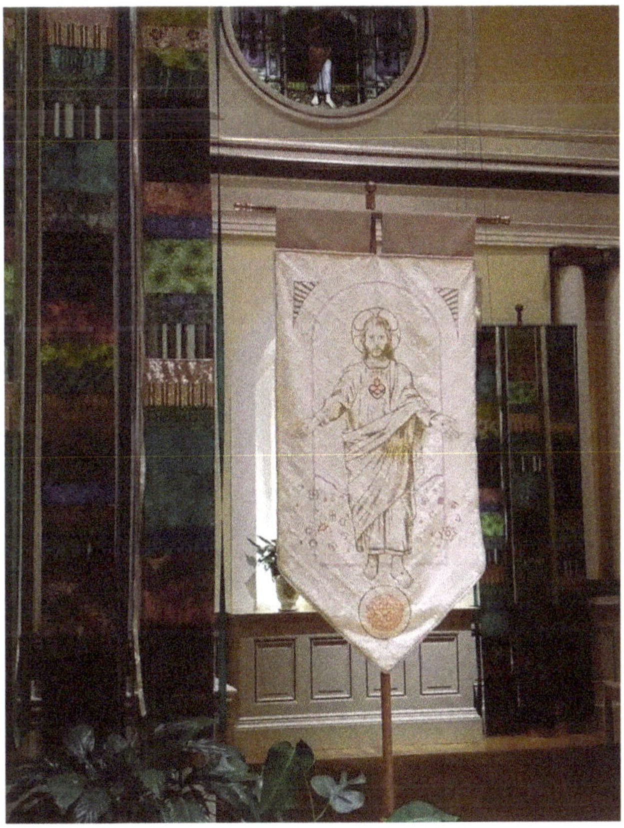

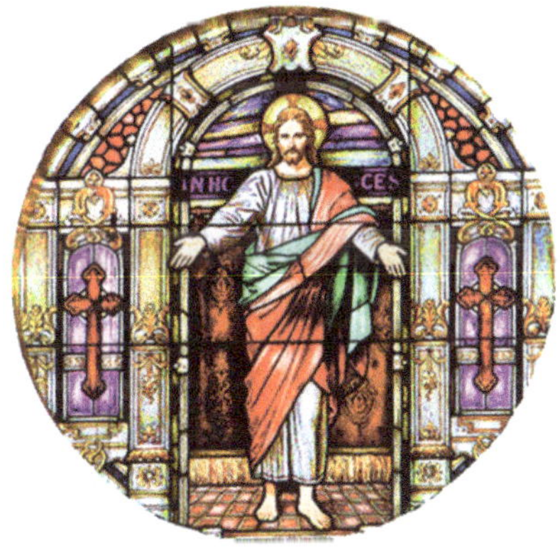

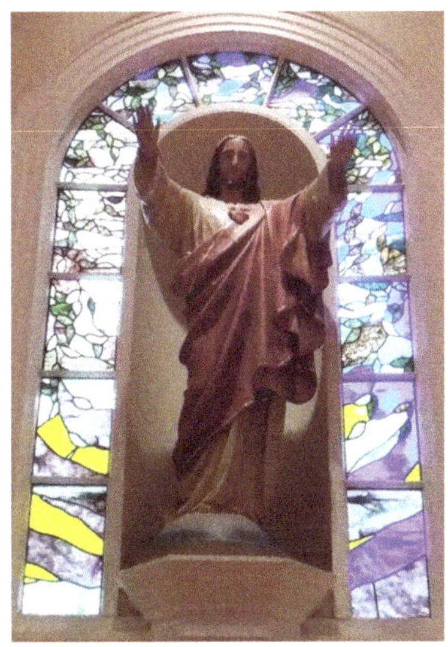

This was a commission by William Mathews, a friend, and a dedicated parishioner at Most Holy Redeemer. Impressed by the banner I created for St. Agnes, he asked that this one feature the risen Christ, as that is in the rose window and a favorite emblem for the parish. After some abstract renderings of Christ, William quested I rely on the representational figure in the window itself. A statue of Christ includes His sacred heart, so I included that symbol. Christ is standing in a doorway; the arch is the church. The radiating lines on the upper corners reference popular architectural details on many Victorian houses in the neighborhood. Nestled between hills, the Castro neighborhood (Eureka Valley) is seen in the background, and the houses and

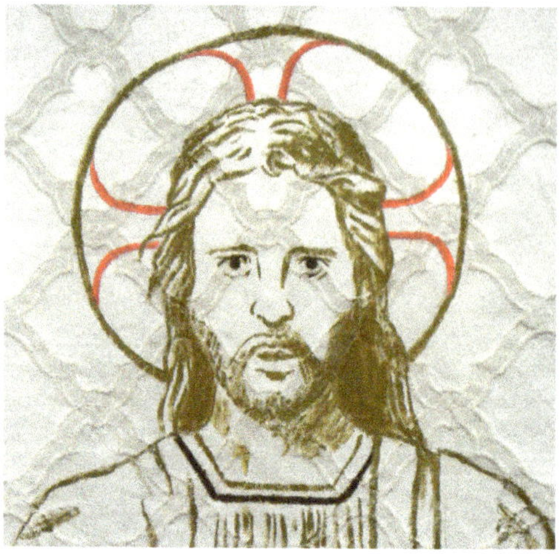
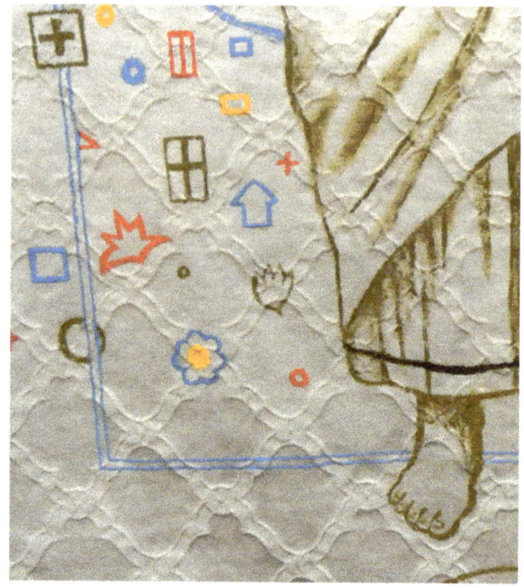
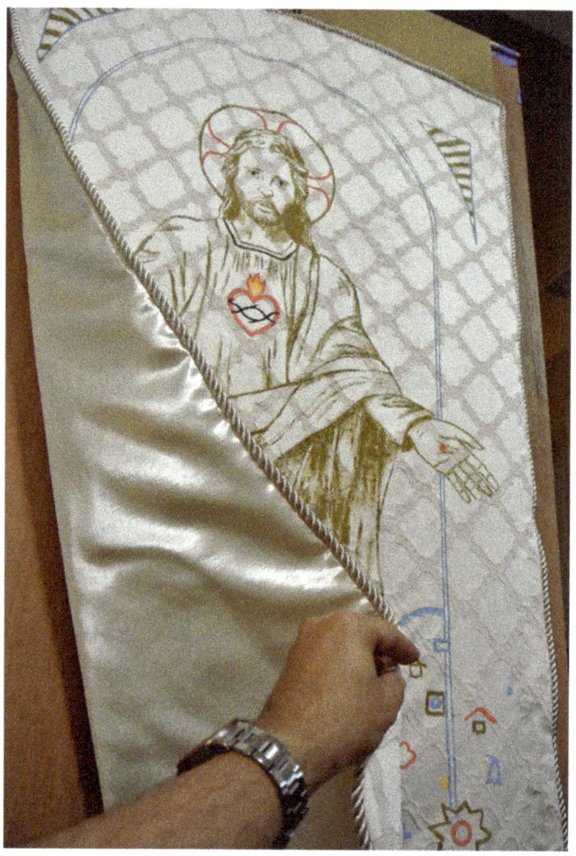
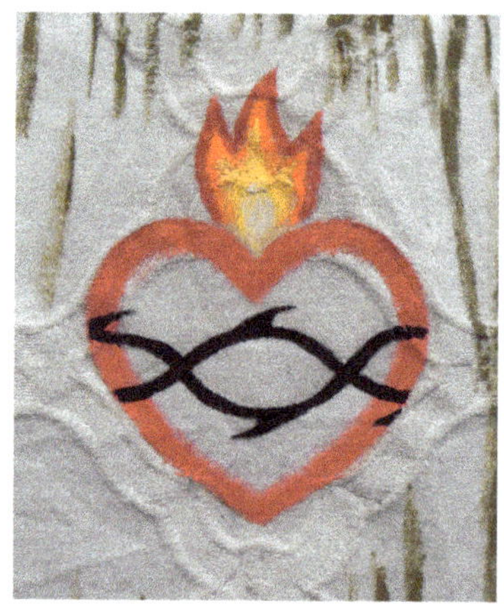
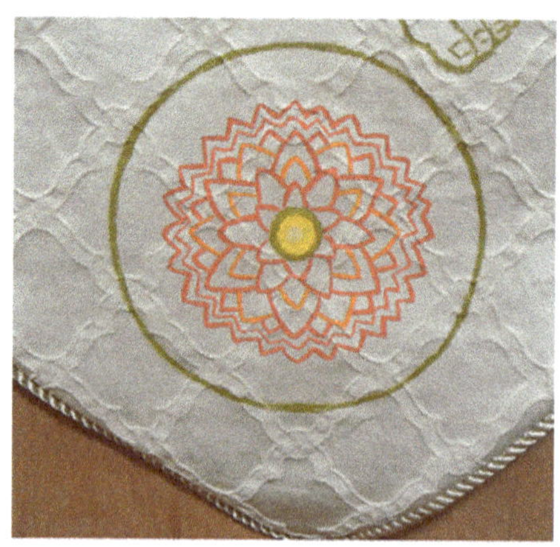

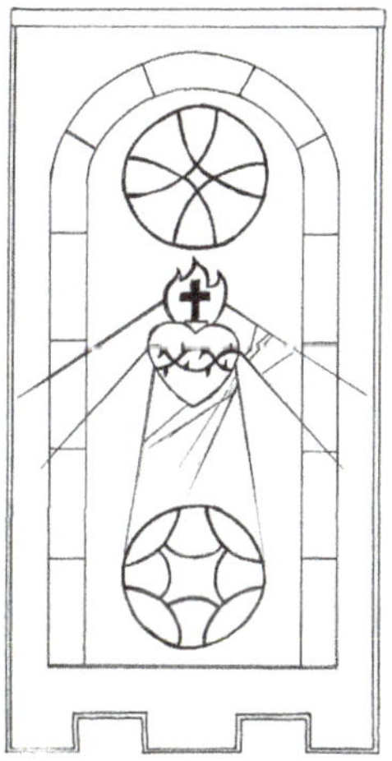
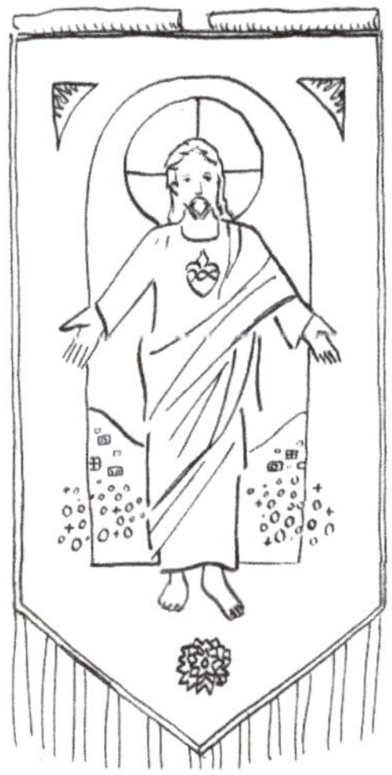
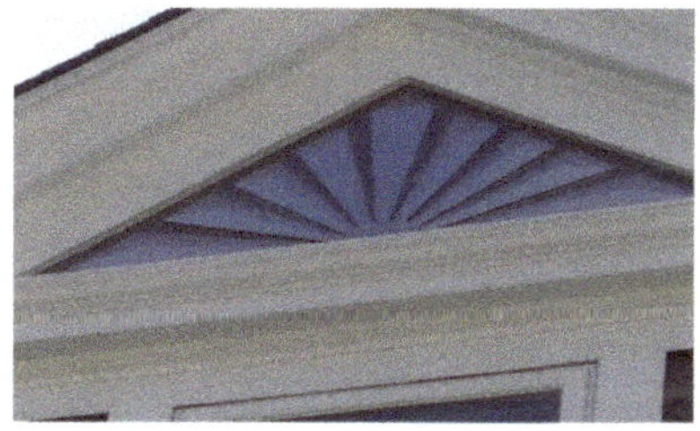

flowers spill into our space. House windows, blossoms, and circles represent the parishioners, and spread out like a field of wildflowers. Thus the parish's diversity is displayed in the variety of different shapes and colors. The crosses stand for the loved ones who have passed on. The Earth below Christ's feet is a dahlia, a symbol of dignity and elegance. It is the official flower of San Francisco, declared by the SF Board of Supervisors and Mayor Rolf in 1926.

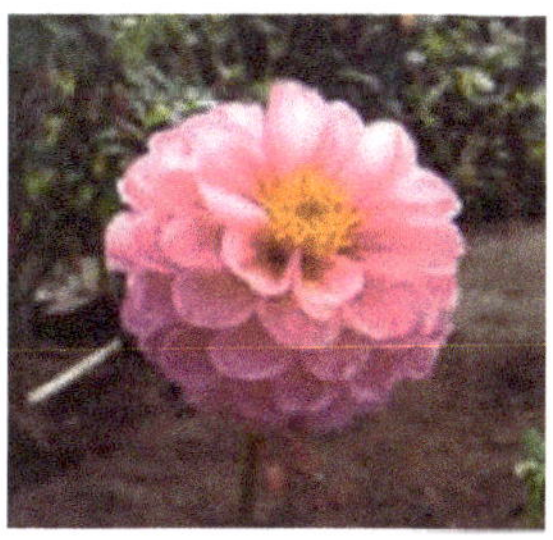

Design advice was also given by Pastor Matt Link.

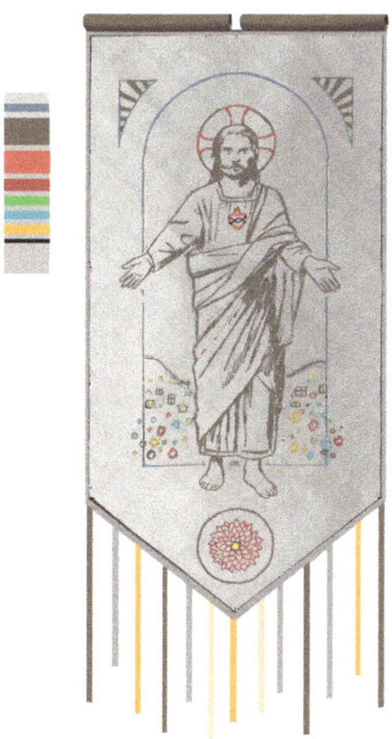
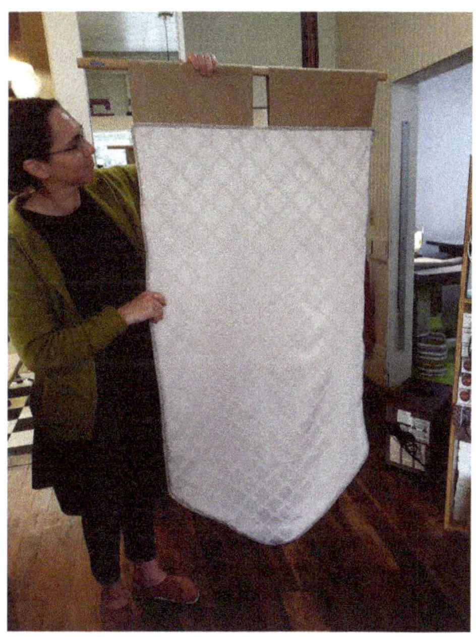

Baptistry Mural
St. Stephen Catholic Church

2019, Gold leaf and acrylic, San Francisco, CA
Gold leaf from Golden Leaf Products, paints from Precita Eyes Muralists
Commissioned by Rev. Tony LaTorre

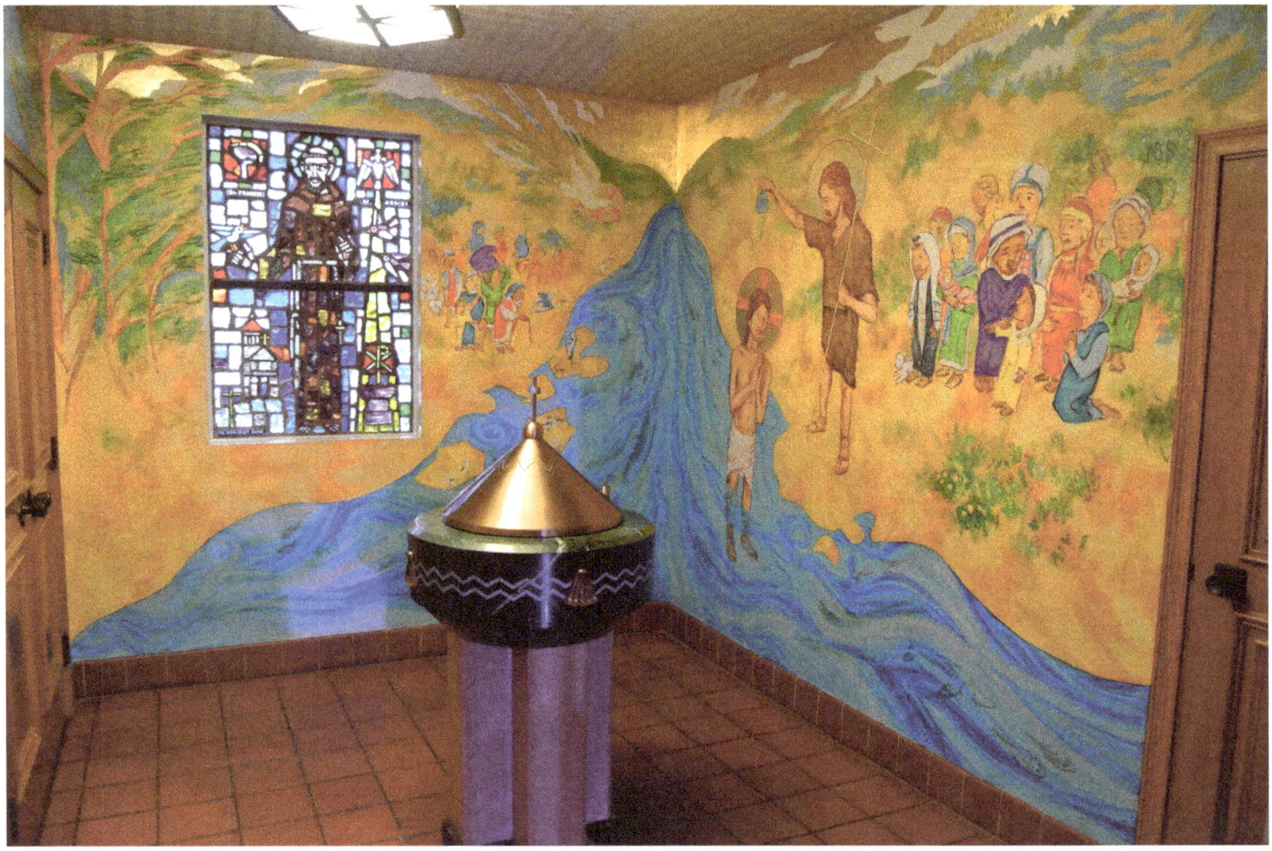

The request from Rev. Tony, the pastor, was to bring to our mind the baptism of Jesus. The elements I drew from included the natural world that makes up the Bay Area, the

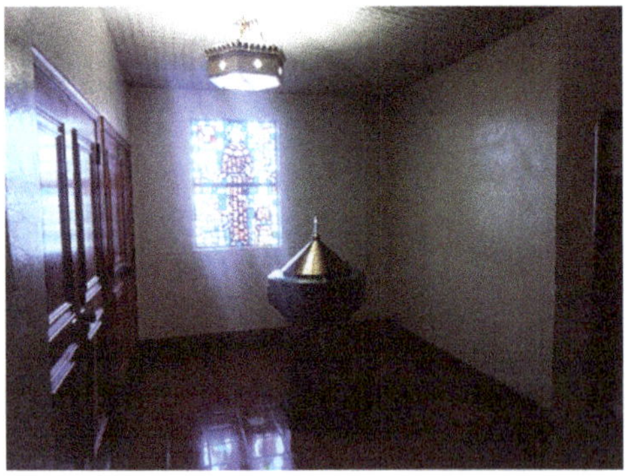

modern design of the baptismal font, the 1960s chunk rock stained glass window of St. Francis, and finally, the church's Spanish Colonial Revival architecture.

A baptism being performed recalls the baptisms of the family and friends present, as well as the baptism of the Lord. Thus, this mural is set in more than one time period. In a sense, it is a timeless room. Christ and St. John the Baptist are depicted in

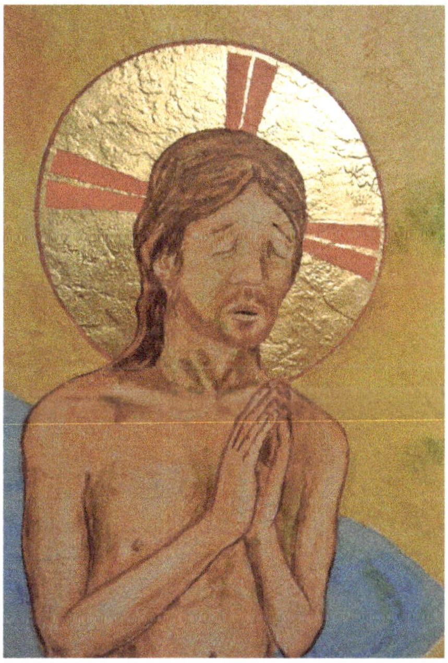
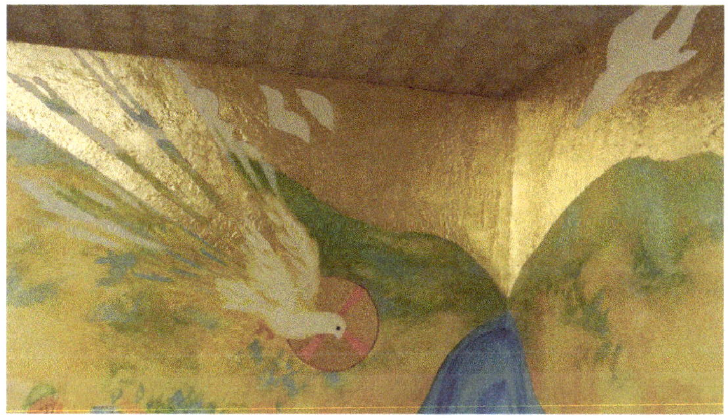
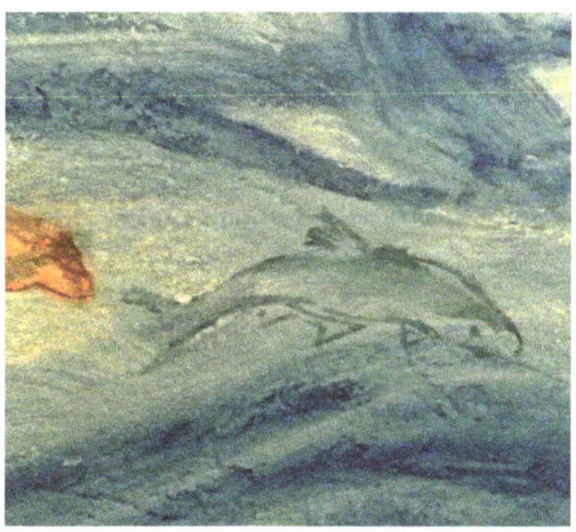
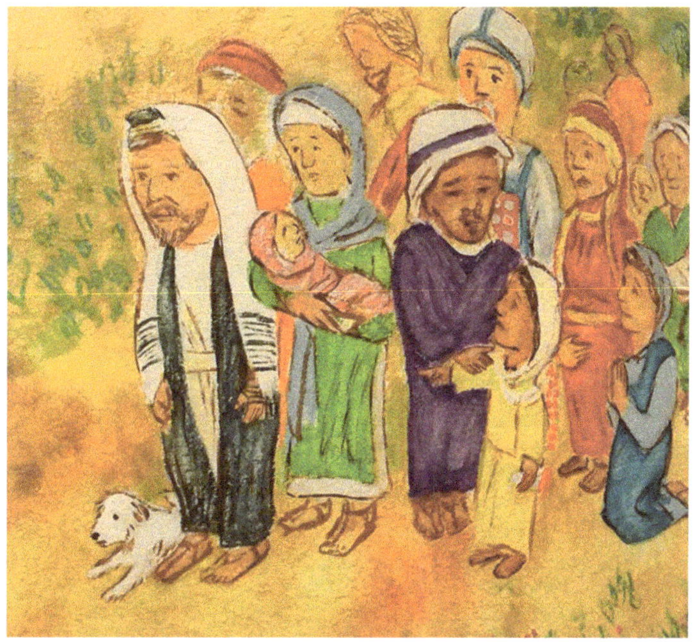
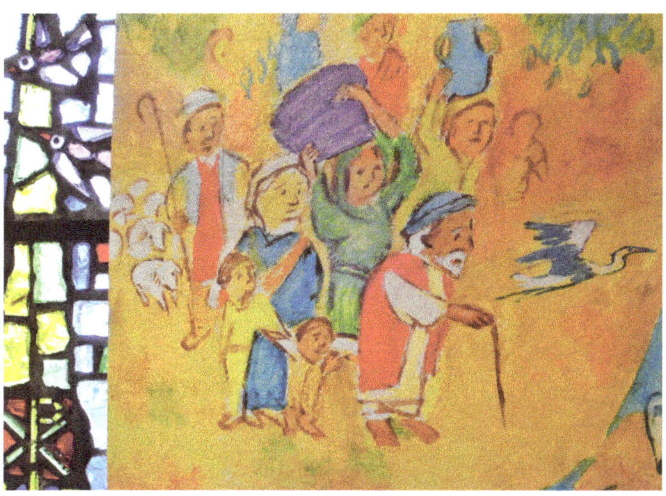
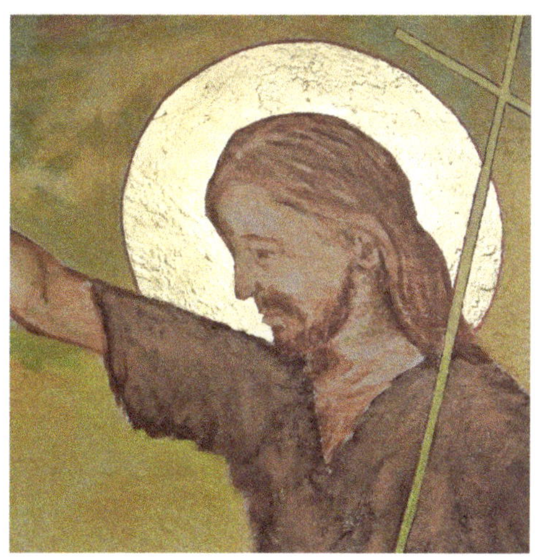

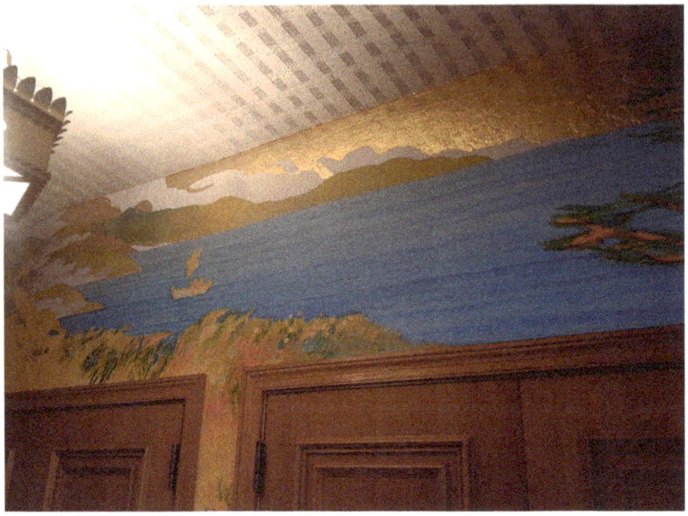

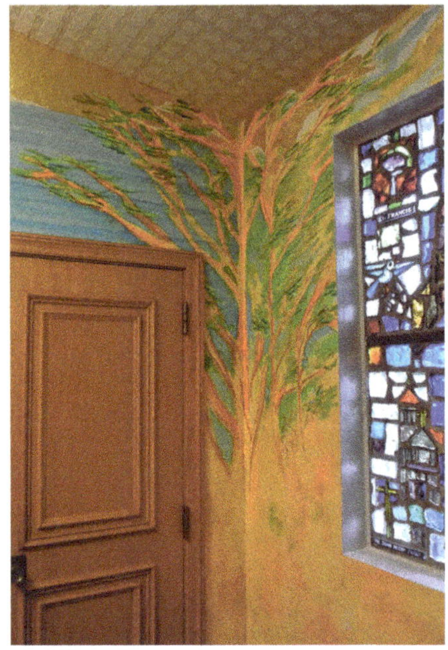

a style lifted from medieval and Renaissance paintings (with a composition inspired by a work by the Baroque painter Bartolomé Esteban Murillo). In contrast, environment is like one out of the late nineteenth and early twentieth centuries Impressionist and Fauvist paintings, bringing it closer to the present. The disciples of St. John the Baptist, to the right, and the villagers on the left, are even more expressively depicted, a nod to the style of the stained glass window. It is as if the people of this very parish,past and present, walked out from the windows and into the mural.

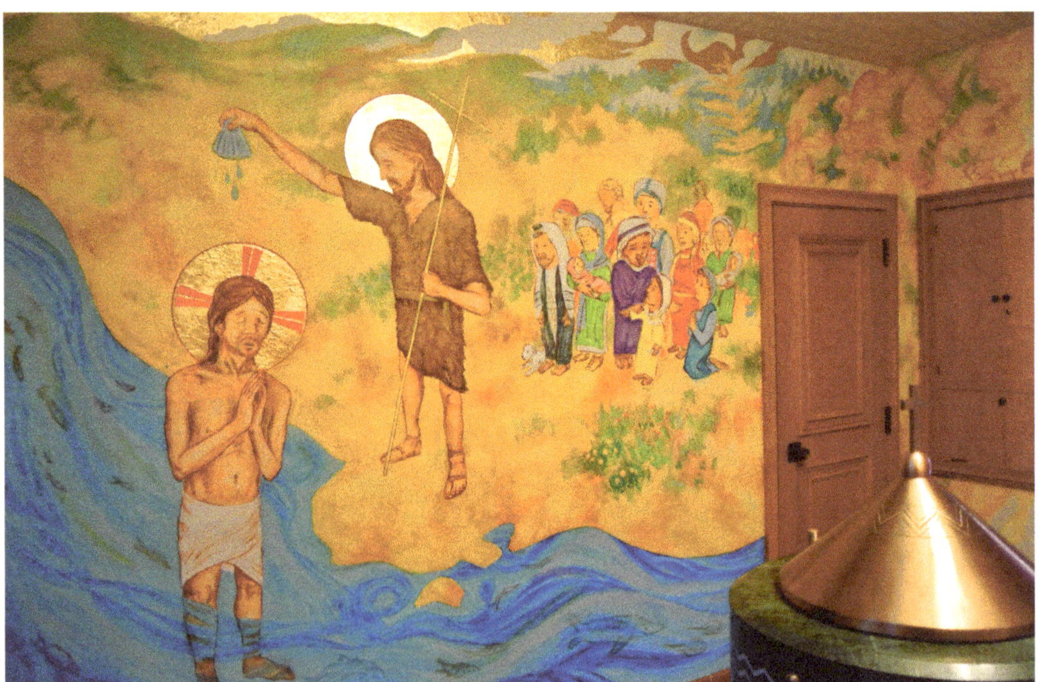

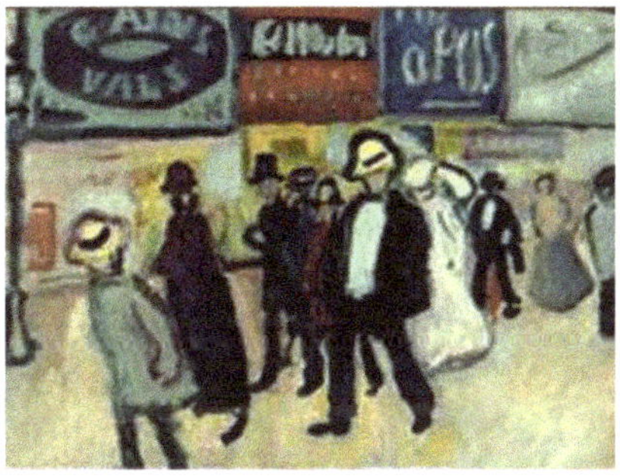

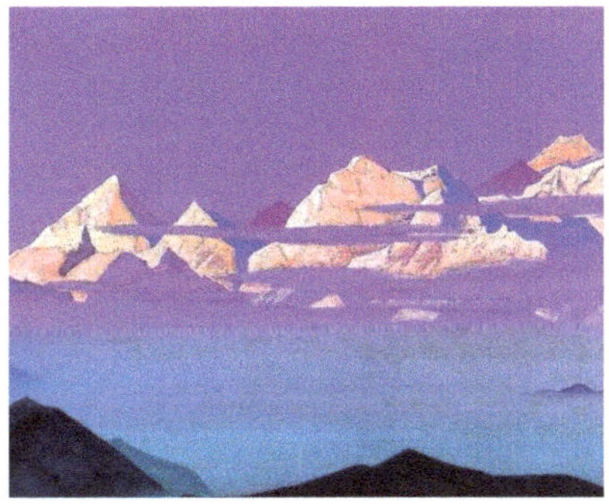

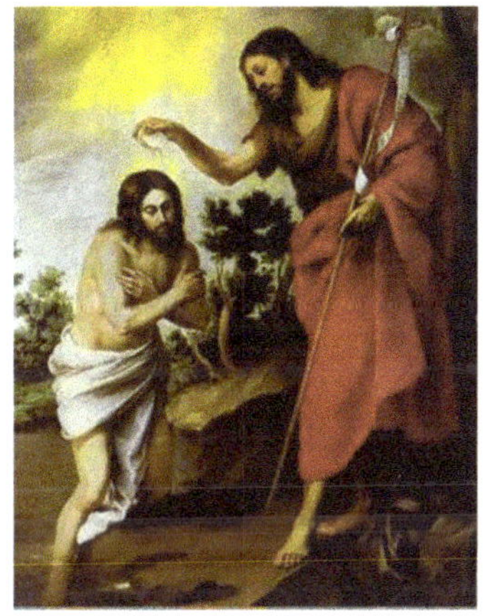

Yes, they are standing beside the Jordan River, but then there are local plants and animals, and even the Pacific Ocean in the distance. And so, we are standing in the Holy Land, and at the same time, we are right here in San Francisco. The styles, bright colors, and gold sky are not a realistic environment but a heightened spiritual landscape. Historically, paintings in churches, especially early icons, were meant to make us feel like we are not on Earth, but almost in a heavenly plane. As for including elements in the local landscape, art history is full of paintings and frescos of Biblical scenes which included architecture and clothing from the eras they were painted.

The tradition during the time of Christ was that the baptizer would also be standing in the water. I took cues from several historical paintings of the scene in which St. John is standing on the bank, as it adds more visual drama and makes Christ's baptism more of the focus. Two of Christ's disciples were fishermen, and so two fishermen are featured, dragging a net ashore, and two more are in a fishing boat in the ocean. The Holy Spirit is coming from the sky, but down at an angle from, and on the same wall, as a window of St. Francis (who spoke to the birds). The pastor asked that his terrier be included, hence the little, white dog, Vito. The Rabbi standing next to him is loosely a stand-in for the pastor. I figured he would have been a rabbi (the Pharisees) rather than the more political high priests (Sadducees). His attire, not that far off from today's Orthodox rabbis, is a visual reminder of Christ's earthly Jewish lineage. The river emerges from a vanishing point on the horizon, and the hills on either side help dramatically emphasize the final place where the golden sky (heaven) dips down to meet the water, which flows forward, down, and spreads out in both directions. Standing in the room, it is as if we are also standing in the water. This is a reminder of our baptism.

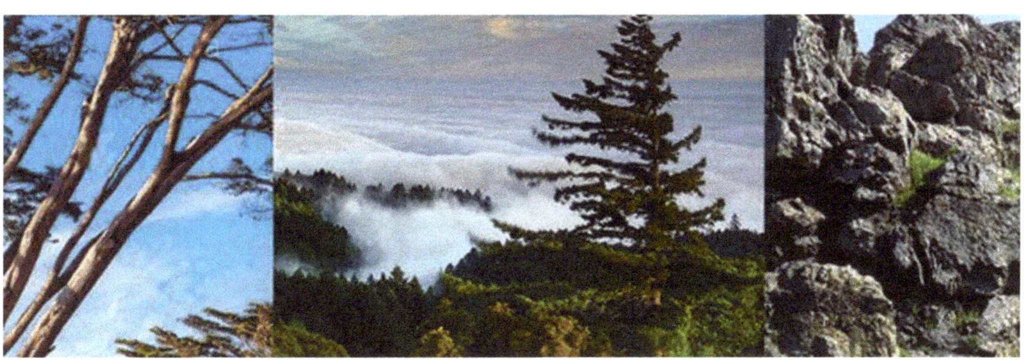

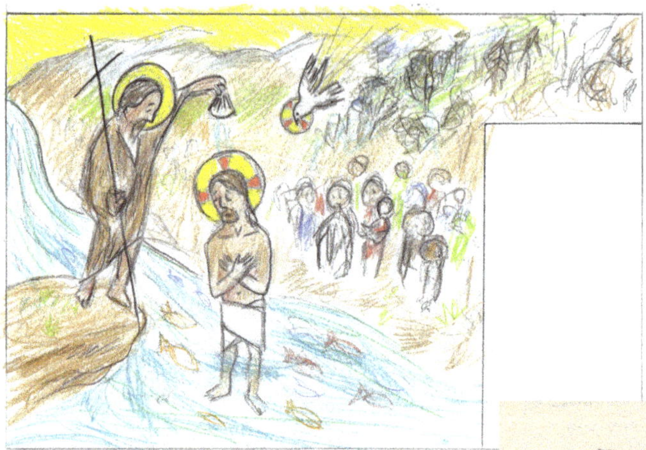

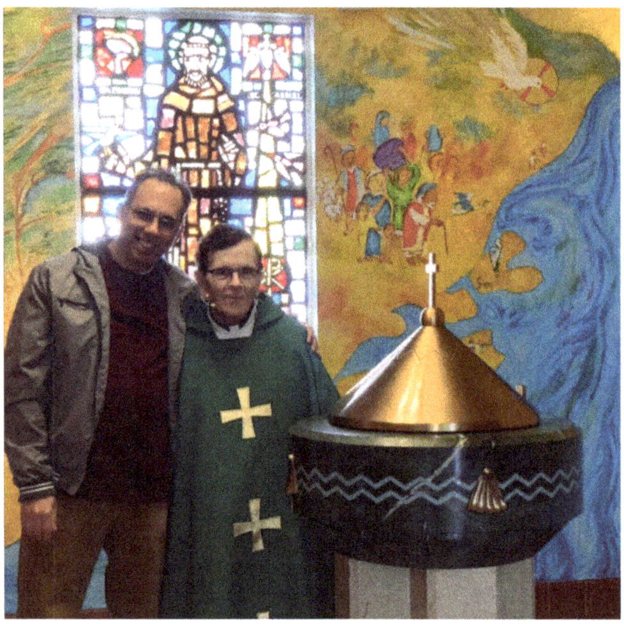

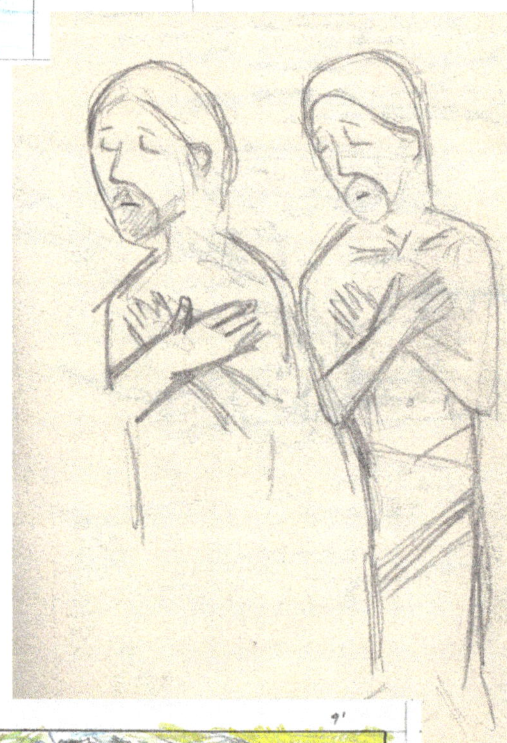

Previous page, top (L-R):

Posters at Trouville
Raoul Dufy, 1906

The Pink Mountains
Nicholas Roerich, 1933

The Baptism of Christ
Bartolomé Esteban Murillo
1655

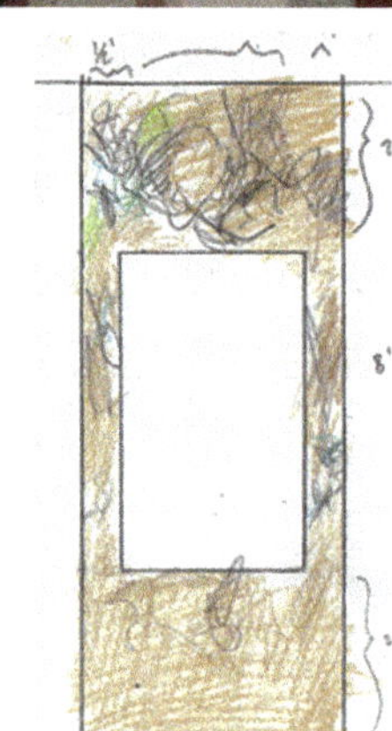

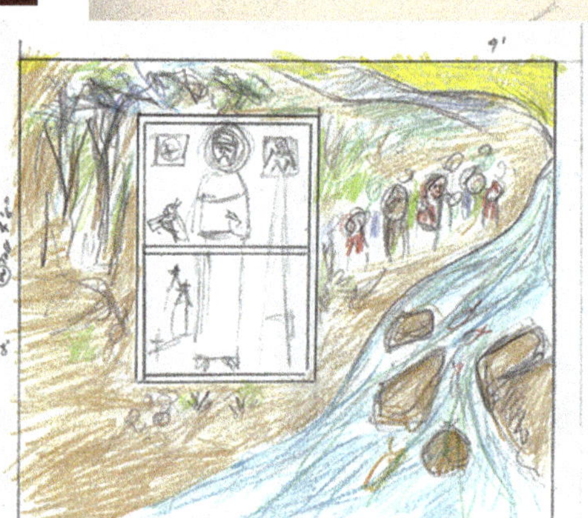

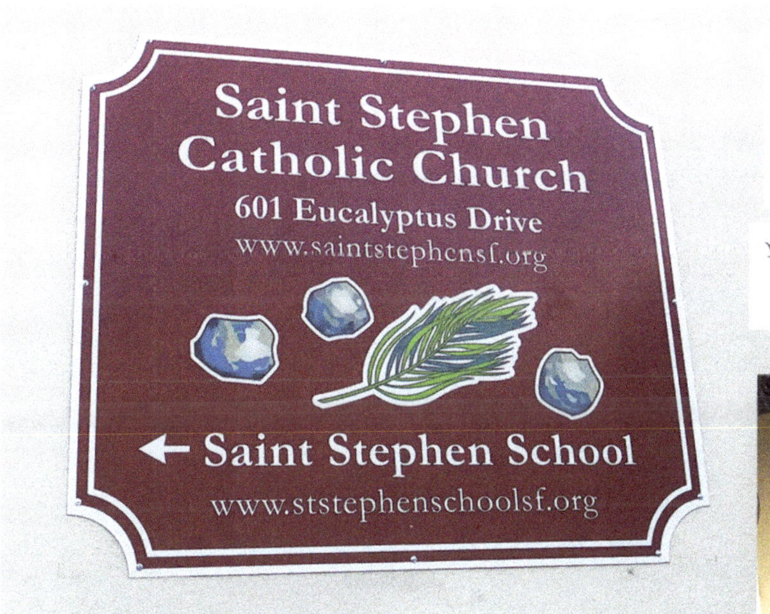

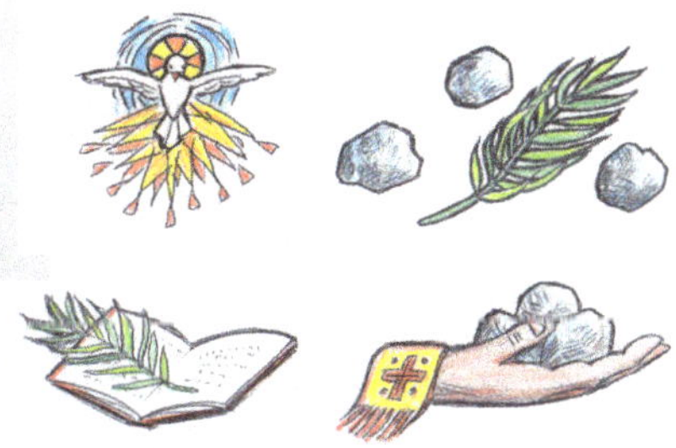

Outdoor Sign for Saint Stephen Catholic Church

2018, Dibond (aluminum sheets
with a solid polyethylene core),
San Francisco, CA
Manufactured by HD Supply, Commissioned
by Rev. Tony LaTorre

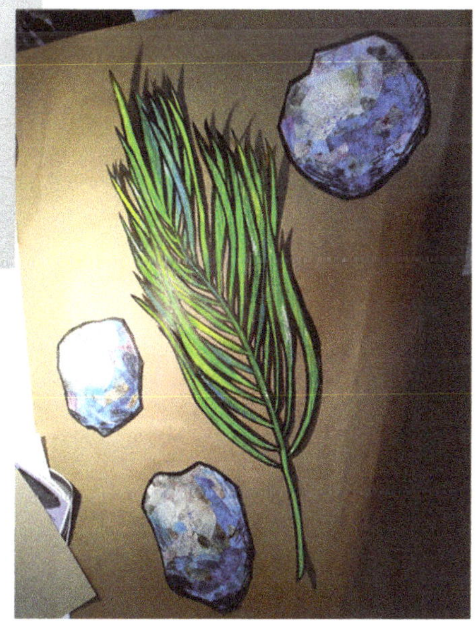

The symbols incorporated are those often depicted with St. Stephen, stones, as he was stoned to death, and a palm leaf, often held by the Church's first martyrs. The bold style they are rendered in was inspired by the stained glass in this church.

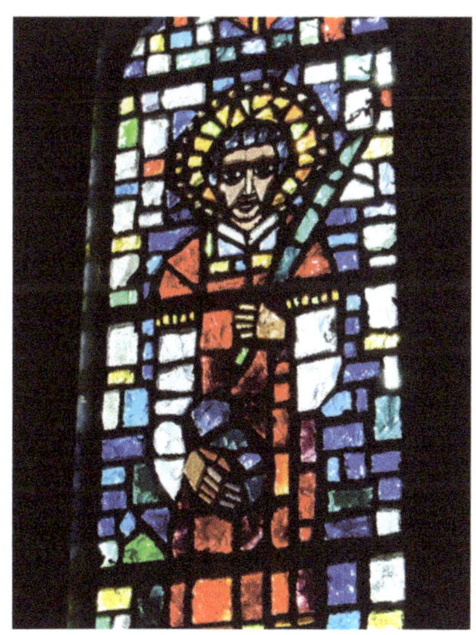

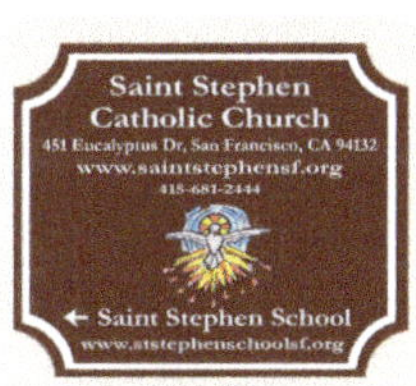

Shape 1 Spirit

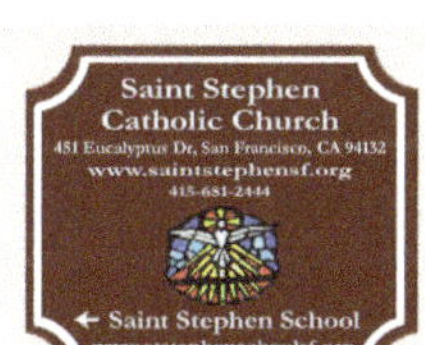

Shape 1 Spirit Stained glass

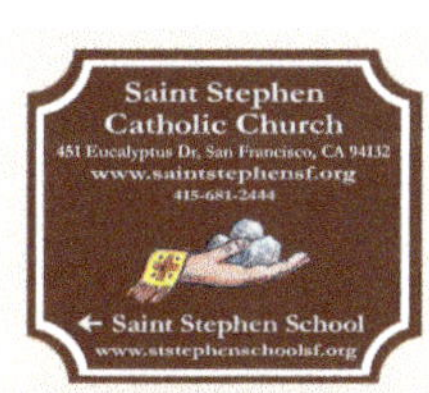

Shape 1 hand/stones

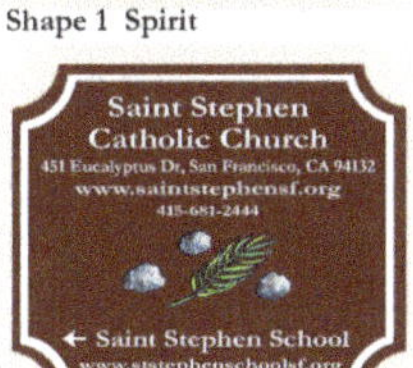

Shape 1 palm/stones

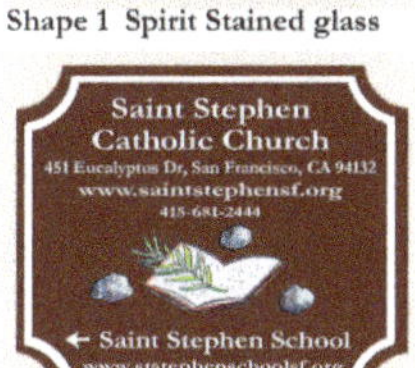

Shape 1 palm/book/stones

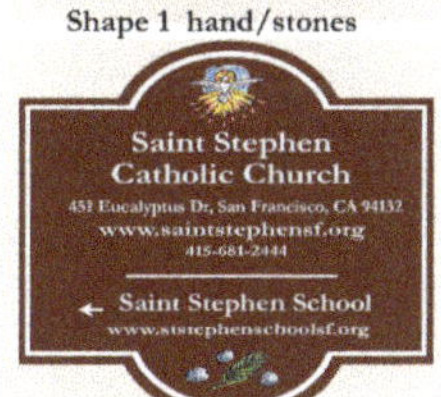

Shape 2 spirit/palm/stones

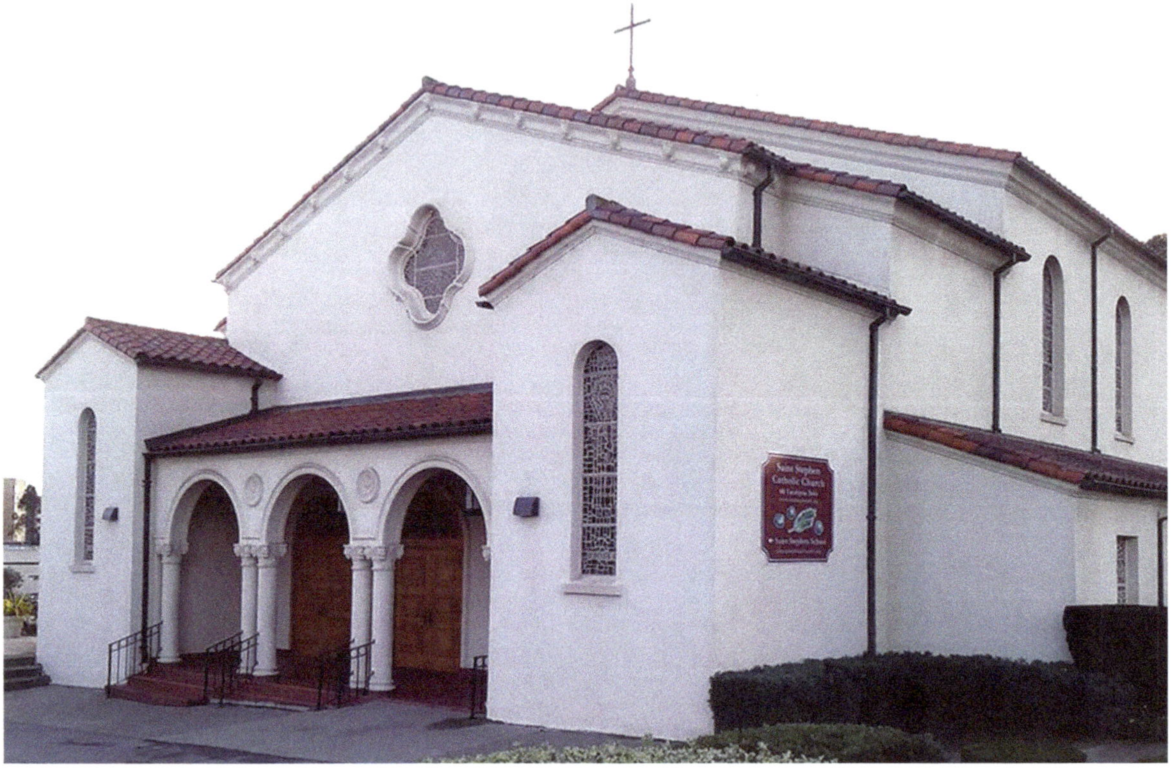

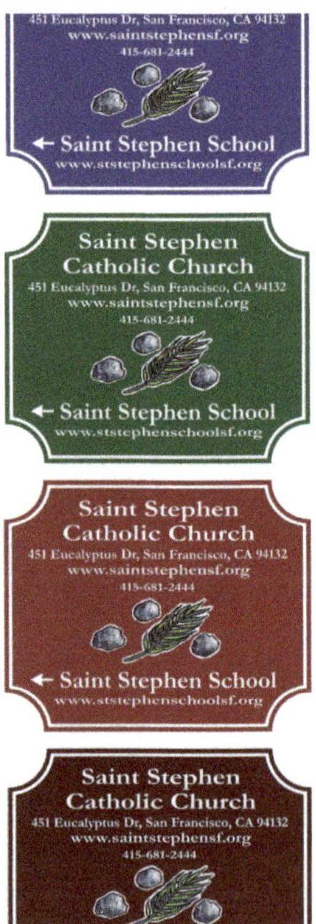
451 Eucalyptus Dr, San Francisco, CA 94132
www.saintstephensf.org
415-681-2444
← Saint Stephen School
www.ststephenschoolsf.org
Saint Stephen
Catholic Church
451 Eucalyptus Dr, San Francisco, CA 94132
www.saintstephensf.org
415-681-2444
← Saint Stephen School
www.ststephenschoolsf.org
Saint Stephen
Catholic Church
451 Eucalyptus Dr, San Francisco, CA 94132
www.saintstephensf.org
415-681-2444
← Saint Stephen School
www.ststephenschoolsf.org
Saint Stephen
Catholic Church
451 Eucalyptus Dr, San Francisco, CA 94132
www.saintstephensf.org
415-681-2444

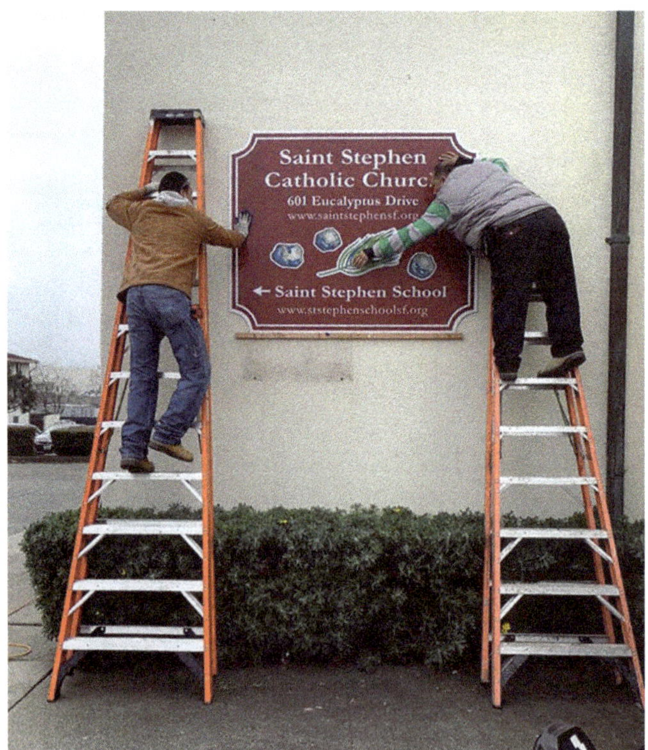
Saint Stephen
Catholic Churc
601 Eucalyptus Drive
← Saint Stephen School
www.ststephenschoolsf.org

Books

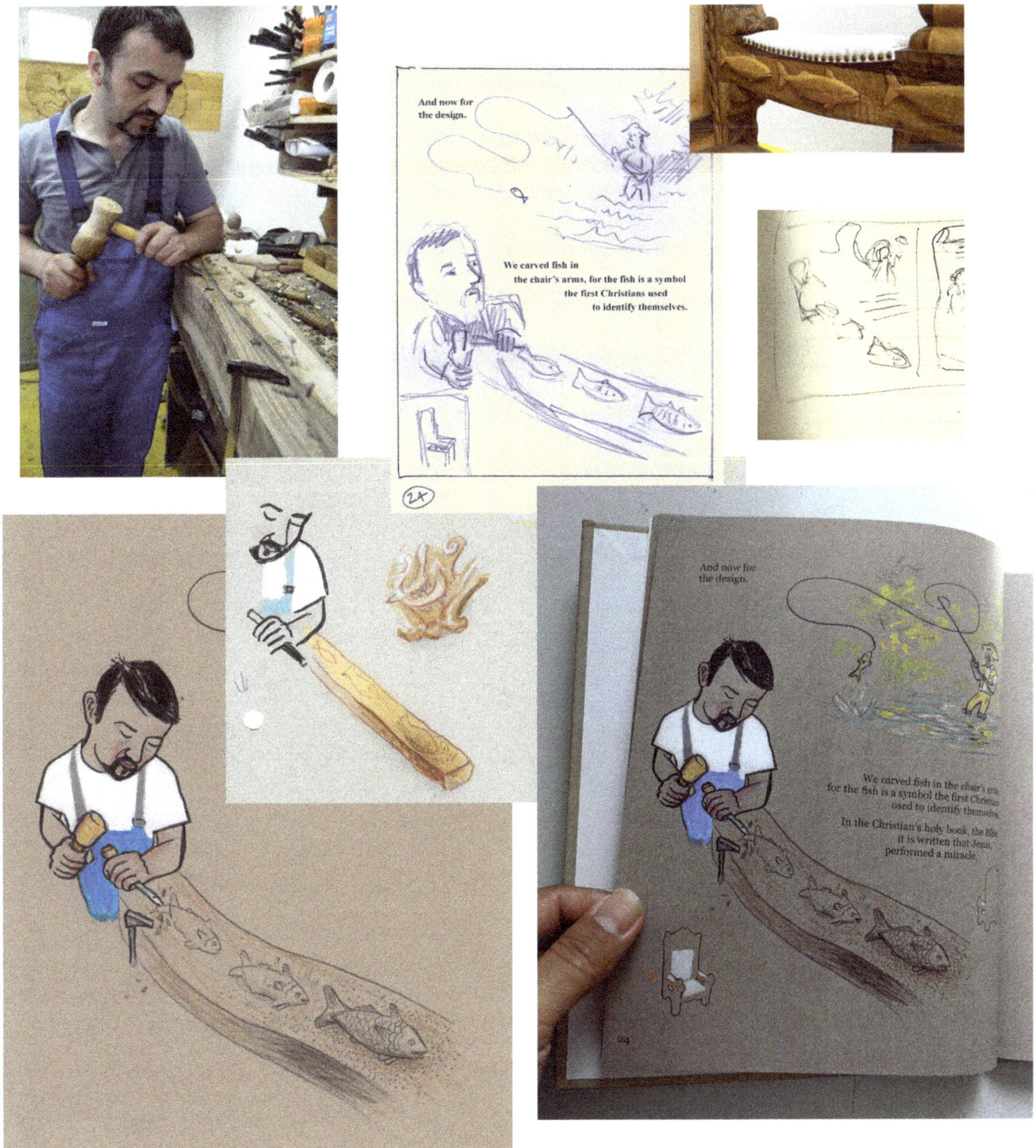
And now for the design.
We carved fish in the chair's arms, for the fish is a symbol the first Christians used to identify themselves.
24
And now for the design.

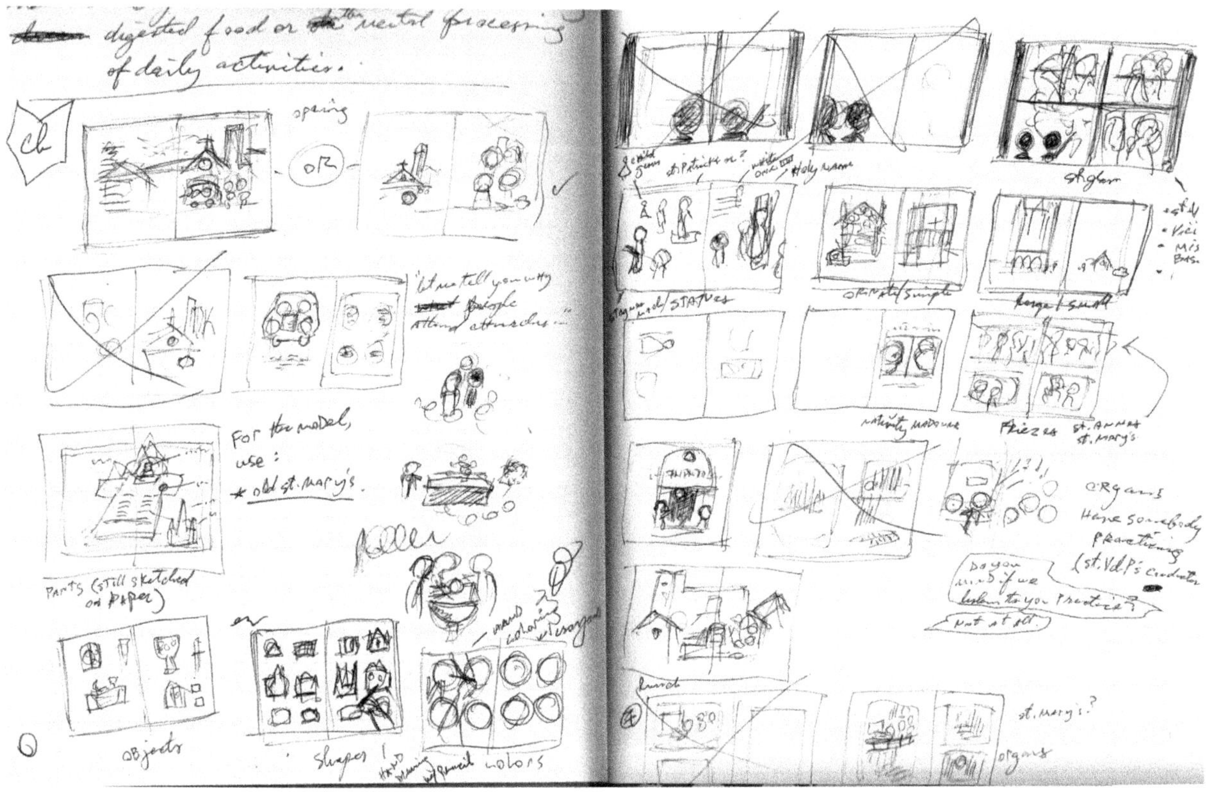
digested food or the mental processing
of daily activities.
Ch
opening
OR
"Let me tell you why people attend services..."
For the model,
use:
* old St. Mary's
Parts (still sketched on paper)
objects
or
shapes!
colors
St. Patrick or?
Holy name
stained glass
ornate/simple
large/small
nativity
Frieze
St. Anne
St. Mary's
organs
Have somebody practicing
(St. V.d.P's conductor)
Do you mind if we listen to you practice?
not at all.
St. Mary's?
organs

One time, during an art critique in college, I mentioned a name of a book illustrator as an influence. That did NOT sit well with the professor! Back then, I began making books out of sight from the painting department - photocopied affairs with linocut-printed covers – which I gave to friends and sold a few at a local museum bookstore. But some of my paintings and drawings developed into series. The downside of a series is that the works are best displayed together in a show; they would be separated like orphans if sold, and the larger picture they paint would be lost. This led me to writing books, besides stories brewing inside. That, and I liked the idea that when one creates an illustrated book, the finished product is the printed book, which can be shared with as many people as you can print books. And its price is usually under $20! Much more affordable than a painting in a gallery. Unless your fame shoots to the roof and the painting gets into a museum, that painting will be bought by one buyer, if at all, and sit in her house, for only her to enjoy. I had ideas to share (or so I believed) and a drive to bring them into the wider world. Why is there any class difference between studio art and illustration? If an artist's work becomes famous enough, most people will still not be able to see it in person, but on the page of a book or a postcard. In the end, the work will be experienced the same way a picture book is. And if the work is much larger than the catalog, as is usually the case, most of the detail will be lost. Book illustrations are made to be viewed at the final scale they are printed.

Thus far, each avenue - whether art made for prints, oil paintings, church installations, or books – becomes its own form of language, with purposes fitting to the medium. For me, working simultaneously on, say, a book and a painting, one can inform the other.

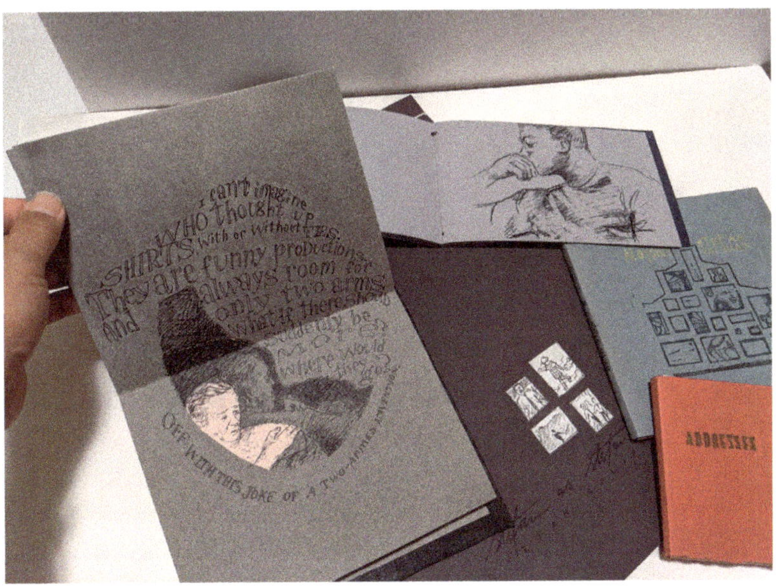

Several books created during the 1990s

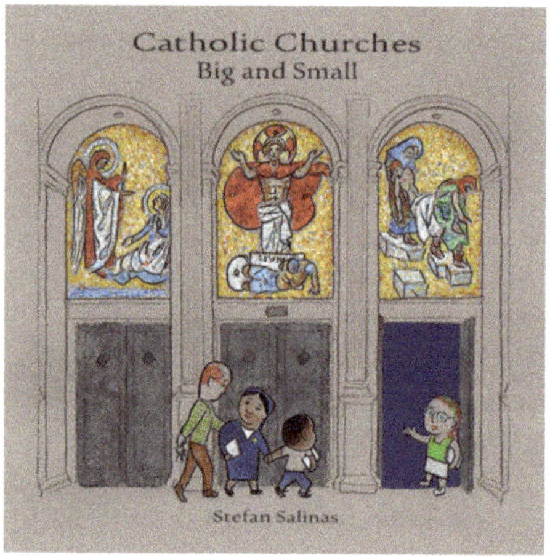

Catholic Churches Big and Small

Camelopardalis, San Francisco, 2014
Acrylic, ink and pencil on paper
Editors: Jack Ronan, Thuan V. Hoang and Tony LaTorre

Travel with a boy, a girl, their father and a nun as they explore the Catholic churches within a single city. A celebration of religious art and architecture - from the historic, to the modern, to the simple, to the ornate. Encounter special furniture, statues, shapes, colors, stained-glass windows, murals, tapestries, various cultures, and much more!

As mentioned before, I have been fascinated by houses of worship all my life. Historian David McCullough once said,"I try to write the kind of book that I would like to read. If I can make it clear and interesting and compelling to me, then I hope maybe it will be for the reader."

Almost half of my friends and associates in San Francisco at the time were Catholic. Aside from my *journey to Rome,* i.e. Catholic conversion, liturgical art was already an expanding rug in my living room. The basic idea for this book was in my mind at least a year before I entered RCIA (The Rite of Christian Initiation of Adults; classes toward baptism and confirmation).

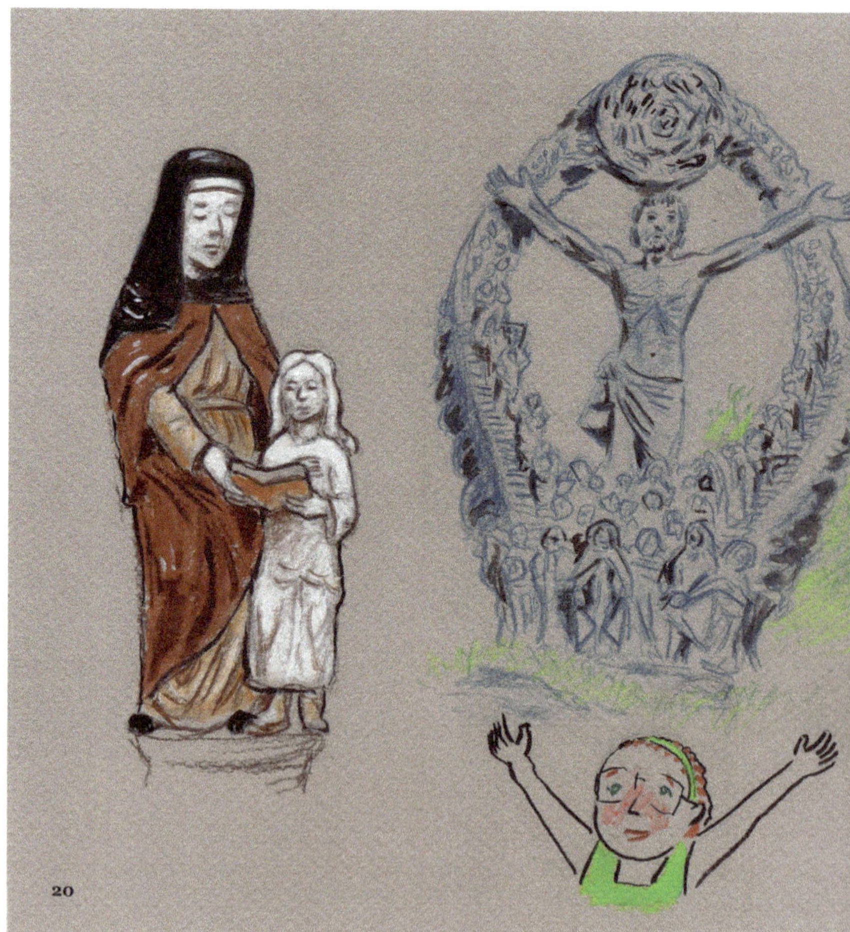

Looking for existing examples of picture-books on Catholic Churches, I found only a few. The Church in the USA claims to have about 51 million members (2018 Pew Research data). There was work that needed to be done!

I saw it as a guidebook to introduce the young to their Sunday surroundings. I learned many adults were just as interested in this book as well, a celebration of our faith's history and culture. Instead of showing grand cathedrals in far-away Rome, I chose a more pedestrian approach – literally. Restrictions can be an artist's best friends, so I limited the churches to be explored to those within San Francisco's city limits. There are forty-seven of them within a seven-mile radius, so a father, two kids, and a nun (our guides) could easily drive to see several within a day. Also, I wanted to physically visit each one, to let my senses take in the character of each space, and find more details than random photos on the Internet could provide.

A pastor commented on my choice of including a particularly minimalist block of a church. He said, "Why is such-and-such church in the book? It's so UGLY!"

I replied, "Some young girl and her family are parishioners there. That single structure is where she received her primary religious instruction, where she was baptized, and where she will have her first confirmation. It is a physical environment in her life in which its sole purpose is to help her connect with God."

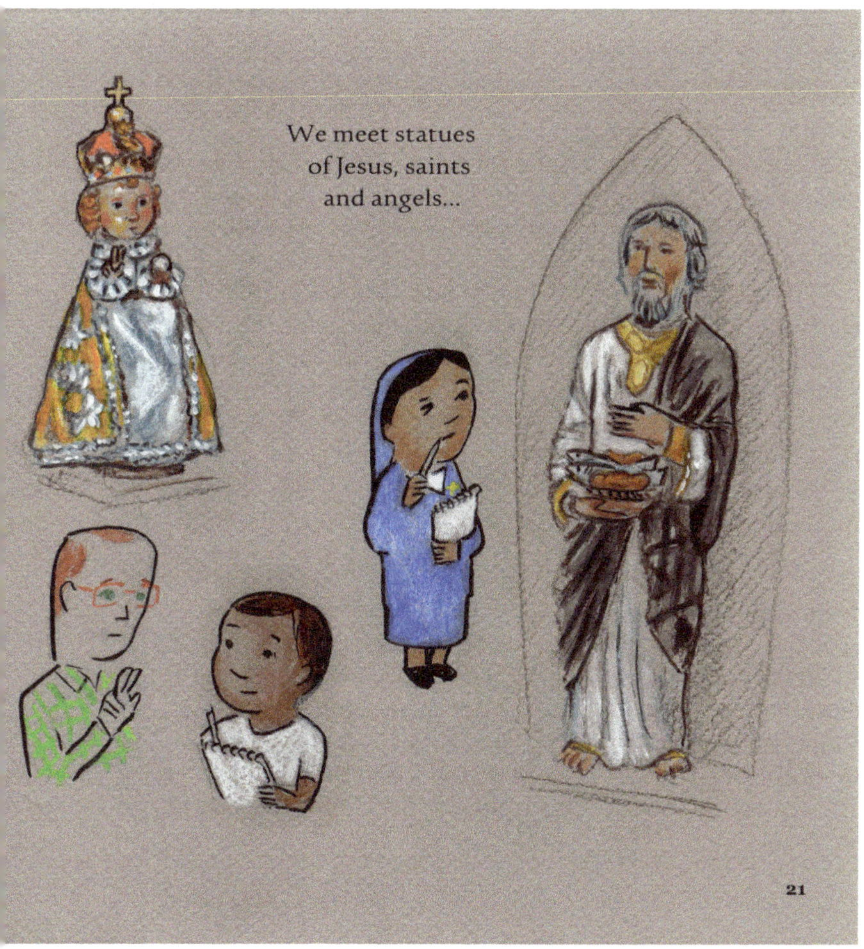

Indeed, a variety of architectural styles reflecting different cultures and ethnicities was important for me to put on display. From a Colonial Spanish-inspired geometric ceiling mural to a statue of an Asian Jesus.Two priests who proofread the manuscript (Rev. Tony LaTorre and Rev. Thuan Hoang) have cameos, along with one who taught and batized me (Rev. Michael Strange, SS), a favorite nun (Sr. Cleta Herold), and a gardener at my parish (Gregory Matracia).

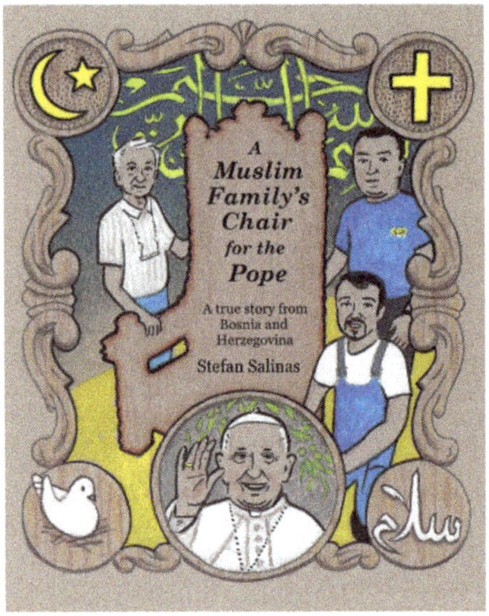

A Muslim Family's Chair for the Pope

A True Story from Bosnia and Herzegovina.

Camelopardalis, San Francisco, 2017
Acrylic, ink and pencil on paper
Editors: Sabrina DeCarolis,
Mohammed Khalid Siddiqi and Michael Strange

In the country of Bosnia and Herzegovina, Muslims, Orthodox Christians and Catholics have been living side by side for many years, but they have not always gotten along. Twenty years have passed since they were at war with each other. How can neighbors of different faiths live together in peace? Pope Francis, head of the Roman Catholic Church, paid a visit to Bosnia on June 6, 2015.
This is the true story of a Muslim family of carpenters who designed and made a chair in honor of this occasion. This book is for children, parents, grandparents, for everyone!

Even though I was swimming in a pool of Catholicism for seven years, my interest in other organized religions remained.

I was being interviewed on an early morning local television show as a promotion for my book on churches. The interviewee proceeding me was an educator of Islam; her focus being on teaching non-believers about her religion and that it is one of peace. She graciously answered each question with a sensitive and open demeanor. We were able to chat briefly before filming. Her segment ended, she left, and then they filmed mine. As the camera and sound man approached me to remove the lapel microphone, he complimented me on my book and praised its role in evangelization, then went on to say something like, "Islam teaches their followers to kill Christians! I do not trust them."

I was taken aback, and the host was uncomfortably quiet. Wasn't the technician listening to the first guest? I, too, stood in silence, allowing the stranger to comfortably speak his viewpoint authentically.

It was at that very moment a seed was planted in the center of my heart, a vow that my very next book must address Catholic-Muslim relations.

Being a convert, I have witnessed, in others and myself, biases and misconceptions those outside the Christian fold have of Christians, and vice versa. After months of searching for a twenty-first-century example of a peaceful, inspirational, Muslim-Catholic true story, an article on Voice of America set in Bosnia and Herzegovina stood out. Salim Hajderovac†, a Muslim carpenter, won the commission to carve a chair for Pope Francis, who was due to visit in the summer of 2015. He, his son, and friends have created wood carvings for mosques, synagogues, and churches.

I have made art for churches. The Holy Spirit has a way of guiding us. After several attempts at reaching the family (they didn't have a website yet), contact was finally established with the help of local Bosnian Muslims Hidajeta Alic, Senad Osmanovic, and Edževit Winkler-Žepčanin, (a friend of the family, who was living in Los Angeles). Salim and I were able to converse, with Edževit as a translator. After a few months of sending drafts back and forth of the story, it was on to illustrating.

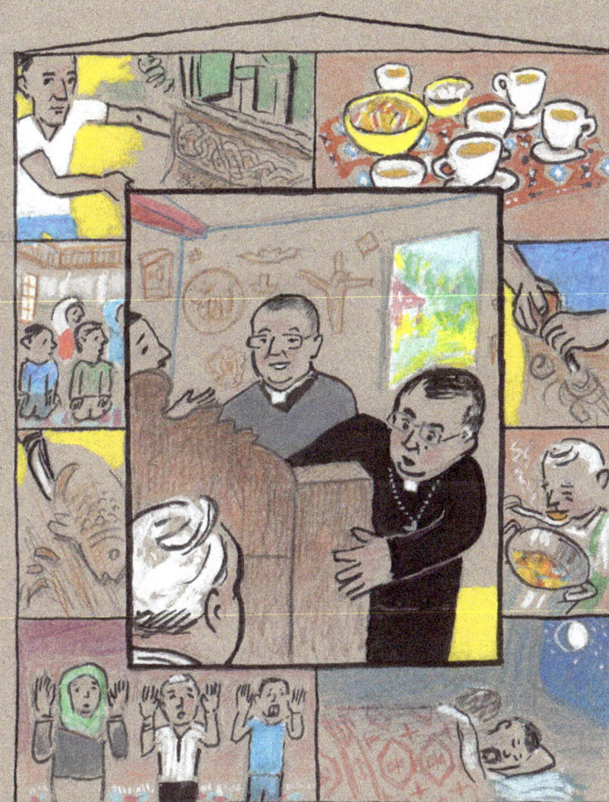

Cardinal Vinko and Monsignor Tomo Knežević stopped in to check on our progress. They were very pleased.

33

Coincidences and blessings dotted the path all along the way. One topic that made me nervous was my homosexuality. There I was, a Catholic American (and the Church has its own rocky relationship with LGBTQ+ people), writing a book set in a visited, from a Muslim person's perspective. Edzevit, it turns out, is not only a proud citizen of the United States and poud of his Bosniak culture, as well as being a faithful Muslim, he is also gay! I asked an imam and priest, Dr. Hafiz Mohammed Khalid Siddiqi and Rev. Michael Strange, SS, respectively, to proofread the manuscript. I didn't want to cross any sacred lines or offend believers of either religion. The journey was quite a unique one.

Sadly, Salim Hajderovac died in April of 2017, just two years after completing the chair. Thank you, Salim, for your creative spirit and giving heart. Blessings to you, as you rest in Paradise.

Ideally, I would have travelled to Bosnia to visit the woodshop, church, mosque, and met the principal players. Fortunately, local and interntional news posted many photos and videos of this project. Google Maps and Earth helped, and footage online of inside the houses of worship, stadium, and the flood the town experienced allowed me to add so many details.

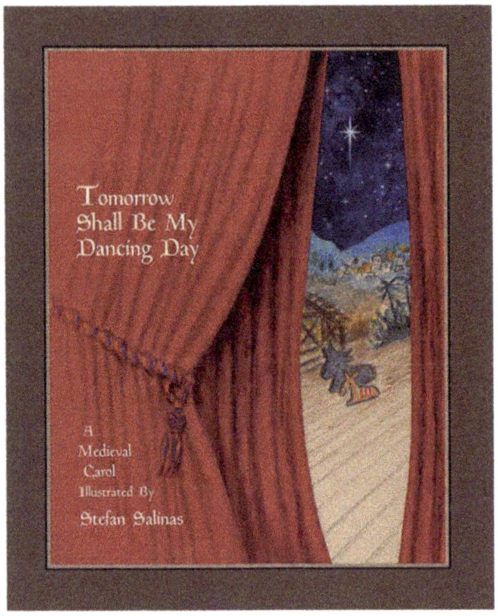

Tomorrow Shall Be My Dancing Day

An Illustrated Medieval Carol.

Camelopardalis, San Francisco, 2018
Pencil, acrylic and ink on colored paper
Editor: William J. Dohar

In an anonymous Christmas carol from the fourteenth century, Christ himself tells us the story of his life, and he refers to it as a play. God came down from above to dance with us... and He is inviting us to dance with him.

The inspiration for this began back in my Unitarian years, while in the church choir. We were singing John Gardner's setting of this carol, which includes tambourines, and has a very lively, driving rhythm. I thought of including the sheet music in the back, and for it to be best read aloud with singing. However, there was not much to it, just the birth of Jesus (ok, that is a ***sizeable*** event, but a story it does not make). Only after I looked up the original full version of the text, years later, did the work on this book officially begin.

The illustrations feature the story as a play, with set and costumes like a drama troupe in Europe in the Middle Ages would design. Here they are players on a stage in a contemporary theater. This is the only carol I am aware of which features Jesus speaking in the first person, so I found it only fitting that the reader's point of view in the pictures is Jesus' (the actor playing Him). The inclusion of modern-day audience members also draws the reader's empathy. Are we the hero as well as the audience? Employing these devices, the hope is to bring the message of this age-old text into our lives.

The color palette was inspired by colors found in illuminated manuscripts. The use of paper cut-outs was meant to evoke the look of shadow box stage set models. My original intent was to construct such models and photograph them, but I did not give myself enough time, as I wanted it to be released just before Christmas. Maybe one day I will re-do it as originally intended. There was no need to have rushed the book. Since it was not a commission, it could have been released the following year. A lesson for future projects. Will anyone realize that the first image of the red curtains opening symbolizes the Son of God's point of view as he is being born, and that the single red and blue twisted rope tie is a stand-in for an umbilical cord?

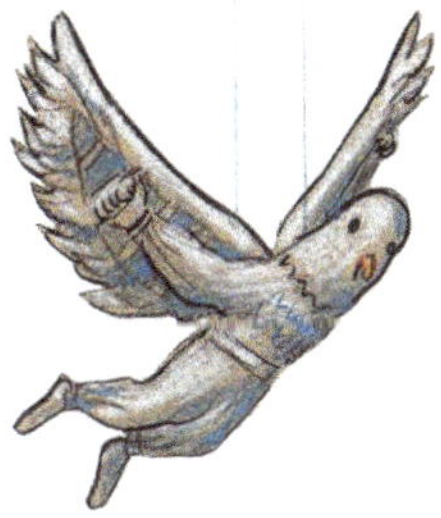

Then afterwards baptized I was;
The Holy Ghost on me did glance,
My Father's voice heard I from above,
To call my true love to my dance.

Sing, oh! my love, oh! my love, my love, my love,
This have I done for my true love.

12

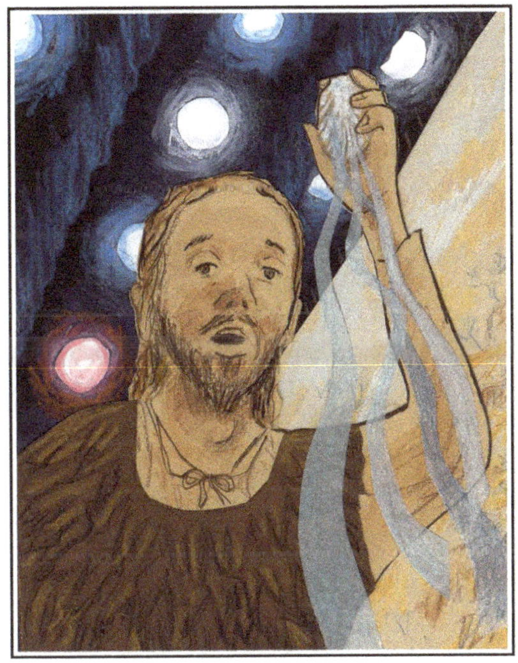

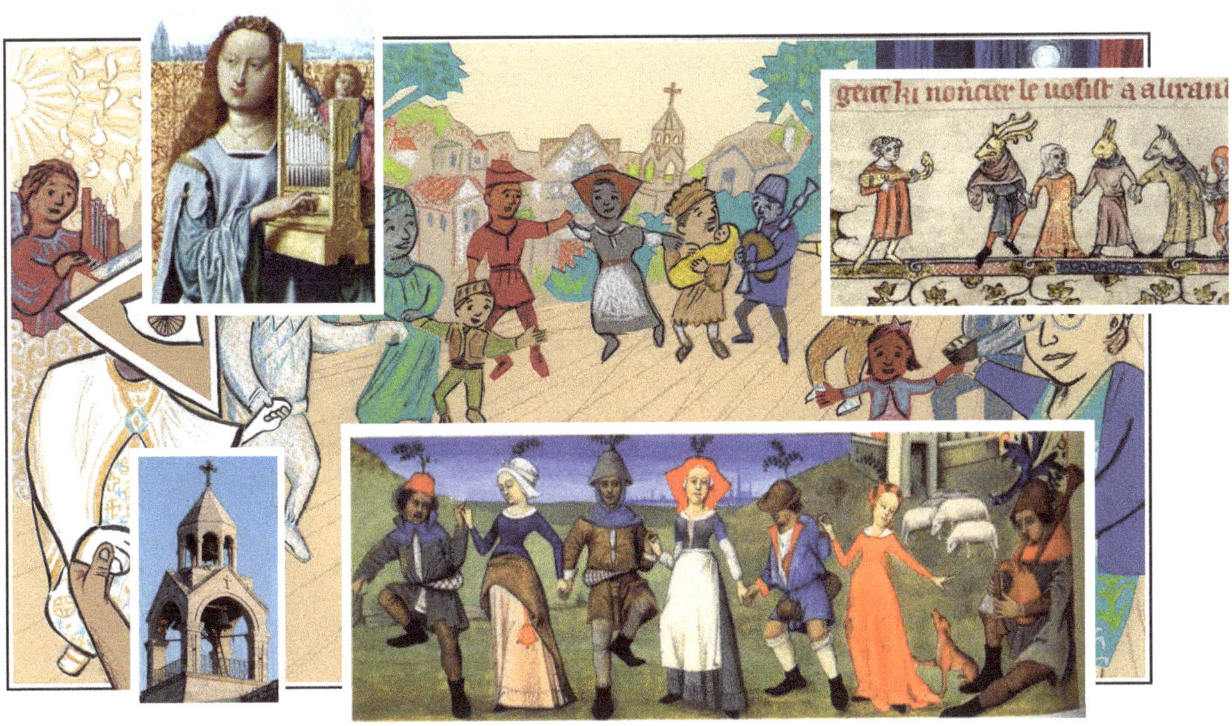

(Below) Art from the book, and reference materials.

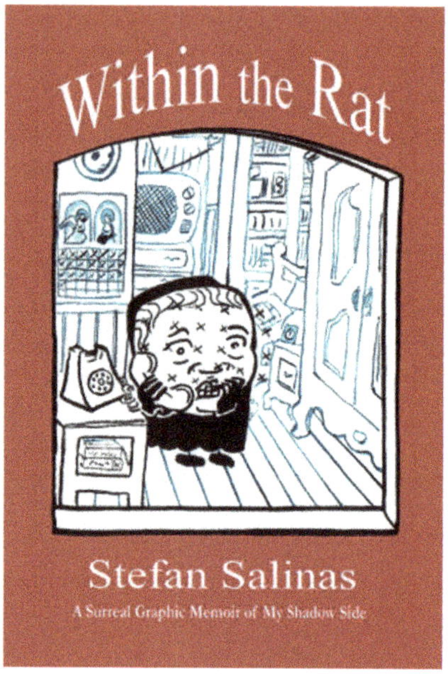

Within the Rat

A Surreal Graphic Memoir of My Shadow Side.

Camelopardalis, San Francisco, 2010
Ink, pencil, grease pencil and linocuts on paper
Editor: Stephanie Martin

Within the Rat *begins with three kids in a tent in a backyard at night. One of them suggests they venture out into the 'dark forest' to find and kill the fabled Mud-crud, a ferocious, man-eating beast. They step into the darkness and the anchor of reason is pulled up...*
This is a journey within - within the subconscious; within memories, family histories, dreams and mental landscapes. We encounter a mother who becomes a horse, a mourner who collects tears, and other manifestations of alcoholism, sexual promiscuity, codependency, anxiety and depression.

This book began as doodles in my journal. Short scenes, some reoccurring characters, surrealistic twists of fate, child-like characters, inspired largely by *Alice in Wonderland*. I was mourning the loss of my mother, and bad habits and depression were teaming up to pull me down. Seeing how cathartic these sketches were to me, friend Bernie Brennan not only encouraged me to work further on them, he gave me the best advice when I decided to piece them together as a printed book: "Don't consider who the audience is and don't worry about how you will market it. Do this for yourself. Otherwise, you may edit out things that need to be addressed with honesty."

I submitted it for a Xeric grant (in Canada and the US, twelve are chosen annually) and won funds for it's printing. The universe had pushed a huge boulder off of my path and seemed to be saying, "Now, what's your excuse?" I mentioned the influence of dreams in the first chapter. While writing this one, a few dreams spelled out my fears and doubts about the endeavor and pushed me to complete the task. There are five poignant, instructive dreams included in the tales, and they are told exactly as they occurred.

My guts, family history, and relationships I laid on the surgical table for all to examine. All were in the language of metaphors and talking animals, thus making the issues universal. It was reviewed in several online publications, and I even scored an interview on TV.

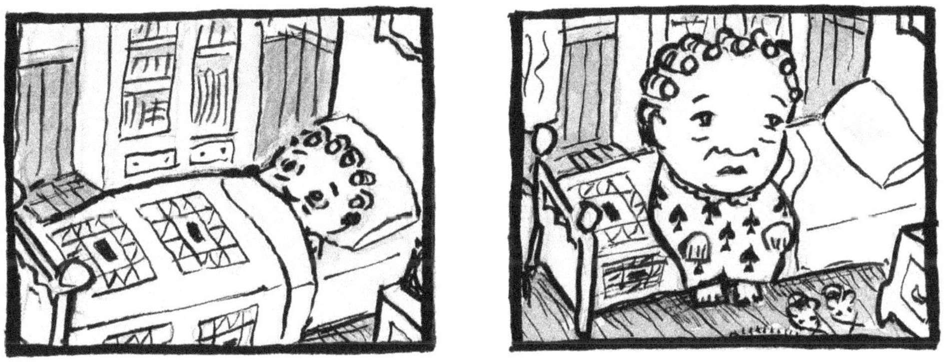

Too late for the laundromat and morning errands - push them to tomorrow. Coffee and an omelet should get me going.

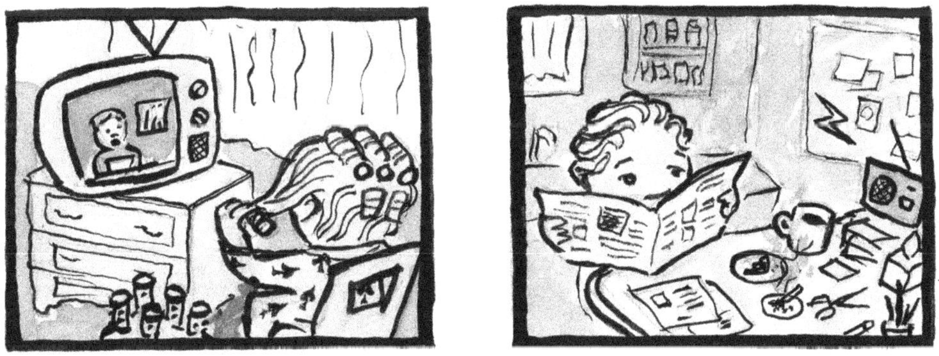

There's so much to get done today. Got to get a better job. Mourning just doesn't pay enough. It's a service of love.

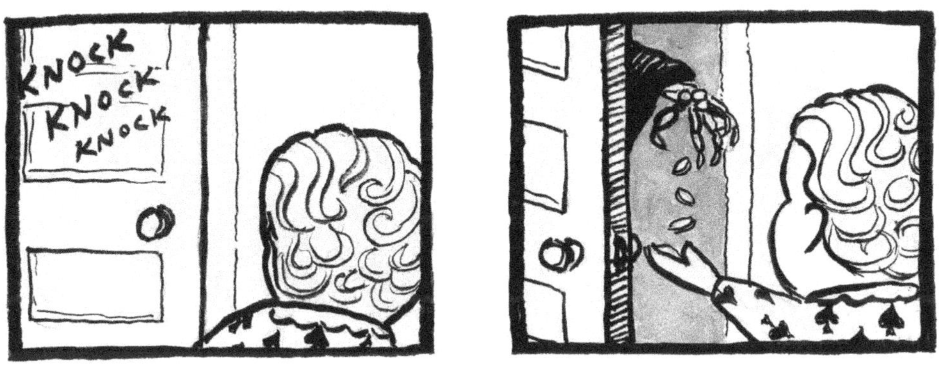

Sometimes I work double shifts - mourning the living *as well as* the dead - and why not? We're all headed in the same direction.

In a twisted way, depression can be a comfortable, familiar couch, even a source of one's own identity. The world's ills can worry a depressive's mind to the point of emotional paralysis. These ideas I explored with a professional mourner character, who cries for individuals, whole swaths of people, and animals facing extinction. We see she gets paid by the skeletal hand of Death.

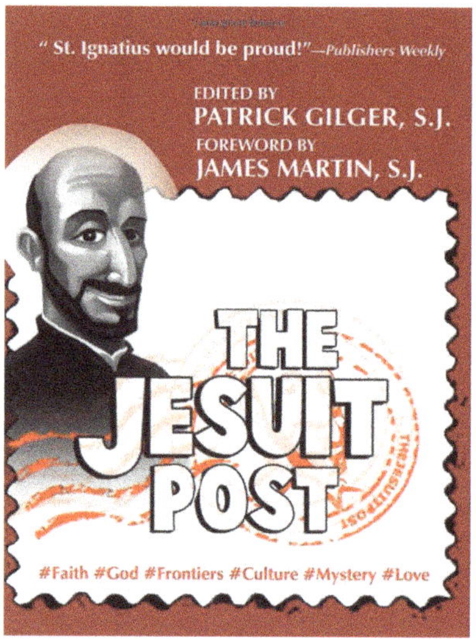

The Jesuit Post

#Faith #God #Frontiers #Culture #Mystery #Love

Orbis books, New York, 2014
Ink on paper

Editor: Rev. Patrick Gilger, SJ
Forward: Rev. James Martin, SJ
Cover Art: Tim Luecke

Following St. Ignatius of Loyola's dictum that God can be found in all things, young Jesuit priests, brothers, and seminarians explore issues of faith, culture, and lives of Christian discipleship in this broad-ranging collection of essays.

When Fr. Patrick Gilger, SJ approached me to come up with illustrations for a collection of essays by American Jesuits addressing religion, society, and culture, I jumped at the opportunity. He wanted something in the style of the art in *Within the Rat*. He gave me the freedom to let my imagination soar, although, like any commission, there were rejections and revisions. *The Jesuit Post* is a blog, and this was their first printed book. I was hoping to have the opportunity to design the cover as well, but in retrospect, perhaps my idea of Jesuit priests sitting in a circle around a campfire would have been a tad too silly. It was an honor and a thrill to be a part of the process.

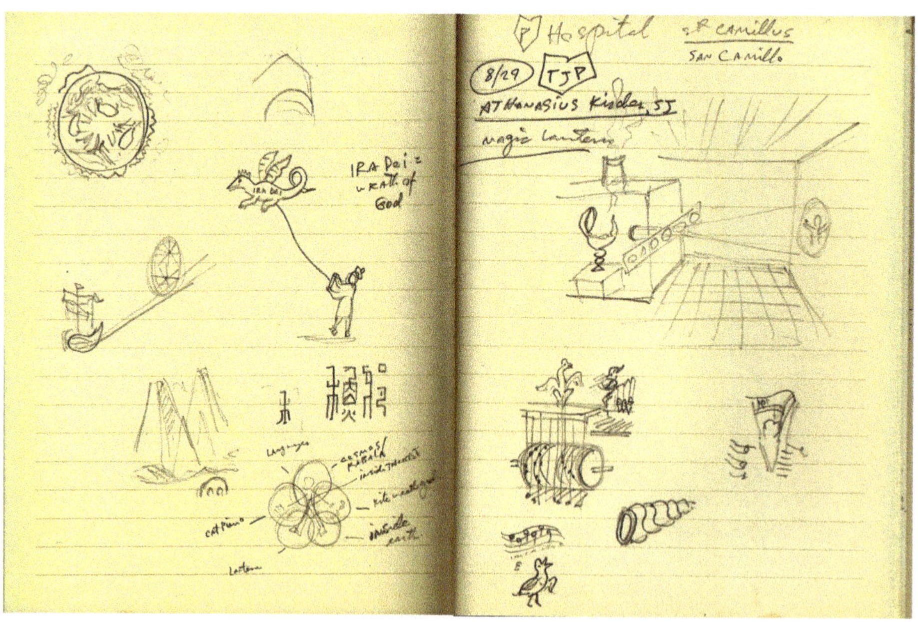

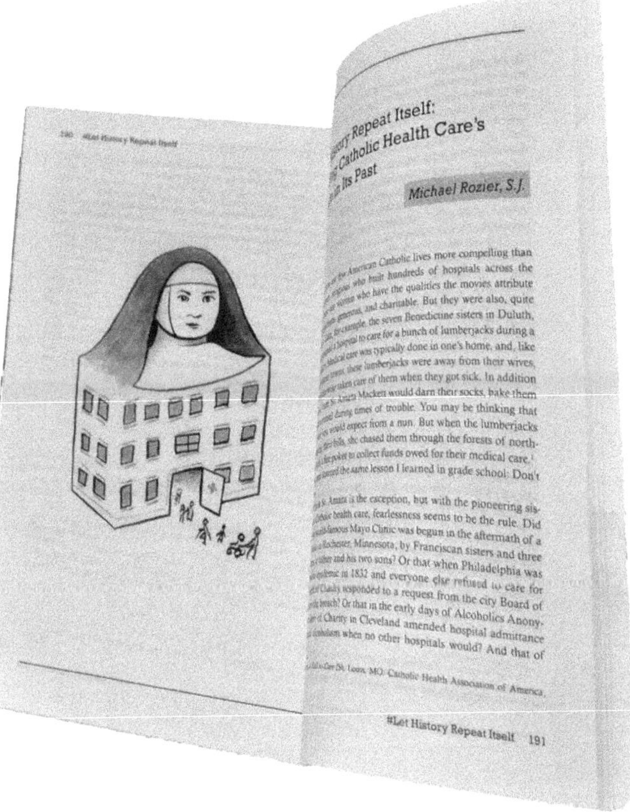
Repeat Itself:
Catholic Health Care's
Its Past
Michael Rozier, S.J.
#Let History Repeat Itself 191

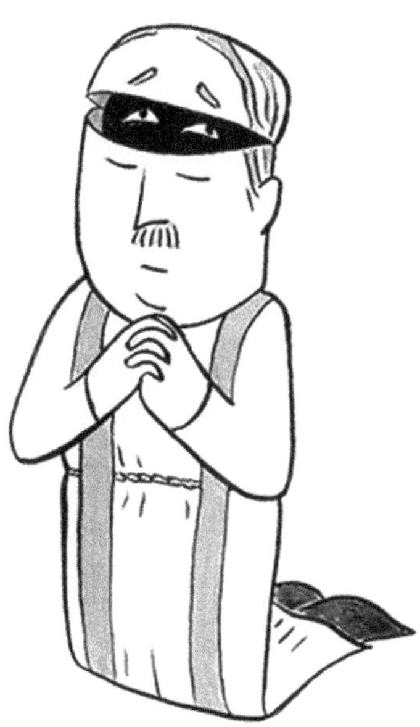

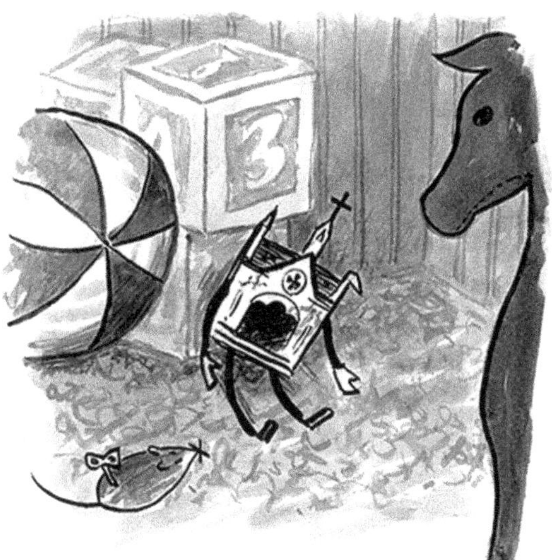

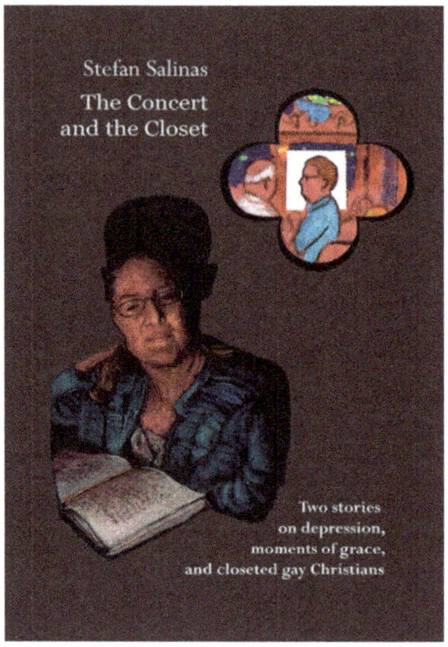

The Concert and the Closet

Two Stories on Depression, Moments of Grace, and Closeted Gay Christians.

Camelopardalis, San Francisco, 2020
Acrylic, ink and pencil on tracing and colored paper
Editors: Stephanie Martin and Jack Ronan

October Recital - *We enter a writer's thoughts, outer and inner experiences. During a single day, a thread weaves through events, emotions, ideas and memories.*
A Parade in June - *Let's go to San Francisco! A man encounters gay Christians - a few who are deeply closeted - as he himself approaches the faith.*

This was a reprint of two comics, printed separately in 2011 and 2012. Both stories were inspired by events and observations that fit together, almost as if the spirits wrote a narrative to reveal truths to me. Or perhaps it was just my brain in search of patterns and meaning in life.

The second one, *A Parade in June*,was kind of written as an ethical deal I made with my LGBTQ+ community. In exchange for entering a religion skeptical of openly queer individuals, I shared a few stories.It is about hiding one's own sexuality, living in layers of secrets, so I included tracing paper in the process. In order to create the rich darker colors, the best outcome resulted by painting from photos which I inverted the colors (the negative of the

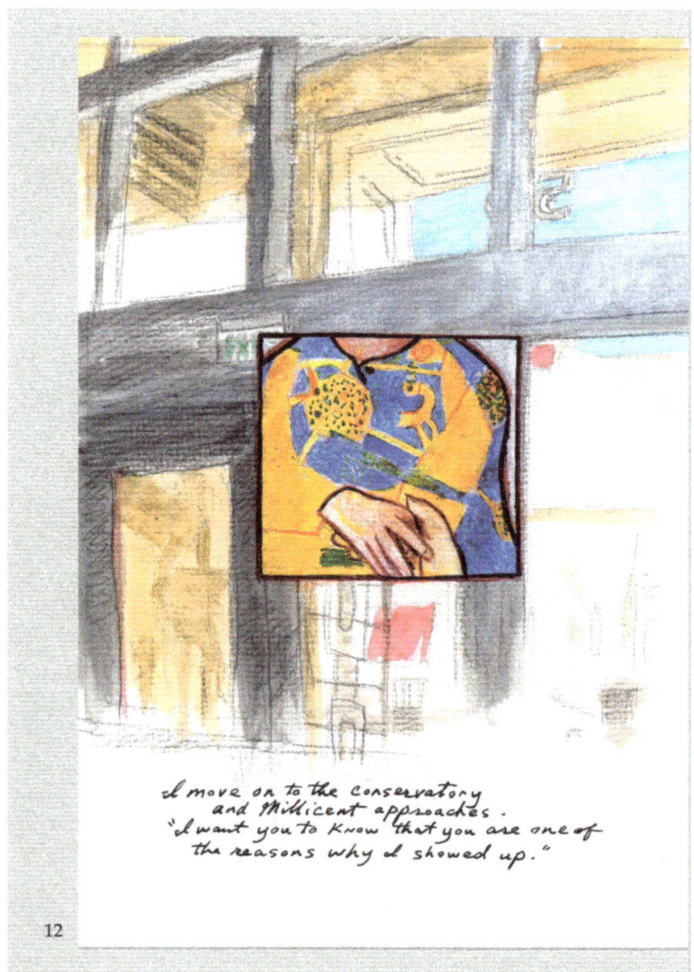

image), then scanned the art and inverted that. Both were to look as if the art and sketches originated in a journal, the second story like a personal travel guide of San Francisco.

Special thanks to Rev. Donal Godfrey for allowing me to include a quote from his book *Gays and Grays,* and to Emily Ezust, for allowing me to include her translation of Gustav Mahler's text to *Die zwei blauen Augen von meinen Schatz.*

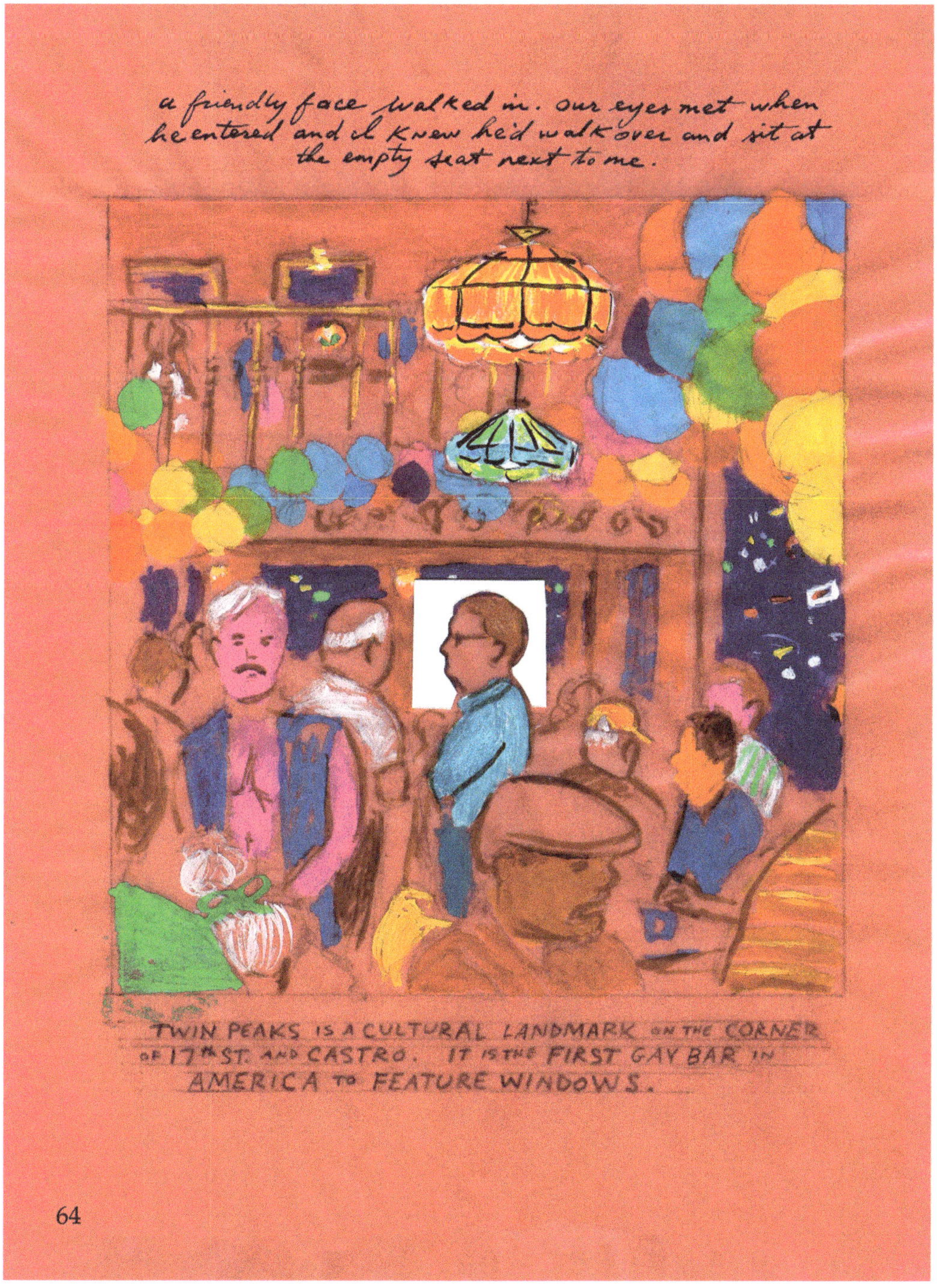

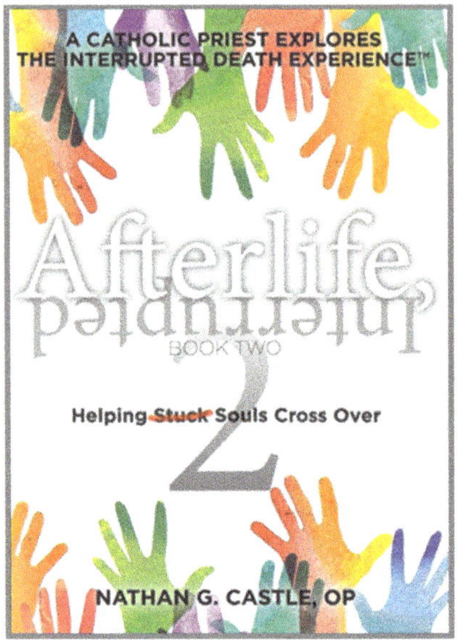

Afterlife, Interrupted Book Two

Helping Souls Cross Over.

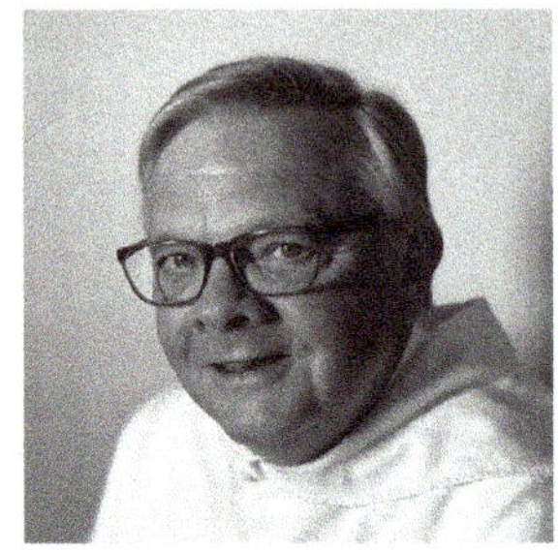

C2B2 Productions, Tucson, 2020
Ink on paper

Author: Nathan G. Castle, OP
Editor: Cathryn Castle Garcia
Cover art: Doreen Hann

This is the second book in the Afterlife, Interrupted *series. Over the past 23 years, Nathan G. Castle, OP, has helped more than 300 "stuck" - and not-so-stuck souls who died suddenly and traumatically adjust to the afterlife. Victims of fires, automobile accidents, shootings, stabbings, drownings - and suicides - come to him in his dreams seeking help to resolve their Interrupted Death Experiences.™ Father Nathan believes that providing such help is something the Holy Spirit has given him and his prayer partners to do. In his* Afterlife Interrupted *books, Father Nathan is quick to point out that not everyone who dies suddenly gets stuck. He also addresses questions like: Is death survivable? What does he do to help people cross over? Does time exist in the afterlife? Do deceased relatives help us adjust to moving through our deaths?*

You never know what will lead to what. After reading *Afterlife, Interrupted*, I wrote to the author, for I had to know how a Catholic priest came to write a book about his communications with angels, spirits, and saints. Being brought up in the Modern Spiritualist tradition, which acknowledges such phenomenon, and moving into Catholicism, which takes a more *cautions* approach to it, my curiosity was piqued.

In the letter, I included a simple drawing of Fr. Nathan. This led to him asking me for a finished version of it, along with a second illustration, to mark the two sections within an upcoming companion book. Then he and his sister, Cathryn Castle Garcia, asked for art to accompany each chapter! I not only read the stories but was asked to dust off my own intuitive cap and open up to inspiration. A blessing of a collaboration, for which I was most grateful for the opportunity.

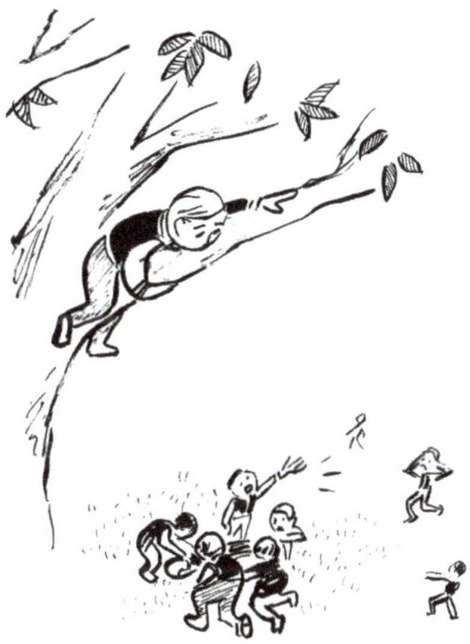

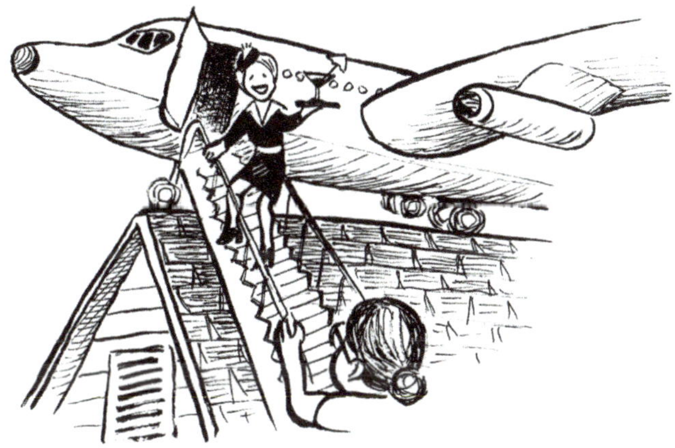

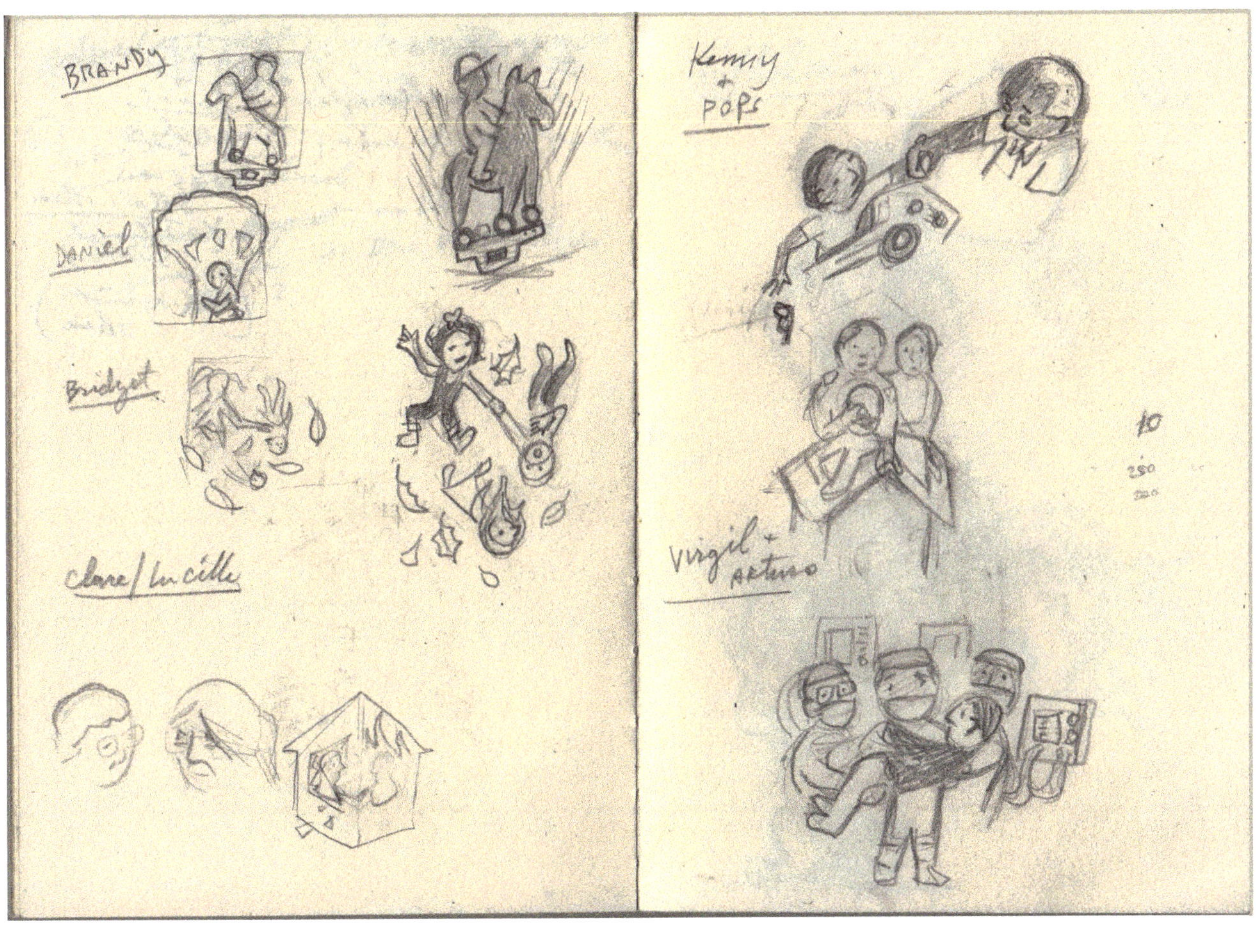
BRANDY
Daniel
Bridget
Clare/Lucille
Kenny + POPS
Virgil + Arturo

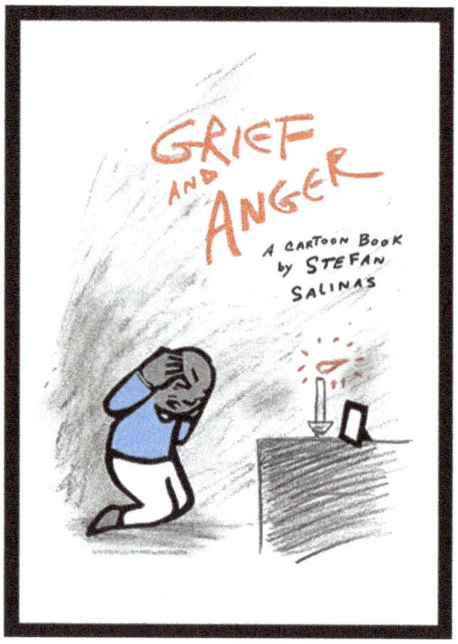

Grief and Anger

Camelopardalis, San Francisco, 2021
Linocut, pencil and acrylic on paper
Editor: Robert Lynn

When we lose a loved one, within our sorrow, there can be anger. Let us take a look at variations of this rage, with eyes of compassion.

My father died in January 2019, and then a dear friend died in July 2020. Dealing with the range of emotions in the stages of grief over both led to the creation of this book.

I took a visual cue from a print by Alberto Beltrán that hangs in my living room (it is important to have good artwork hanging around). Linocut prints, pencil, and acrylic paint, along with rough, handwritten text, combine on the pages with immediate, raw emotion. My goal was for it to appear as if they were pages from a distraught person's journal. The rough cartoons and touches of levity sprinkled throughout keep us moving through the heartache explored.

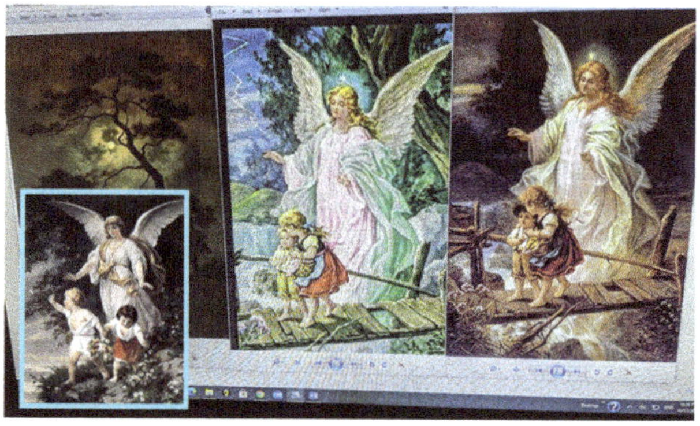

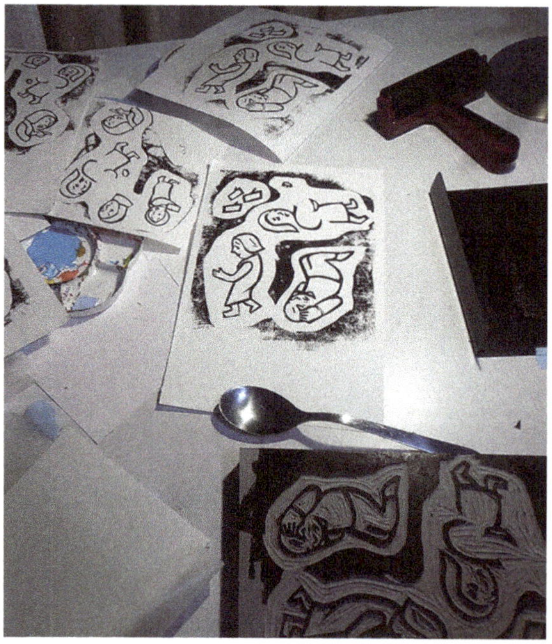

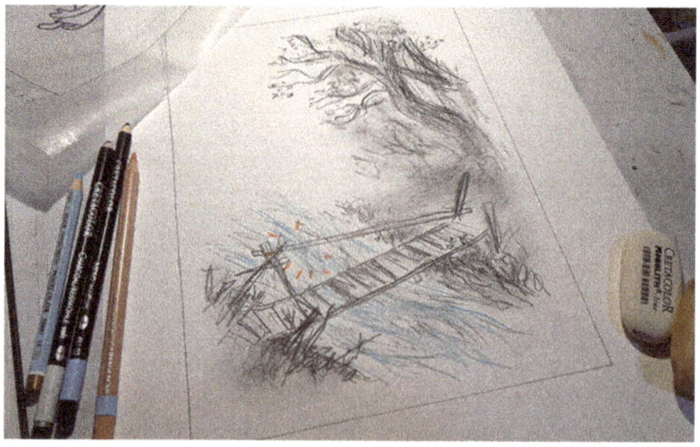

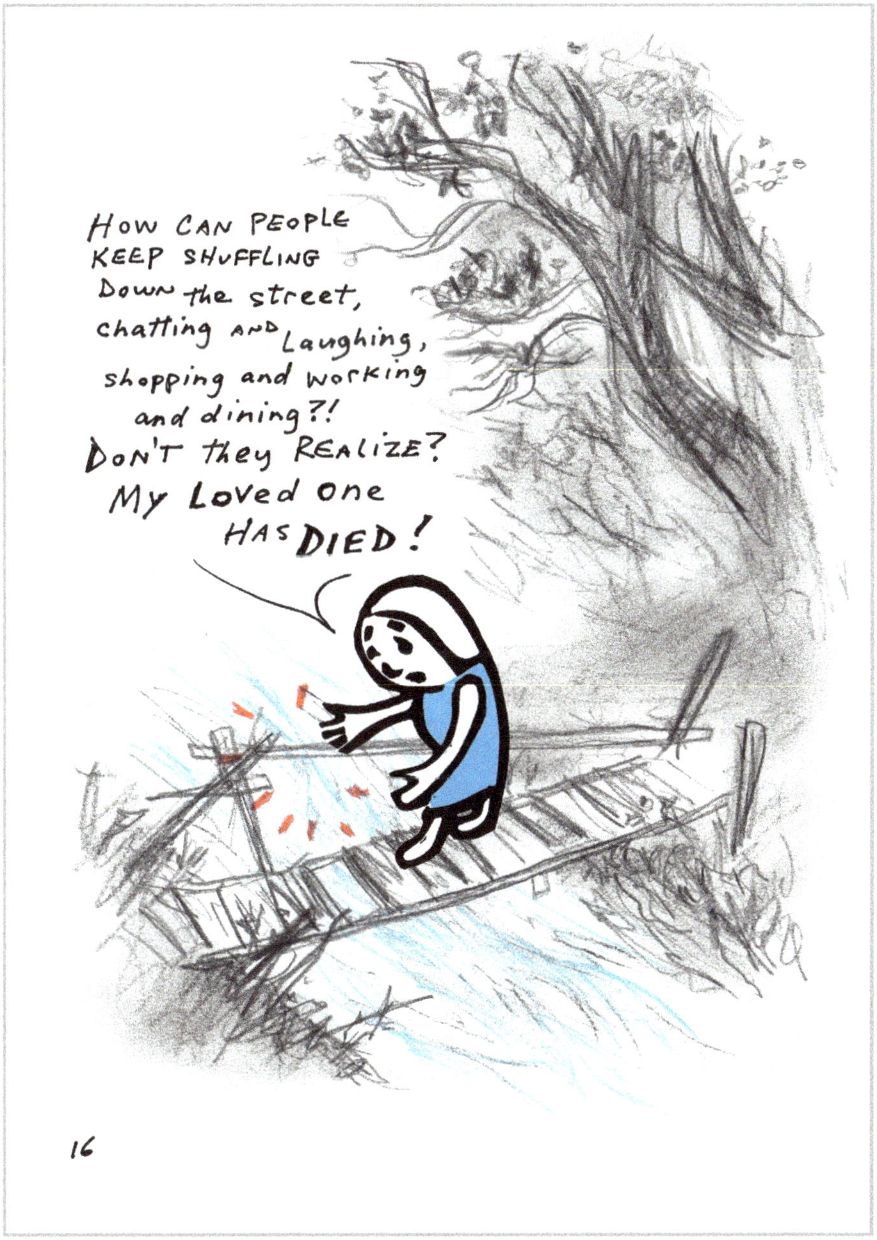

On the previous page, the woman in this book confesses that she could not take her sick husband to the ER in time to save his life. To place the viewer into her emotional state of angst and sorry more deeply, I borrowed the setting found in the famous German painting of a guardian angel, repainted and made famous by Bernhard Plockhorst. She stands where the girl is, but the guardian angel is absent. Her husband, which was where the boy in the painting stands, has vanished. ...Or has he fallen down the hole in the bridge?

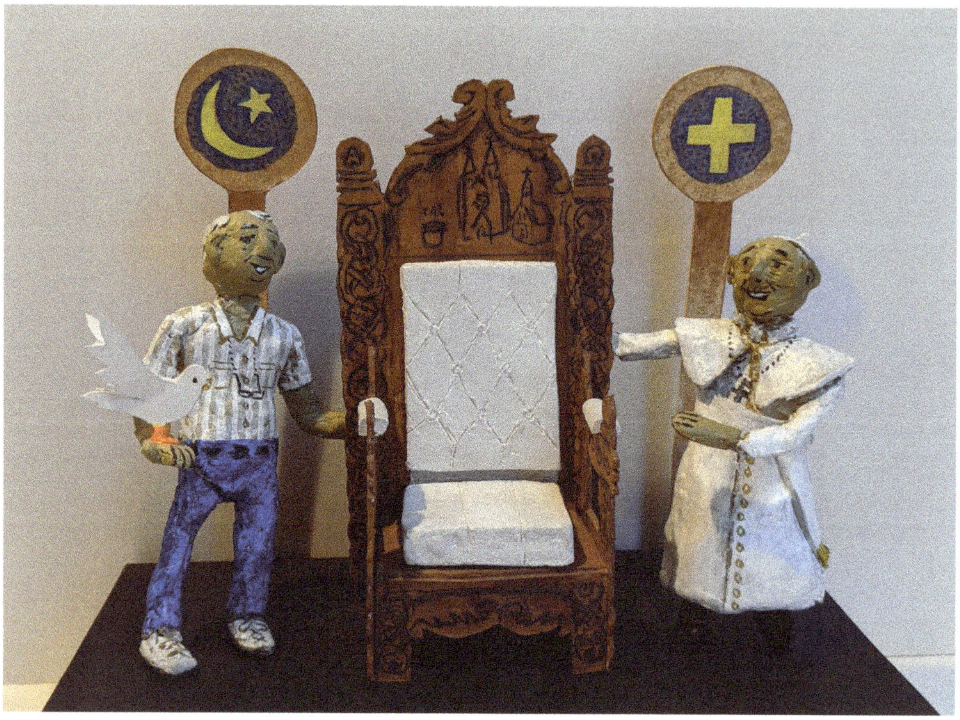

Promotional sculpture for *A Muslim Family's Chair for the Pope*, 2017
Papier-mâché, tape, wire, board & acrylic, 8"h x 8"w x 4d"

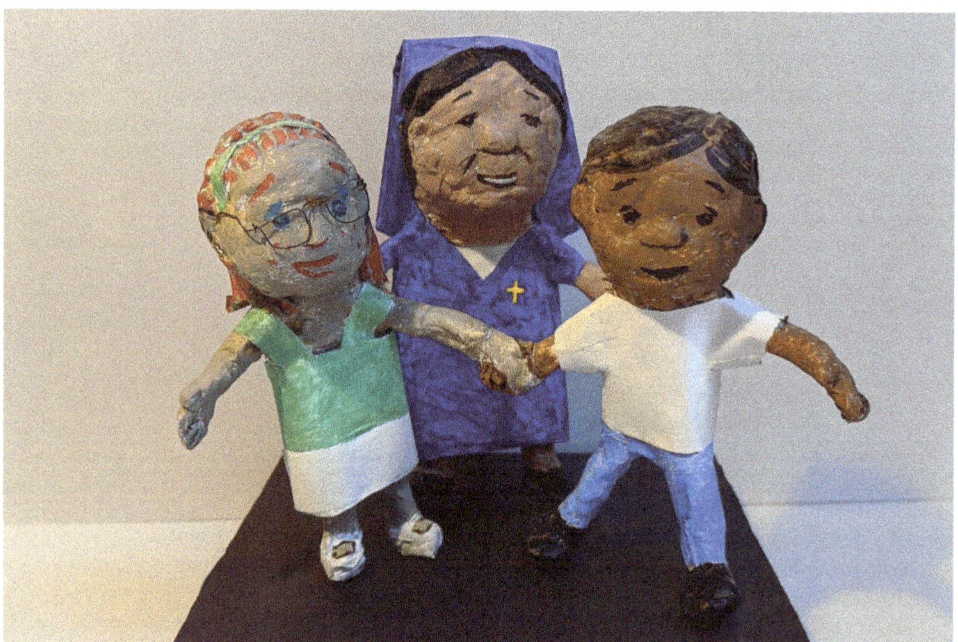

Promotional sculpture for *Catholic Churches, Big and Small*, 2014
Papier-mâché, tape, wire, board & acrylic, 6.5"h x 7"w x 6d"

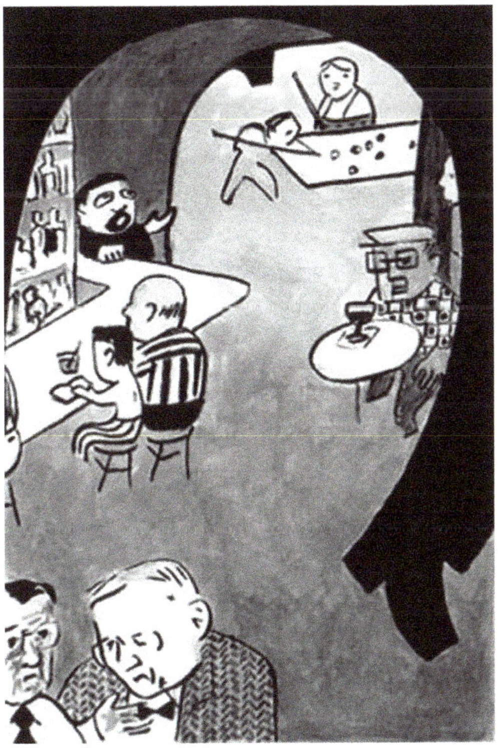

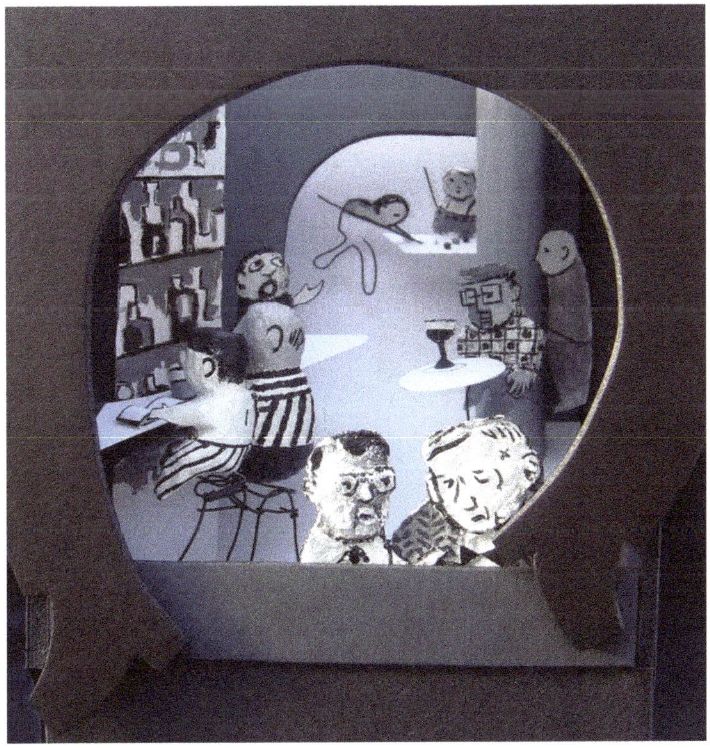

A Den of Comfort, 2011
A diorama of a page from *Within the Rat*
Papier-mâché, tape, wire, board & acrylic

Books Never Realized

Out of dozens of book ideas never completed, here are some samples.

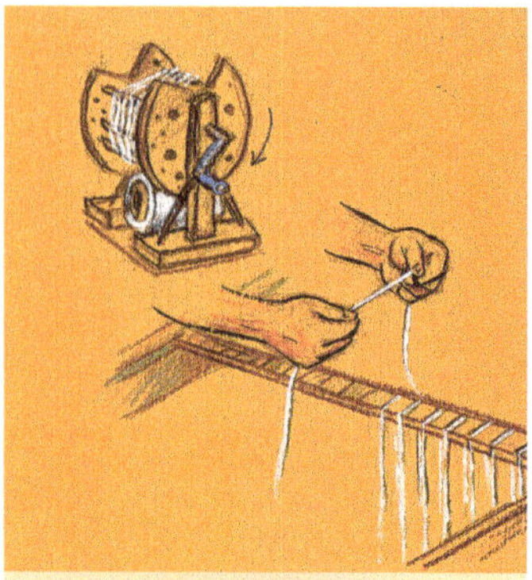

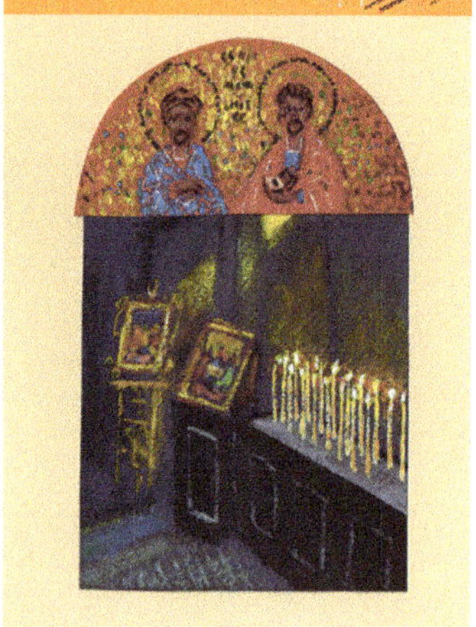

Portrait of a candlemaker at a Greek Orthodox church. Acrylic on paper.

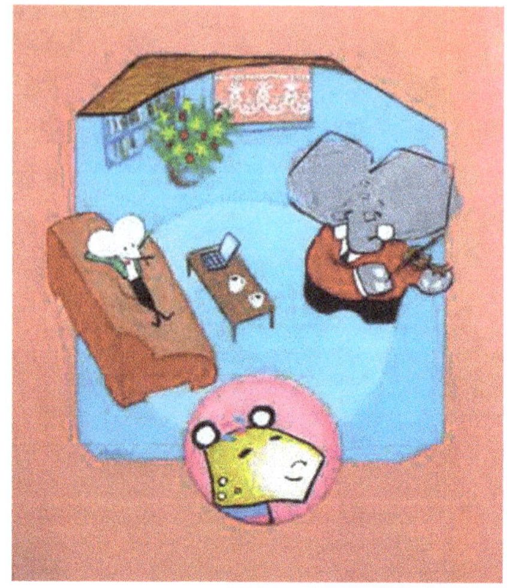

Happy and Jolly, about a mouse and elephant couple. Acrylic on board.

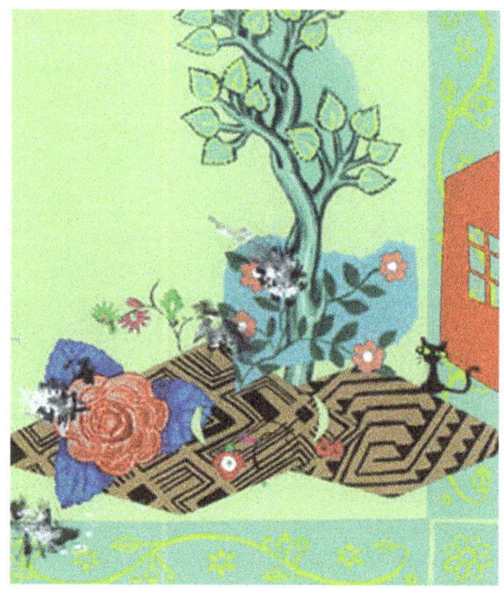

Soup and Roses, about a grouchy neighbor who falls ill. Acrylic on paper.

Rosa's Hat, about a boy who witnesses flowers supernaturally blooming on a dying woman's hat. Acrylic on paper.

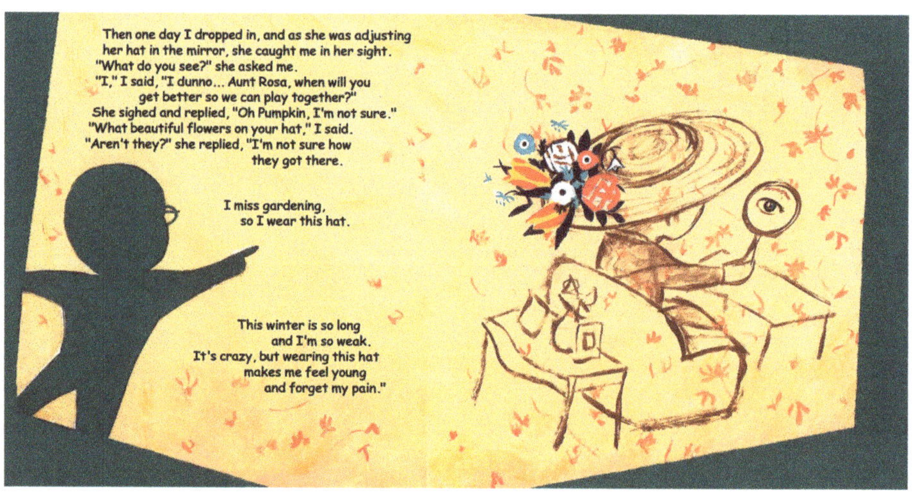

Webcomic

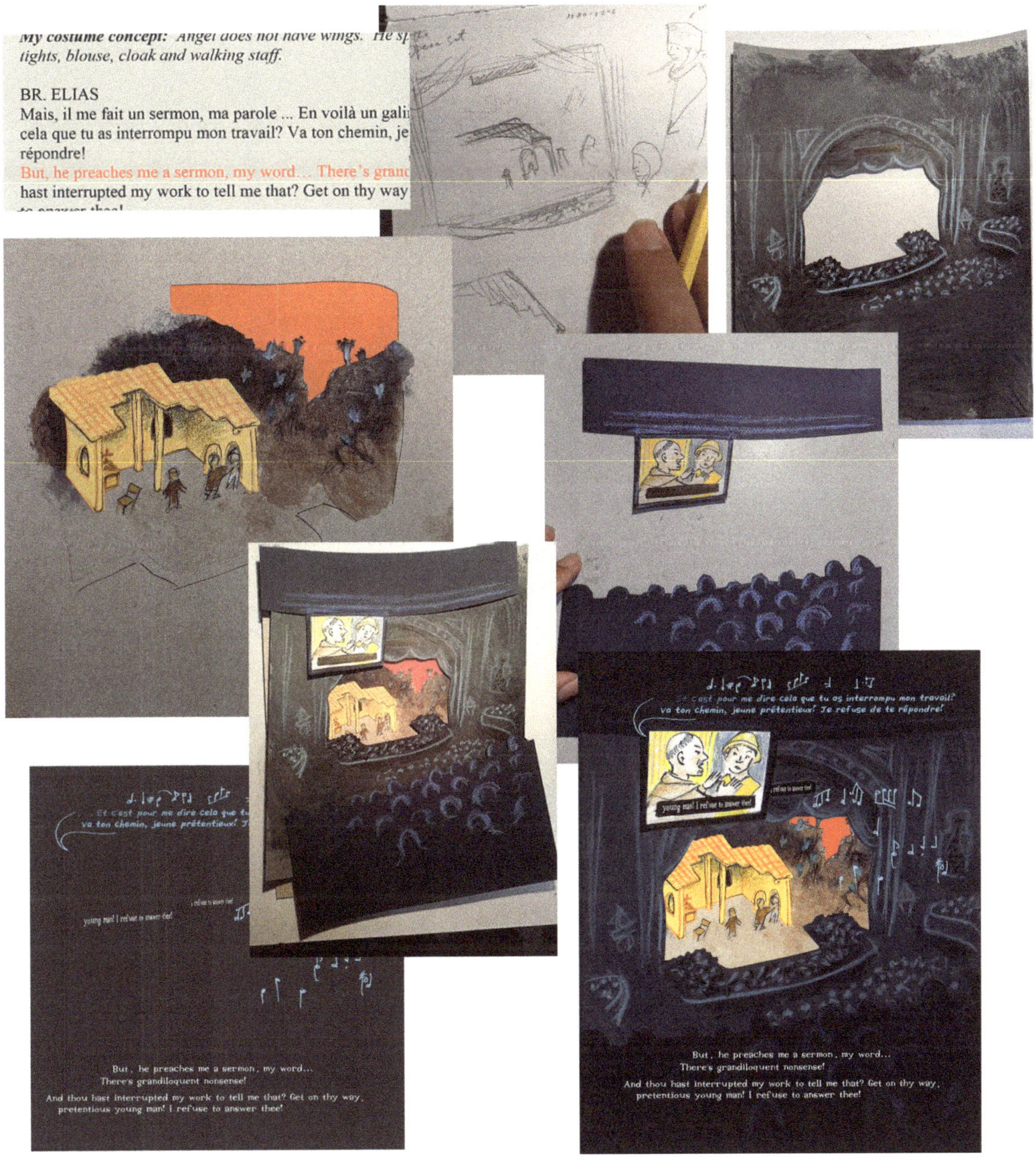
tights, blouse, cloak and walking staff.
BR. ELIAS
Mais, il me fait un sermon, ma parole ... En voilà un gali
cela que tu as interrompu mon travail? Va ton chemin, je
répondre!
But, he preaches me a sermon, my word… There's grand
hast interrupted my work to tell me that? Get on thy way
c'est pour me dire cela que tu as interrompu mon travail?
Va ton chemin, jeune prétentieux! Je refuse de te répondre!
young man! I refuse to answer thee!
But, he preaches me a sermon, my word...
There's grandiloquent nonsense!
And thou hast interrupted my work to tell me that? Get on thy way,
pretentious young man! I refuse to answer thee!

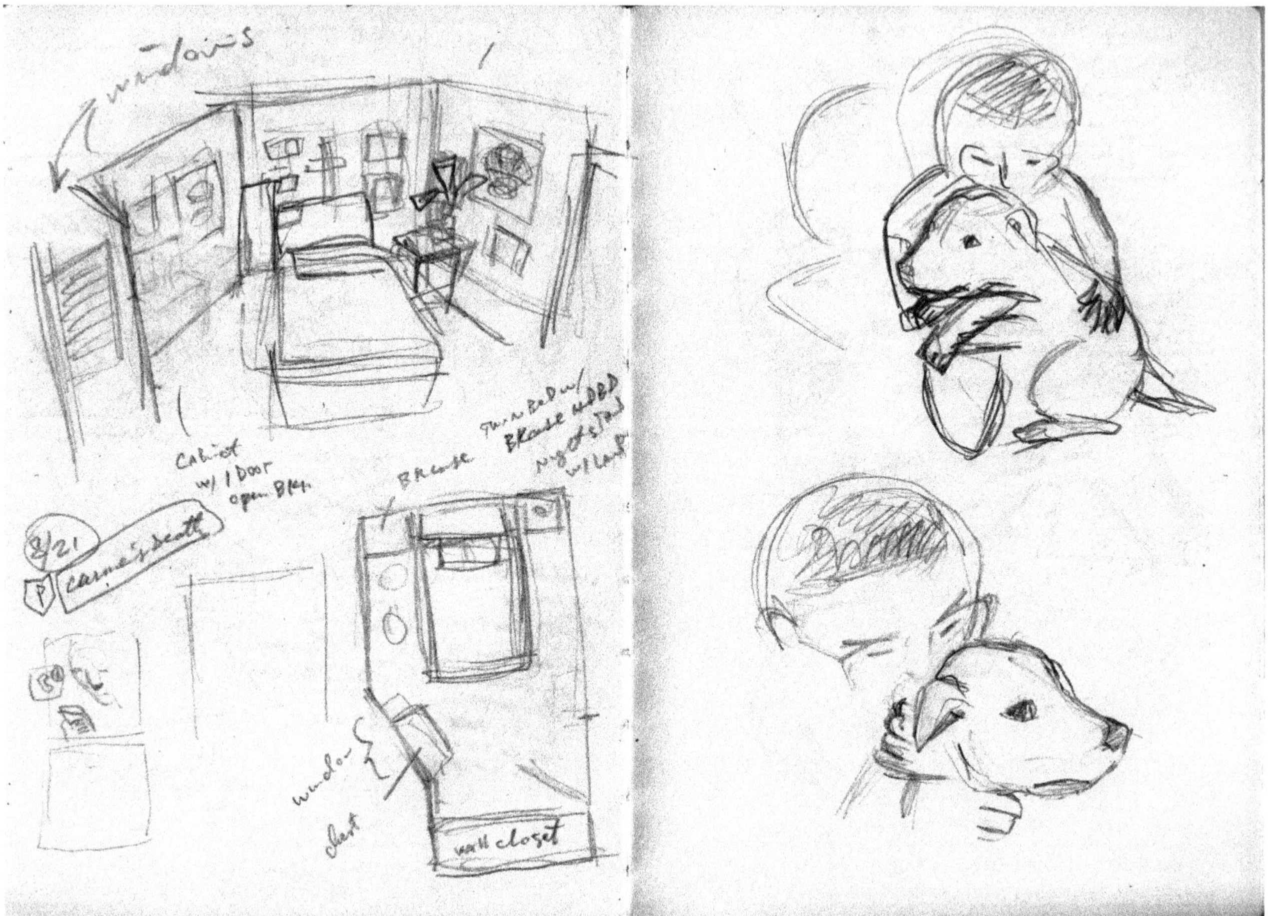

P — pizza pete's scene

Funny Host stories

(H) So, the other Day, A handicapped man in the communion line was in the wheelchair. He didn't seem to have much motor control over his limbs, only right hand working. Anyway when he received the Host, his fingers snapped it to pieces.

(We see he's in a wheelchair, so no need to mention)

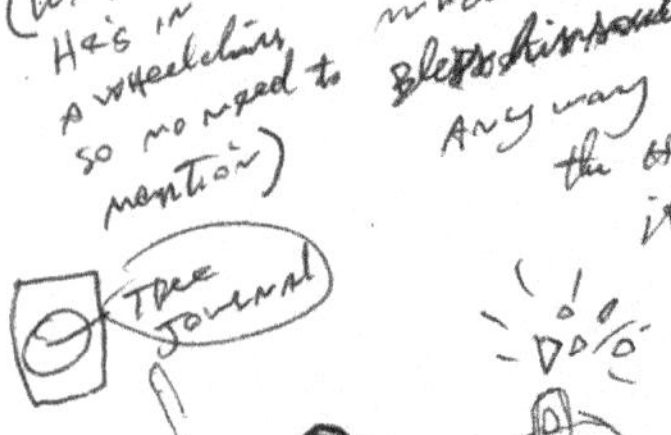

(D) & (F) Laugh (L) covers mouth & wide eyes

(H) (giggles kind of nervously) You guys take these things much too lightly!

(Foreshadowing?)

(D) Oh A-HA HA HA HA HA HA Dear little Brother,

(H) I was on my knees, trying to rescue all the pieces.

(Show this. - Alert a man behind from stepping back on the last piece)

D: Remember what Chesterson said: "Life is much too important to be taken seriously"

(L) Wasn't that Oscar Wilde?

(D) "The reason angels can fly, is because they take themselves lightly"

The Sacramental Father Dom

Posted on SmackJeeves, Tapas and Webtoons, 2019-2020
Acrylic, pencil and ink on paper + digital

Early within Pope Francis' reign, in a city in Northern California, amidst our modern secular society - alcoholism, politics, sex abuse scandals, plight of the poor, and isolationism - how does a Catholic priest navigate through all of this? Walk alongside Fr. Dom, a 65-year-old diocesan parochial vicar, during six months of his life, as he goes through a bit of an existential crisis. Step into his thoughts, memories and dreams...

Nine years from inception to completion translates as 7- 1/2 years of research, writing, and rewriting, then sixteen months of illustrating (and still revising) the final pages, resulting in 68 episodes, 426 pages in total. This story was drawn from research, as well as from the lives of actual priests. It is as honest a portrayal as I could make it and has been a true learning experience and labor of love.

Since my move to San Francisco, I have gotten to know a few priests, working alongside them and sharing time and ideas with them as friends. Understand that I grew up outside of any major established religion, especially one with a set of a strictly defined hierarchy of religious leaders. I was not raised with the idea that a minister is not just a man but an intercessor between the rest of us and God. I did realize they are expected to follow a strict code of ethics in their daily life. Hearing of the joys and frustrations, some of which are unique to that vocation, sparked a flame inside. Being a convert to Catholicism and working alongside clergy may have helped me see the profession from a different angle. My goal was to give people outside of the faith, devoted believers, and all in between, a peek inside the vocation and a gained appreciation for it. Like my book on the Bosnian Muslim, my challenge was to get inside the hero's head. Besides research in books, films, and essays, I anonymously interviewed a dozen priests and some people who work closely with them. I fielded additional questions from some of them as the project progressed.

I did not want the characters in my comic to be clones of those I have gotten to know, so I pulled from the anonymous interviews and research. Stories heard while visiting different parishes, voices present and past, events and observations, were still basically lifted from real life. Details, places, and names were shuffled to make it a work of fiction,but know that the more fictional a spoken phrase or action in the story seems, the more likely it actually happened. The other priests in the story, and even some of the non-clergy, represent alternate points of view. They are like facets to a larger diamond; alternative paths Dom can take. It is a portrait of many priests.

Similar to *Within the Rat*, I had no idea what the plot was going to be or what shape the story would take. As scenes and characters came to me, symbols and themes emerged, and it felt like it flowed as if the tale was writing itself. It amazed me how many times I would

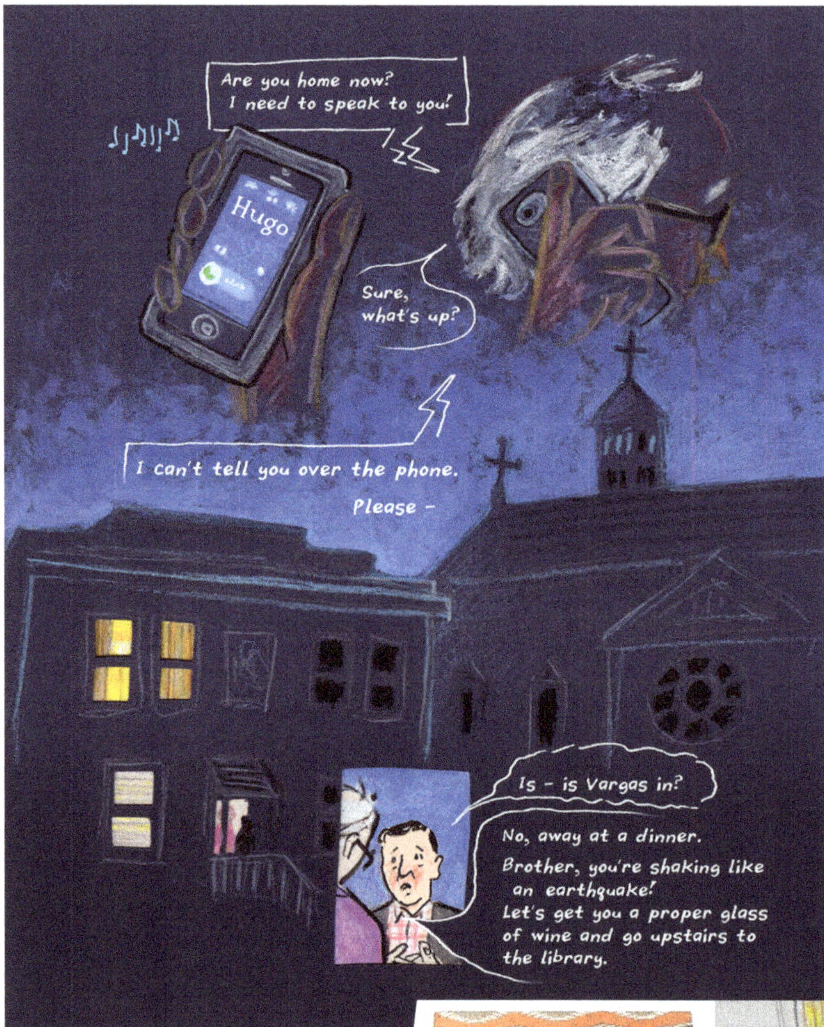

be just at the right place, at the right time to observe, hear, or learn about a detail that further informed and enriched the story. When seeking knowledge about something for a project and being open to receiving information (not always in the form you expect), I have found it can be akin to a call and response with the Holy Spirit (the Greater Consciousness, Allah, or the Universe, if you prefer).

Sacramental objects are defined early on. They joined other symbols and themes. Music also plays an important role. Dom is a lover of classical music, and his café buddy is a flutist.

The locations, buildings, churches, furnishings and clothing were carefully chosen to fit the characters and atmospheres sought. Fr. Dom's suite has a Mid-Century modern aesthetic (Vatican II highly influenced Dom). The simple egalitarian pieces hint at his character.

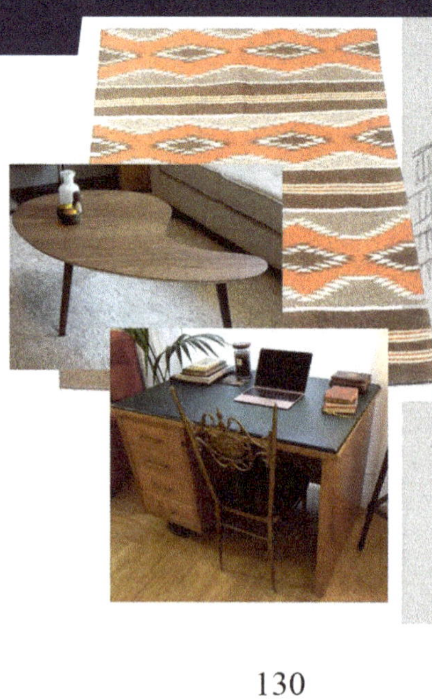

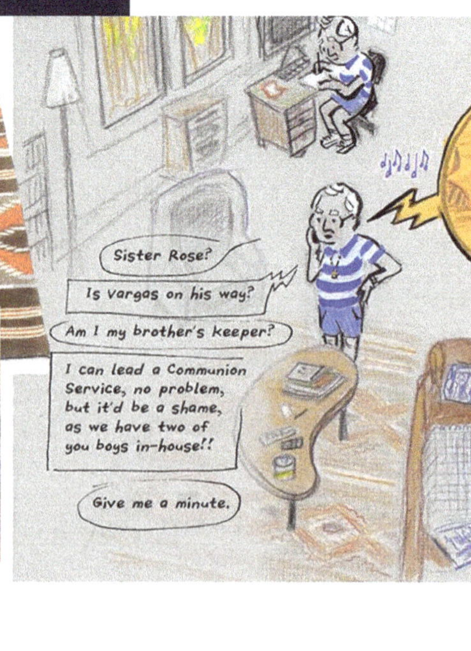

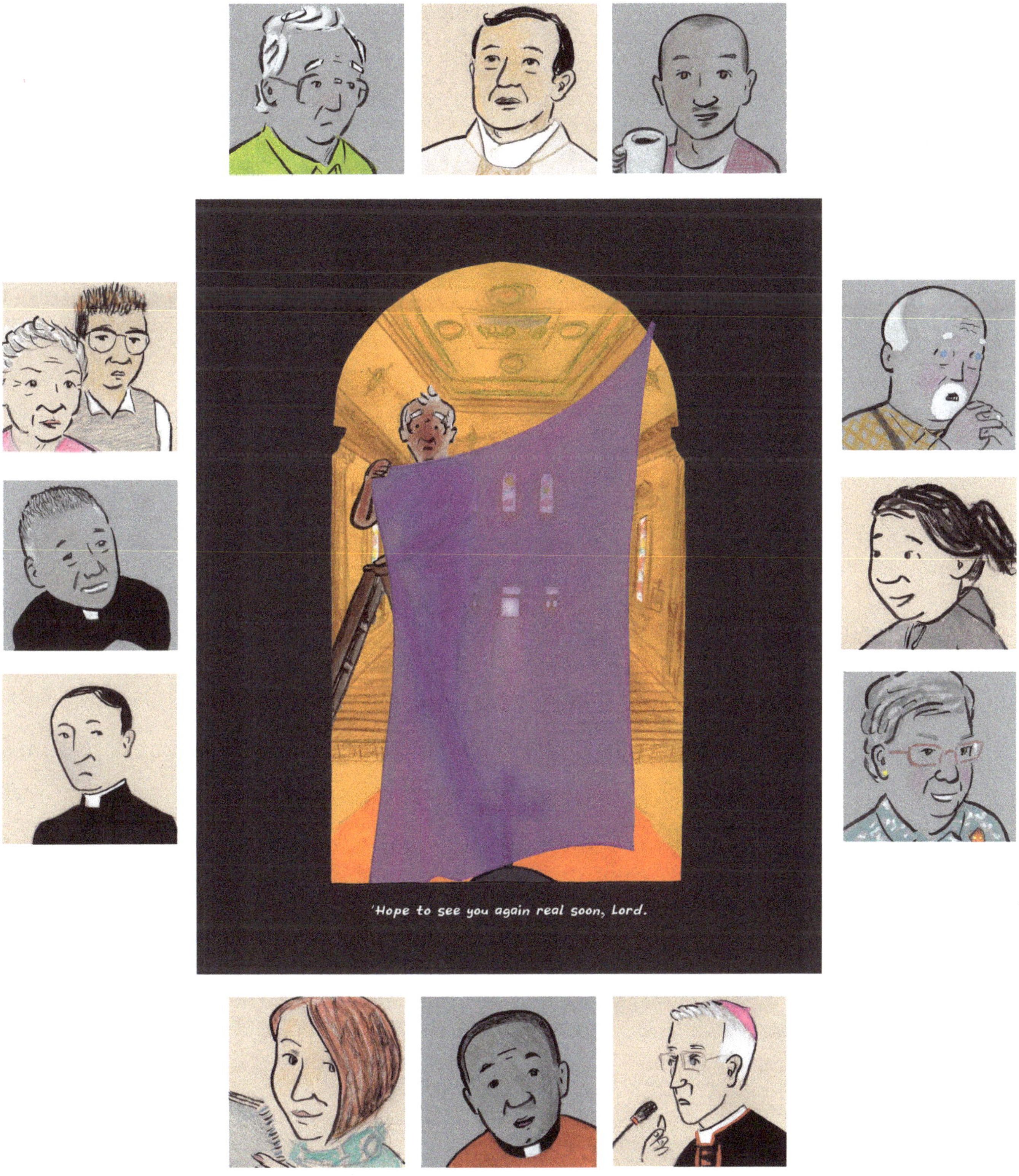
'Hope to see you again real soon, Lord.

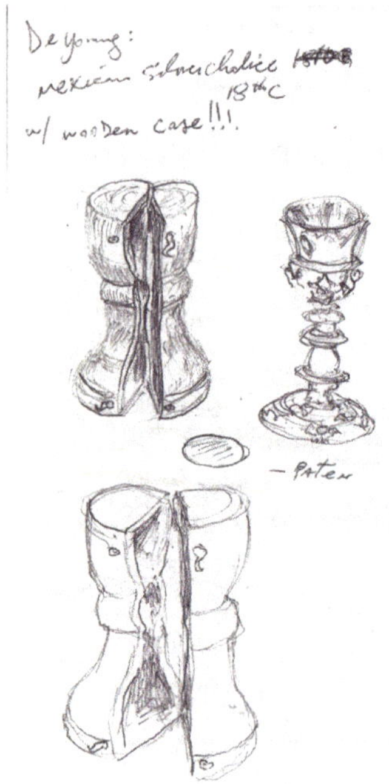

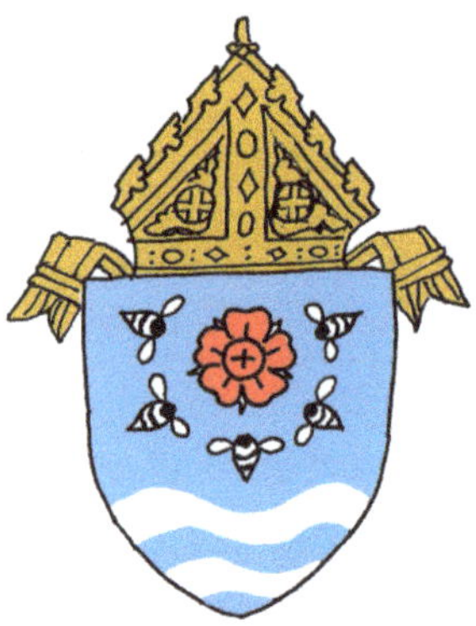

Archdiocese of Santa Rita

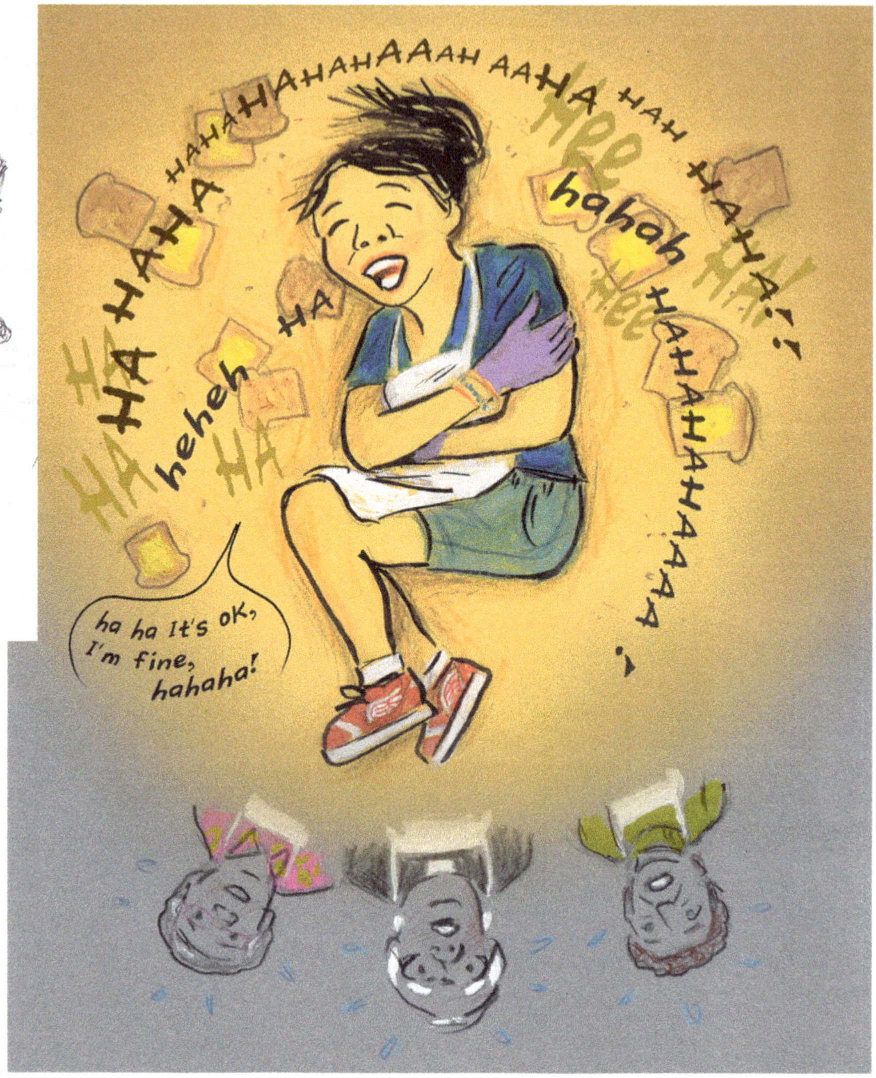

Pay attention to where the music is set and how it helps the story along.

The final sixteen months, when I was rewriting, illustrating, and posting the weekly episodes online, forces of creativity, focus, and drive were flowing through me like never before in my life. I missed a lot of sleep, neglected house upkeep (a jungle of dishes, clothing, and papers everwhere!), only saw friends on occasion, yet still managed to hold a full-time day job. As of writing this book, it is still just a webcomic, but I hope to get it in e-book and/or print someday. It was a rewarding journey, full of deeply heartfelt emotions, and it opened me to a larger world of knowledge and spirituality.

I am sincerely grateful to all of the anonymous men and women I interviewed and drew inspiration from. Thank you Rev. Lyle Beckman, the Center SF, William Dohar, Michael Evernden, Katie Lacz, Patrick Michaels, David Miles, Sr. Maureen O'Brien†, Michael Pappas, Robert Pierson, Sr. Mary Frances Seeley, Barry Venditti, Tom Wade, and Felicia Woods. You all helped this come to life. Thank you.

Graphic Art and Illustration

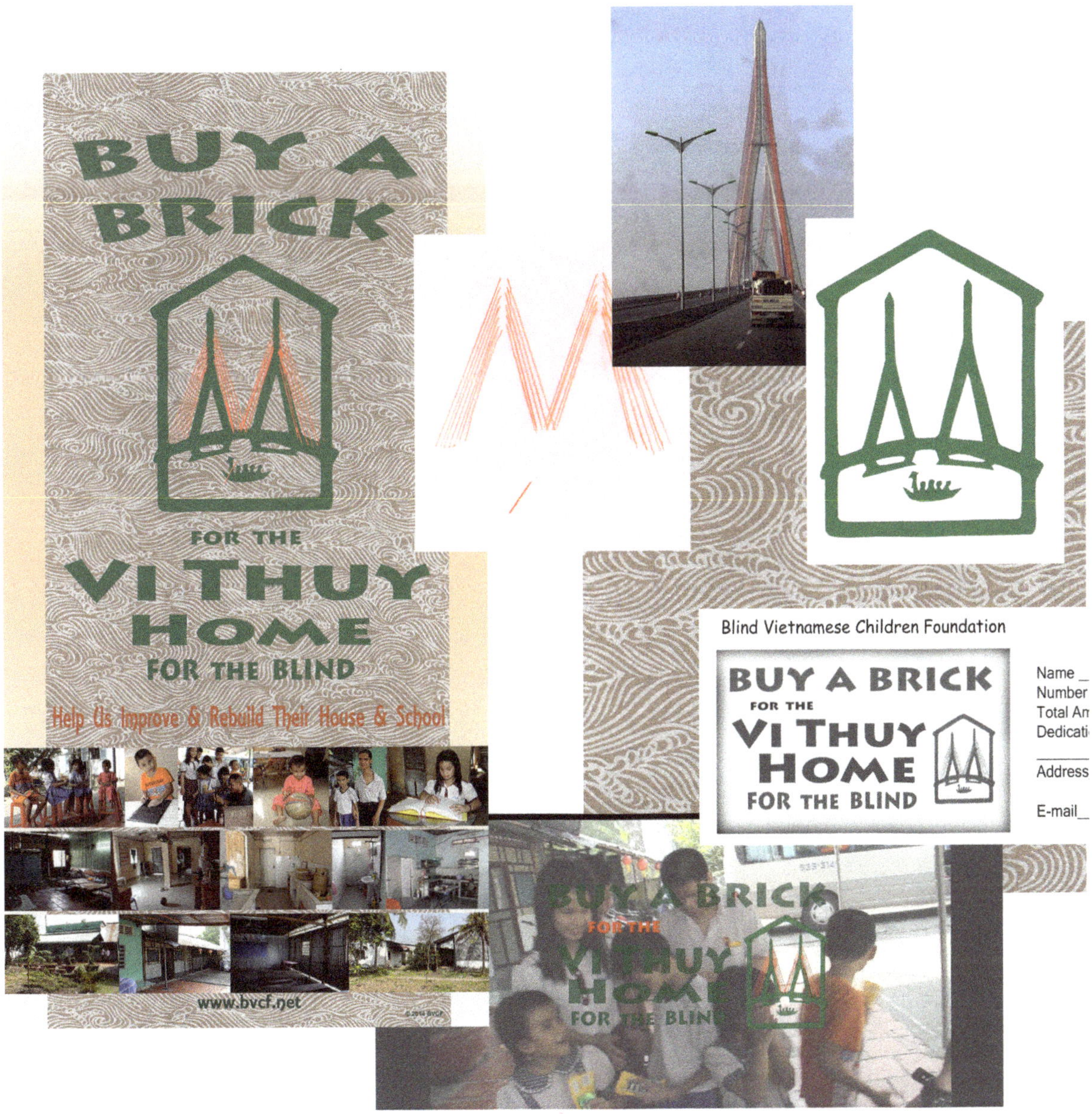

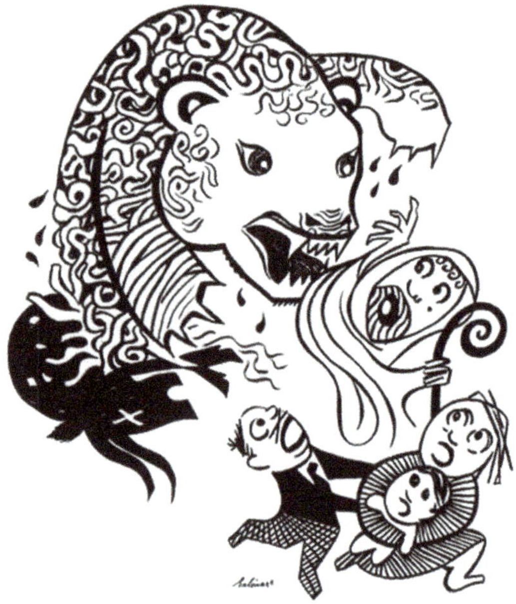

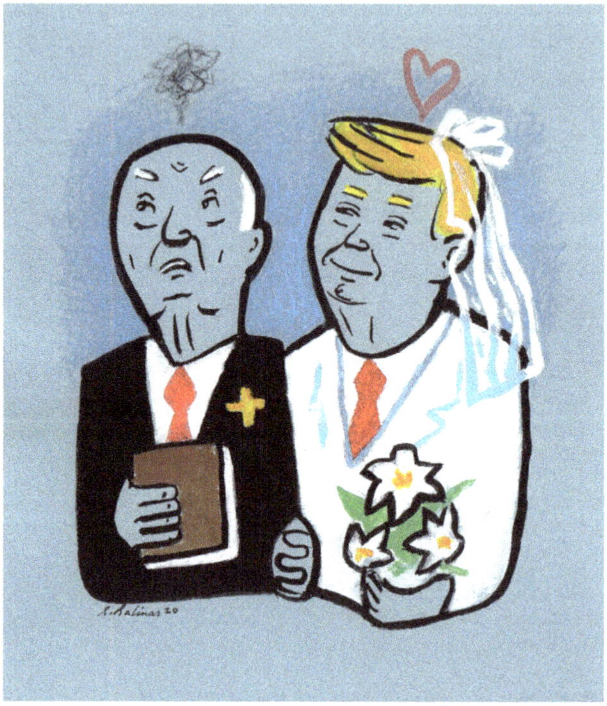

Clockwise from top left:

Illustration for *The Progressive* Magazine, 2008, ink on paper

"Last Call for Aging White Evangelicals" article by Alan Bean
Friends of Justice blog, 2020, Acrylic and ink

BVCF fundraiser theme, 2014, Acrylic on paper + digital

The Church in Surgery, 2020, Acrylic on paper + digital

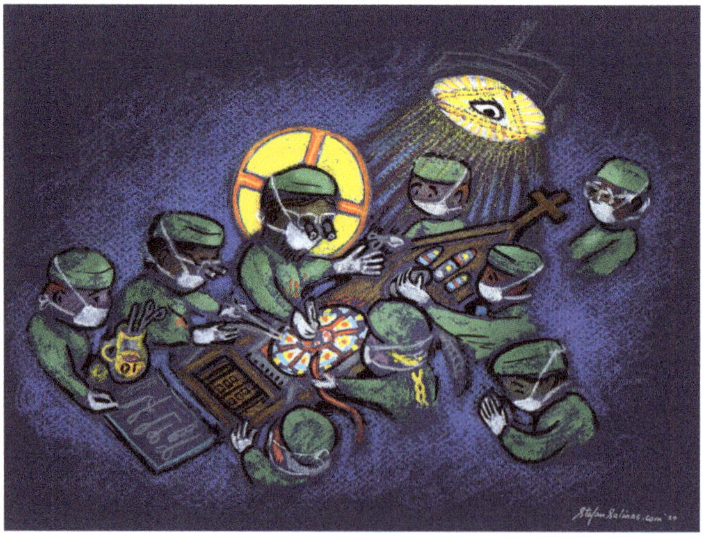

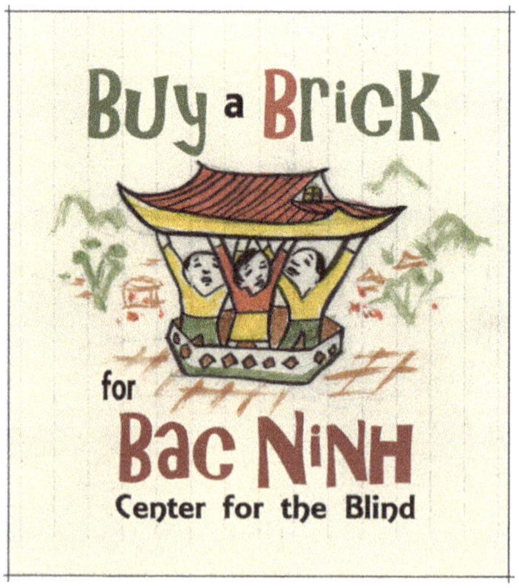

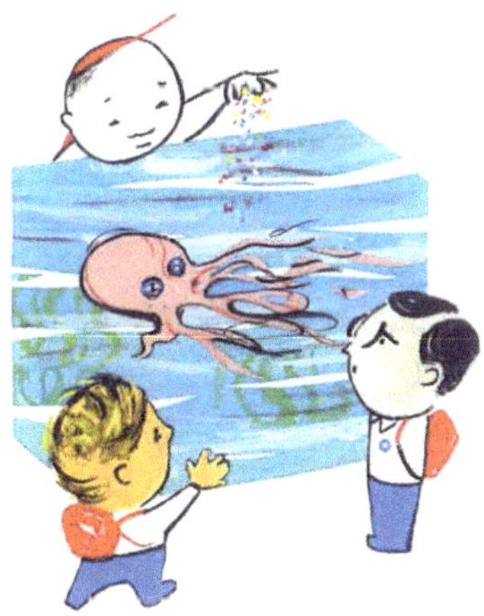

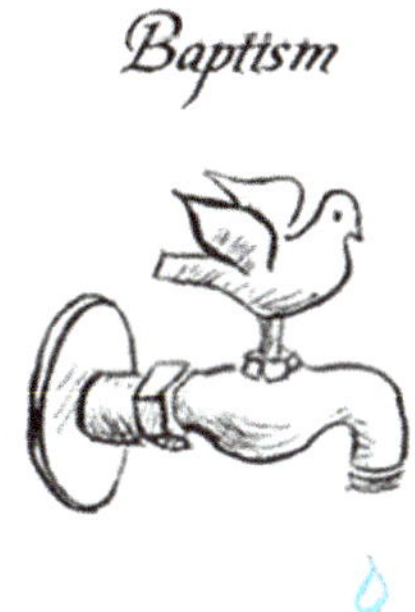

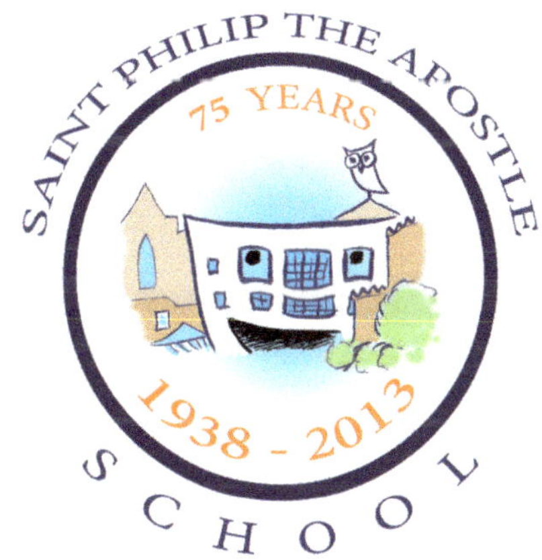

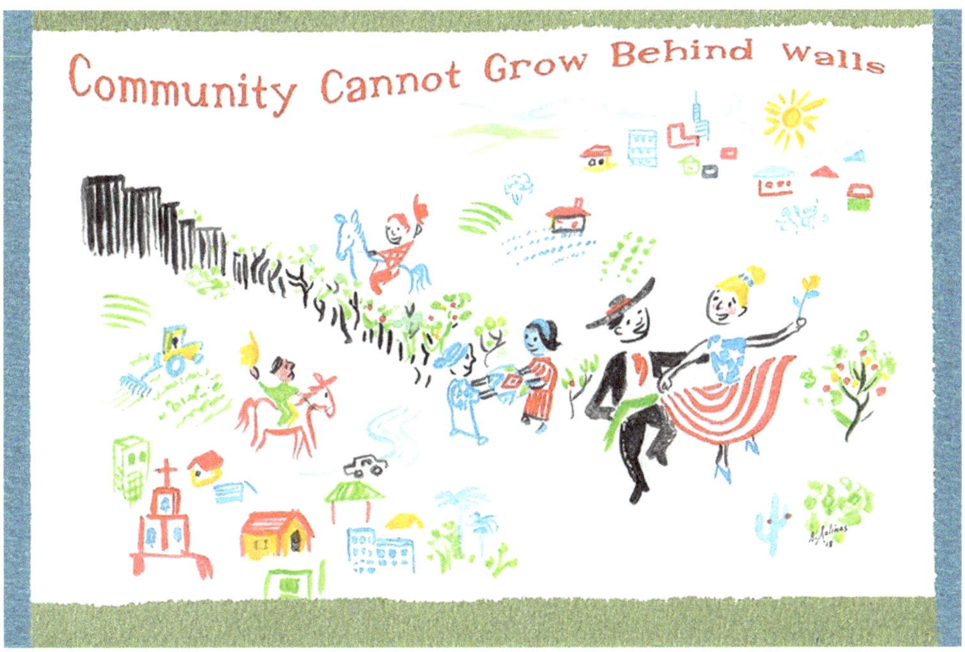

Graphic for a St. Philip the Apostle banner, 2013, Ink and digital
Illustration for *Connection*, Network's quarterly magazine, 2018, acrylic and ink

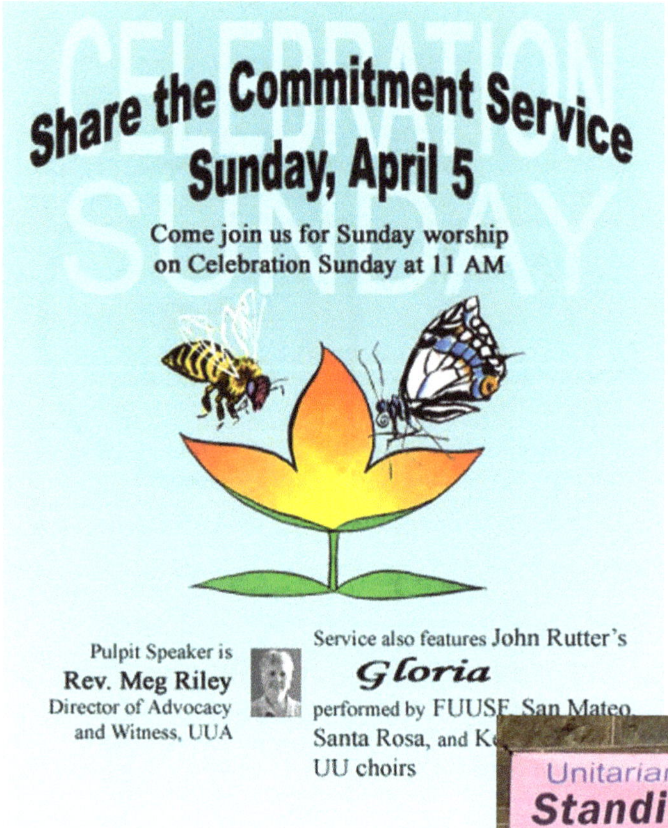

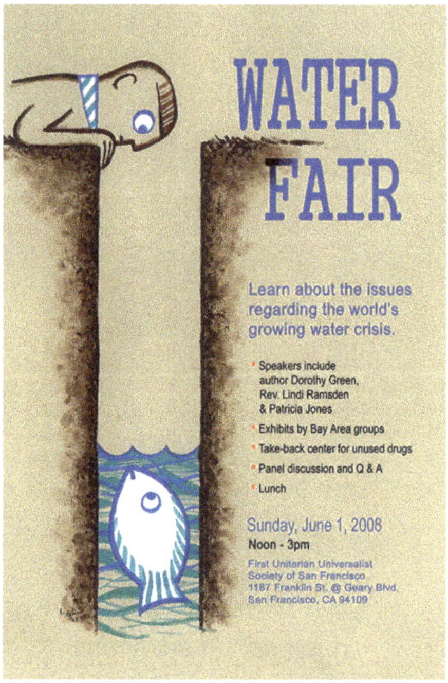

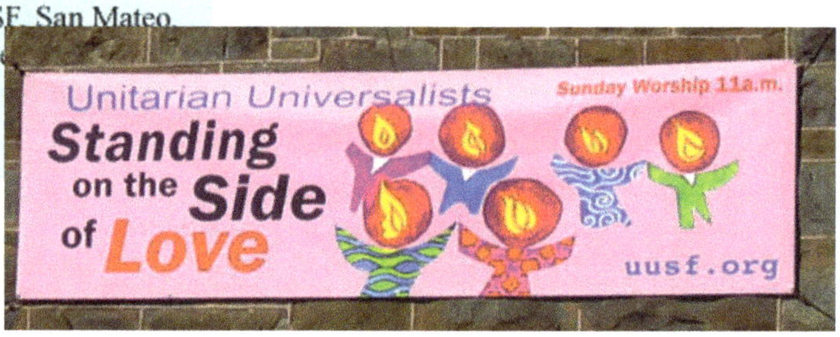

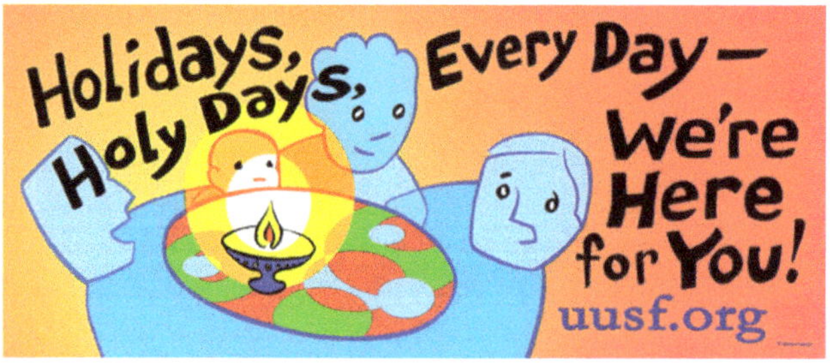

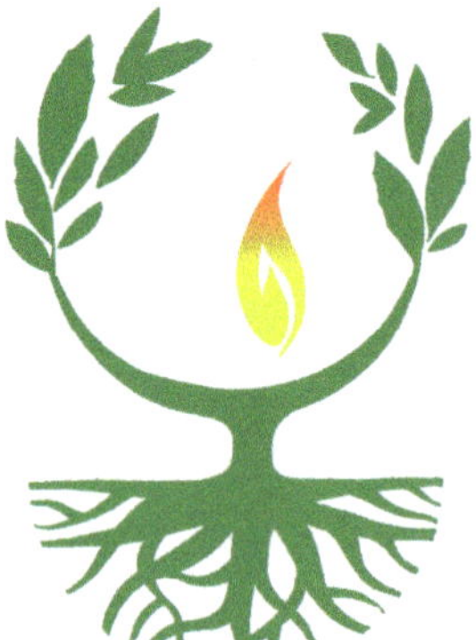

Designs for the First Unitarian Universalist Society of San Francisco
2000 - 2009

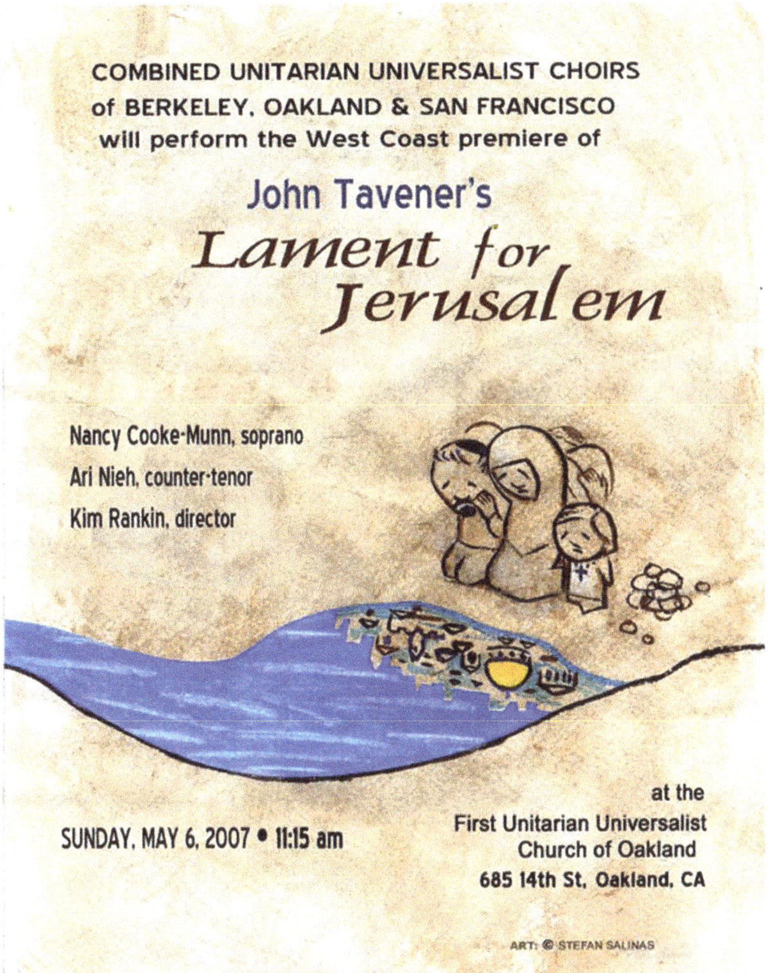
COMBINED UNITARIAN UNIVERSALIST CHOIRS
of BERKELEY, OAKLAND & SAN FRANCISCO
will perform the West Coast premiere of
John Tavener's
Lament for Jerusalem
Nancy Cooke-Munn, soprano
Ari Nieh, counter-tenor
Kim Rankin, director
SUNDAY, MAY 6, 2007 • 11:15 am
at the
First Unitarian Universalist
Church of Oakland
685 14th St, Oakland, CA
ART: © STEFAN SALINAS

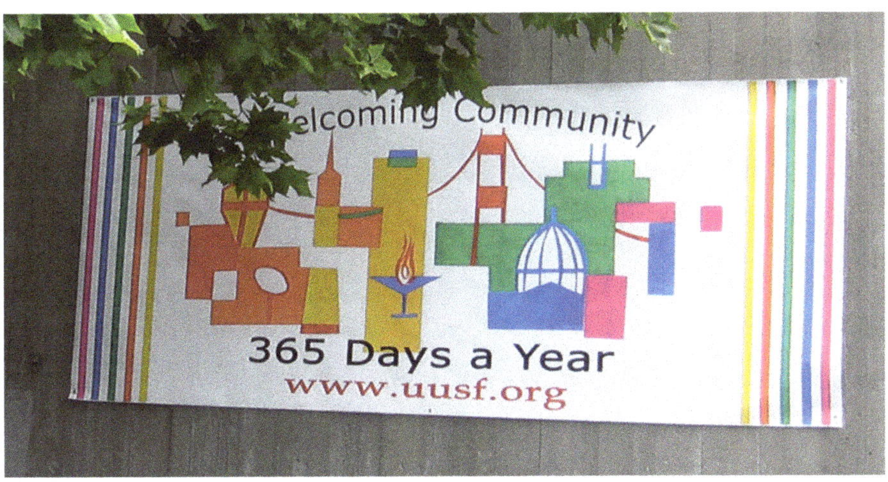
365 Days a Year
www.uusf.org

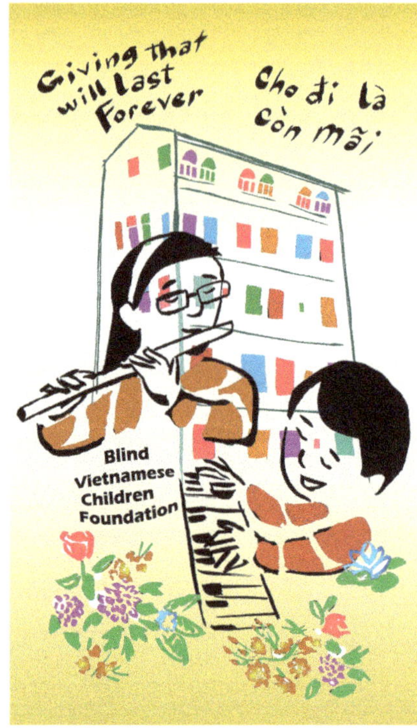

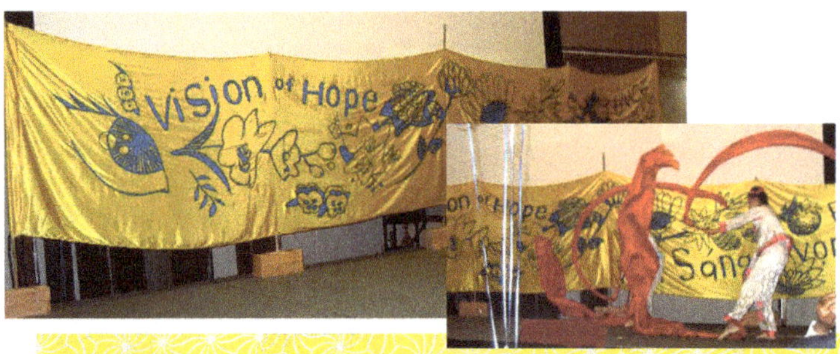

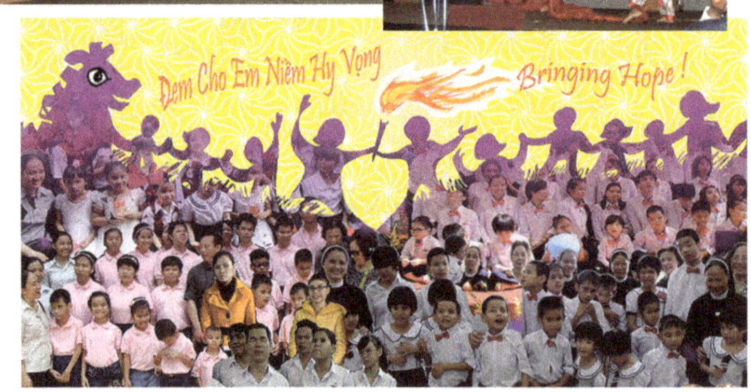

So far, most of the graphic art I have made for the *Blind Vietnamese Children Foundation* ranges from visuals for their annual benefits, hall décor, stage backdrops, to their website, brochures, thank you cards; the works. Thanks to a friend of the foundation, Annie Huong Truong, I was fortunate to accompany the president and patrons on a few trips to the sponsored schools and homes in North and South Vietnam as a photographer and videographer. What awe-inspiring and mind-expanding experiences they were!

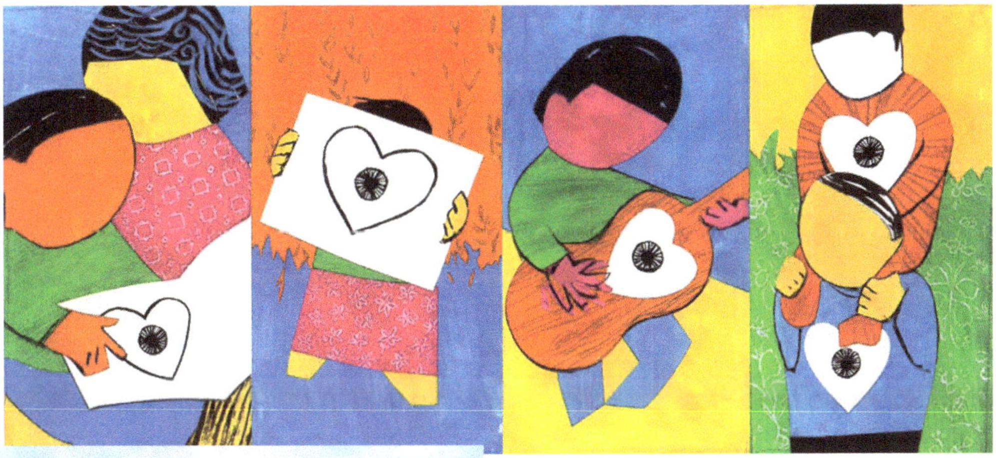

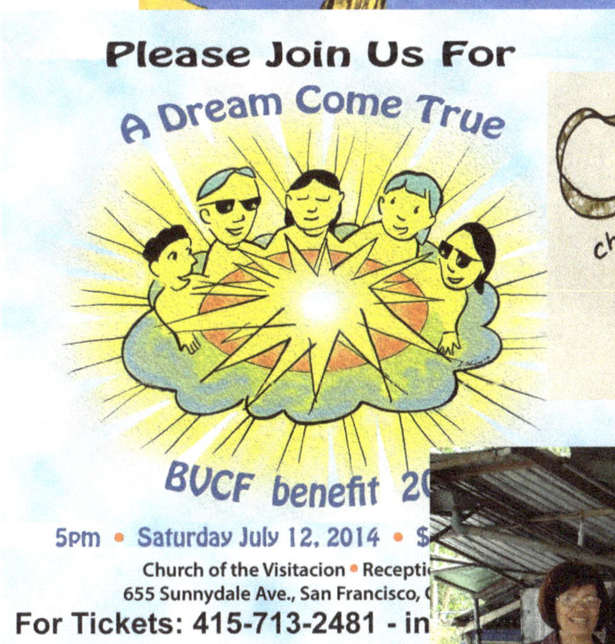

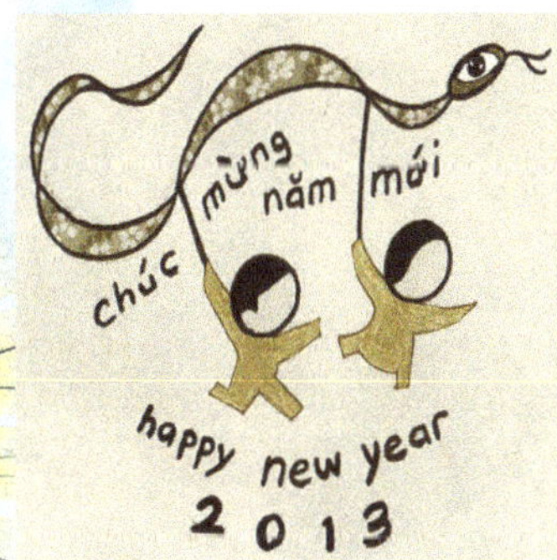

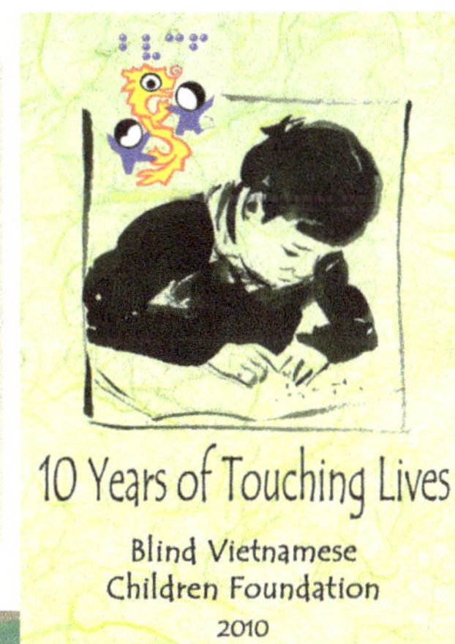

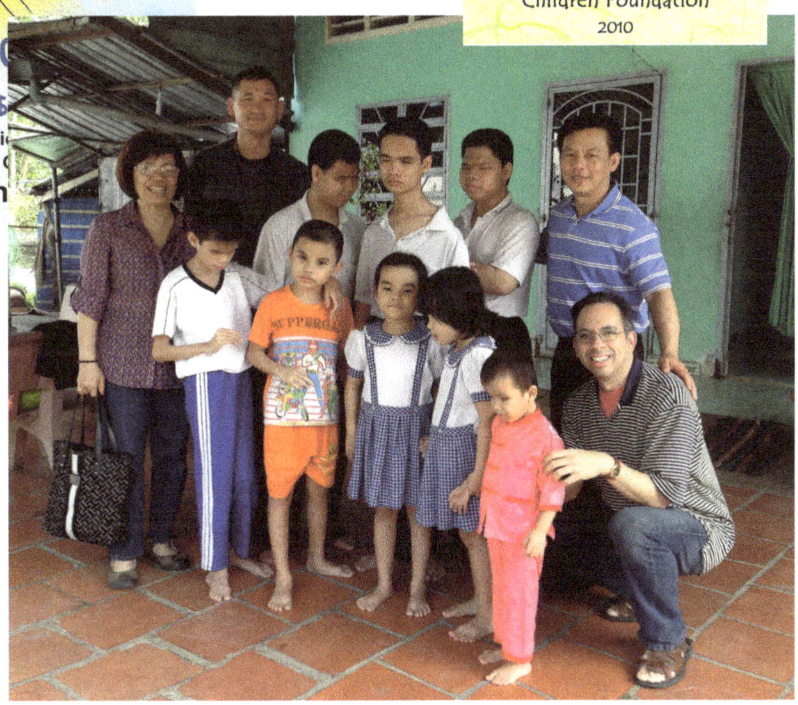

In their logo, I depicted a golden dragon, which according to cultural legend, is a stand-in for the island nation.

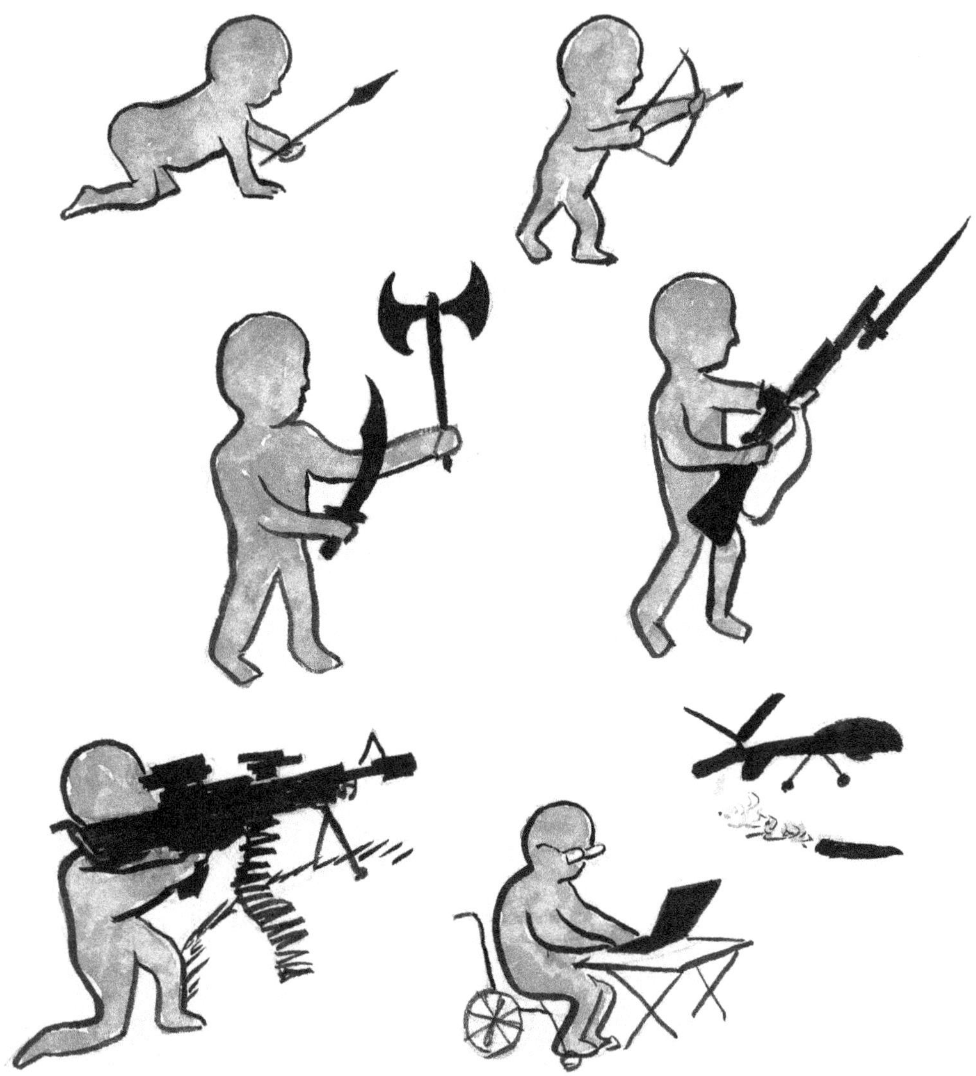

From the comic *Original Sin*, 2018
Ink on paper

Lessons and Insights

Limitations and boundaries can be an artist's best friend. Limited supplies, workspace, time, the subject matter; whether due to a client's guidelines, self-imposed, or lack of availability. Half of my paintings were stretched and painted within a 10' x 12' room, which including a futon mattress, desk, drafting table, and everything else I owned.

The illustrations I made for prints on wood, then paper, were all 9" x 12" or less to fit on a scanner's glass. Time constraints can force the creative to exercise the spontaneous and improvisational sections of her brain. Some believe the first solution that comes to mind is the best. I enjoy hand-making cards for friends and associates, and often I conceive what would be most appropriate to draw for the person, only five or ten minutes before I put pencil or brush on paper. These become perfect mini-exercises. The *Fr. Dom* webcomic needed to slowly simmer on the backburner, as I was collecting anecdotes, bits of information, and experiences while working on other projects and going about my daily routine. An advantage to working on more than one project at a time, especially if they are different in nature, is ideas and discoveries from one can inform the other. Some decisions are transformed or swapped for other ones during a long hike across the city.

So far, all of the books I wrote *and* illustrated I have self-published. This was not my intention, and to set the record straight, I have consistently sent all of their proposals to publishers, hoping for a bite. The children's book on churches, was in fact chosen by a religious publisher. They sent me a questionnaire to fill out, and a contract was on the way; however, in light of new information (that they chose not to discuss), their decision was reversed a few days later. It could have easily been the *Rat* graphic novel, or discovery of my TV interview about it, or the brief review of the gay-themed *October Recital* in the SF Chronicle (which I later republished in 2020). It was a blow to my ego, but it put me on the path of learning about peparing files, registering with the Library of Congress, acquire bar codes and ISBNs, marketing,and many other aspects of publishing one's own book.
Full creative control. Another helpful result of the curt rejection was it gave me permission to be more fearless with any future subject matter personally explored. I have to keep reminding myself of this! Of course, if it's for a client, every artistic decision should be made with the nature of the commission or purpose of its existence in mind.

When I set out to make a children's book on Catholics and Muslims, I still planned on sending it to various publishers but forged ahead with the option to make it a reality all myself, if necessary. Sadly, none of the schools I visited to read my Church book returned my calls for the interfaith one, and public schools shied away, dare I mention religion in their classrooms. Breaking new ground is not a walk in the park. Some adults said interfaith relations is not appropriate to teach little kids. But is the alternative to wait until they reach young adulthood, when prejudices solidify in their hearts? It did sell well at book festivals, got me invited to a multi-cultural event with a Sufi rock band, and the display for it at the main library here in San Francisco caught the eye of a board member of St. Agnes parish who commissioned me to create a processional banner. The audience may be small, but who can see the future?

When choosing a subject to write a book about, chose something that will NOT bore you easily, for not only will you invest from one to several years in the writing, but then you must add a few years promoting it; promoting it with a smile and a spring in your step. See? All my years working as a retail slave have come in handy at book festivals, gallery openings, and conventions. You never know when skills you have acquired for one job or project may aid another. Also, life is too short to beat yourself up for still having a "day job" and not "making it" in the art world.

Allow ideas to flow *through* you. Big or small, if they really ring true to you, and you carry them out to the populace, it will ring true for someone else. The pastor of Church of the Visitacion told me that on several nights, where my Visitation tile mural faces the street, he spotted a man standing in front of it. He was standing and praying. The aim of that project, all the time designing, all the labor, raising funds – was it worth it? A man sees before him an image; a *sacramental*; an instrument to help him pray to the Divine Mother. Shouldn't that be enough?

Although you may write a book for a particular intended audience, a different demographic may be more moved by it. Be open to that. I mainly wrote the Catholic-Muslim book to speak to Catholics, but many Muslim parents and children valued the message of peace, and delighted in the positive portrayal the people of their faith have in the pages. At one interfaith event, I learned that most of the audience were Sufi Muslims. Since it is set in Bosnia and Herzegovina, it should have not been a surprise when an interfaith choir reached out to me from Sarajevo, wishing to print a version of the book there, in the Bosnian language. After translating and updating the pages, it is now on hold due to the non-profit's reorganizing. We have our fingers crossed!

The webcomic about the priesthood I wrote primarily for the Catholic laity, former Catholics, and non-believers, to give them a glimpse of the joys, struggles, and challenges involved in such a vocation. And yet, priests have taken comfort in seeing their lives represented with compassion. One pastor in his mid-60s asked me, "How have you, a convert in your 40s, been able to get into the head of a priest in his 60s?"

No matter the extensive research spent in books, periodicals, and online, an essential element is to actually speak with and observe people related to the topic, if you can. Plus it can help you with motivation, as some of those people may later ask you how your project is progressing. This is a way of realizing that the topic is an important one to be explored for not just you alone. For *Fr. Dom*, I had the naïve intention going in that I should not bring up any "hot button" issues, but take the charming, light, slice-of-life approach. Those heavier concerns and fears kept creeping up in the research, in the interviews, and personal experiences. As I drove up to the subject of present-day American priesthood, it said to me, "Thank you for showing up, Mr. Salinas. Now kindly move over to the passenger seat. I'll take the wheel." As this was becoming a story to give voice to the voiceless, the whole endeavor would be useless if I neutered the touchy topics.

Are you aware of the message behind the art piece you are bringing to life; the wind blowing it forth; the telegram that asks to be transmitted? The ego will want to take full command and claim ownership. The ego is a useful servant, but not the Master. This is the balancing act. Granted it depends on the nature of the project. A self-portrait can be as improvisational and introspective as the imagination can take it, but a commission to paint a saint, in keeping with a style within a particular church, is a different matter.

Still, when a decision about composition, color, or other aspect *sings* to you, listen. The juxtaposition of the gothic style of painting and expressionistic impressionism within the mural at St. Stephens was not my goal from the start, nor did it seem so awkward when I was working on it; the mix just made sense as I sketched and painted.

I do not possess synesthesia (seeing colors as musical notes); however, sometimes, when something feels right to me, a note will play in my head. At times, as if by an organ or a choir, sometimes high, sometimes low. Or I will hum (an inner movie soundtrack?). Does this happen to you when you are standing in front of an astounding work of art or a scene in nature?

As mentioned before, dreams and s*trings of coincidences* have aided in art production. This will be explored in a future book, God willing.

Friends, may we be kind to ourselves and to one another.
We can either learn how to live together, or we will die apart.

The Kingdom of God is within you. - Luke 17:21 (GNV)

Open the Kingdom.

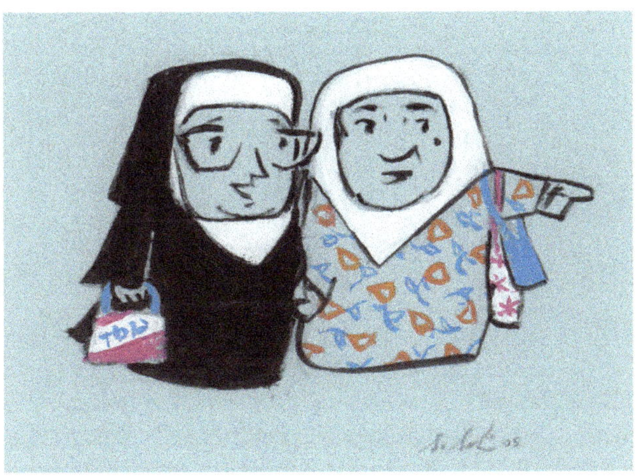

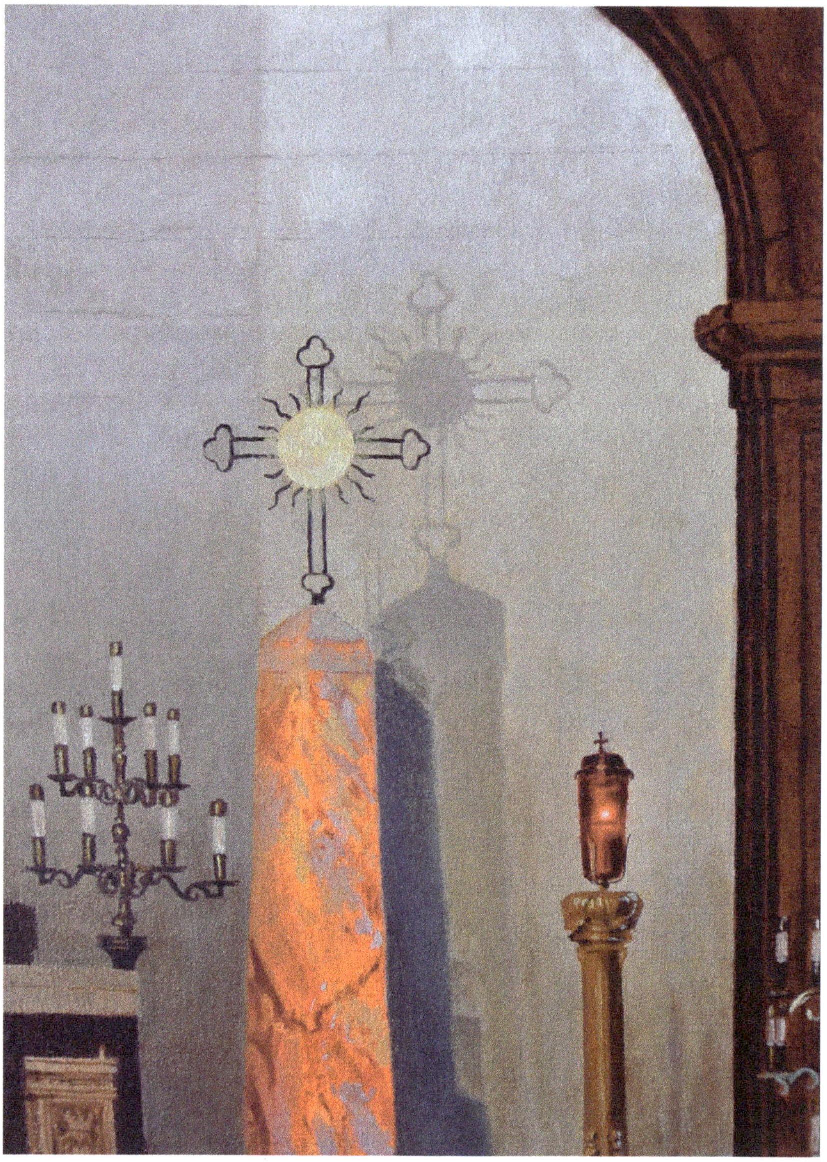

Sun Cross, 2015
Oil on canvas, 14"h x 10"w

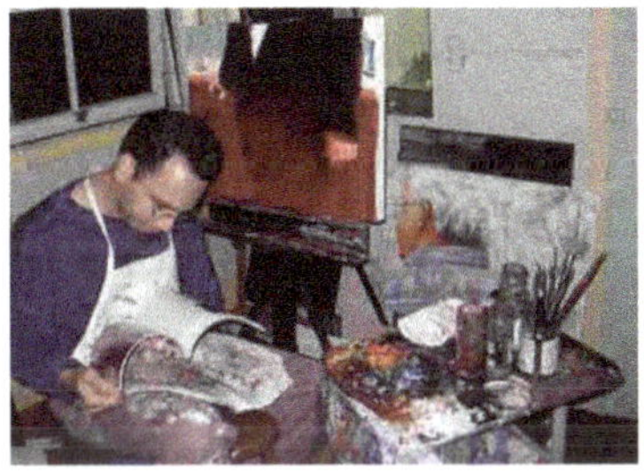

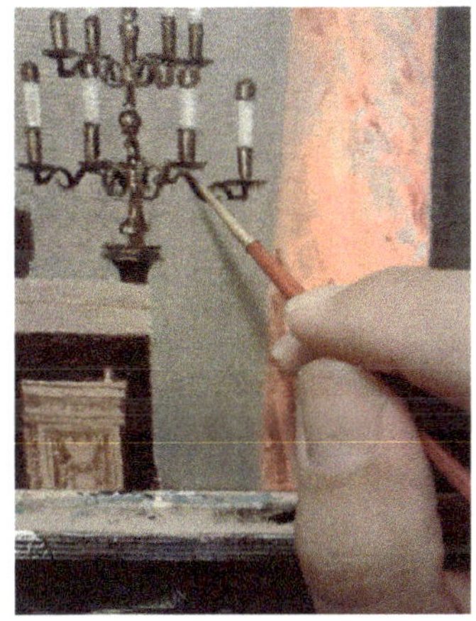

Biography

1972 Born in Houston, TX.
1997 Bachelor of Fine Arts from the University of Houston, TX.
2000 Moved to San Francisco, CA.

SOLO EXHIBITIONS

1999 *The One Who Sits and Waits*. Commerce St. Artists Warehouse, Houston, TX.

2002-2003 *People/Personae*. Beyond Expectations Café, San Francisco, CA.

2004 *Spirits and Archetypes*. Kings Gallery at First Unitarian Universalist Church, San Francisco, CA.

2004-2005 *Representations*. UCSF Alumni House, San Francisco, CA.

2006 *Nocturnes and Anthems*. Beyond Expectations Café, San Francisco, CA.

2016 San Francisco Public Library, Main Branch, San Francisco, CA.

2017 San Francisco Public Library, Main Branch, San Francisco, CA.

2017 Red Hill Station, San Francisco, CA.

GROUP EXHIBITIONS

1993 12-Person Show at Commerce Street Artists Warehouse, Houston, TX.

1994 *The Big Show.* Lawndale Art Performance Center, Houston, TX.

1996 *Hope and Horror in the Ashes of Yugoslavia.* Bosniac Cultural Center, New York, NY.

1998 *Main Street Voyeur (in correlation with Fotofest).* Not Su Oh, Houston, TX.

1999 *Multimedia 99.* Commerce St. Artists Warehouse, Houston, TX.

1999 *The Big Show.* Lawndale Art Performance Center, Houston, TX.

2002 *Gods and Goddesses.* First Unitarian Universalist Church, San Francisco, CA.

CHURCH COMMISSIONS

2013 Icon of the Holy Spirit Descending. Church of the Visitacion, San Francisco, CA.

2014 Altar Rails featuring the Four Evangelists. Constructed with Toan Tieu, Church of the Visitacion, San Francisco, CA.

2014 St. Francis Stained Glass Window. Constructed with Hogan Studios, St. Philip the Apostle Parish, San Francisco, CA.

2015 Catholic School Processional Mural, St. Philip the Apostle Parish, San Francisco, CA.

2015 Tile Mural of the Visitation. Constructed with Tile Mural Creative Arts, Jesus Lara & Miguel Campos, Church of the Visitacion, San Francisco, CA.

2018 Processional Banner. Constructed with Quong Sing Shop, St. Agnes Parish, San Francisco, CA.

2018 Processional Banner. Constructed with Liz TerboLizard, Most Holy Redeemer Church, San Francisco, CA.

2018 Outdoor Sign. Constructed with HD supply, St. Stephen's Church, San Francisco, CA.

2019 Baptistery Mural. St. Stephen's Church, San Francisco, CA.

CLIENTS INCLUDE:
The Jesuit Post, The Progressive Magazine, Network Lobby, First Unitarian Universalist churches in Houston & San Francisco, Blind Vietnamese Children Foundation, St. Vincent de Paul Society, St. Philip the Apostle Church, Church of the Visitacion, Most Holy Redeemer Church, St. Stephen's Parish, St. Agnes Parish, St. Philip the Apostle Church, San Francisco.

Bibliography

BOOKS
Titles written and illustrated by Stefan Salinas

Catholic Churches Big and Small. San Francisco, Camelopardalis, 2014.

The Concert and the Closet. San Francisco, Camelopardalis, 2020.

Grief and Anger. San Francisco, Camelopardalis, 2021.

A Muslim Family's Chair for the Pope. San Francisco, Camelopardalis, 2017.

Tomorrow Shall Be My Dancing Day. San Francisco, Camelopardalis, 2018.

Within the Rat. San Francisco, Camelopardalis, 2010.

AWARD: 2010 Xeric Grant for *Within the Rat.*

Titles illustrated by Stefan Salinas

Castle, Nathan G., OP. *Afterlife, Interrupted, Book Two.* Tucson, Fluid Creations, Inc., 2020.

Patrick Gilger, S.J., editor. *The Jesuit Post: #Faith #God #Frontiers #Culture #Mystery #Love.* New York, Orbis Books, 2014.

WEBCOMIC

The Sacramental Father Dom. San Francisco, Camelopardalis, 2019-2020.

TELEVISION

Mosaic. Burroughs, Hugh "Interviews of Ameena Jandali and Stefan Salinas" Hugh Burroughs, host, CBS. Aired June 8, 2014 on CBS KPIX 5, San Francisco. http://archive.org/details/KPIX_20140608_120000_Mosaic/start/1020/end/1080

Novi Dan. "Knjiga o Hajderovcima obavezan udžbenik u SAD-u? (A book about the Hadjerovacs is a mandatory textbook in the USA?)." Faruk Međedović, writer, United Group. Aired June 13, 2017 on N1 Sarajevo. https://ba.n1info.com/kultura/a169134-hajderovac-o-izradi-papine-stolice/?fbclid=IwAR1

Ten Percent. "David Perry speaks with Stefan Salinas." David Perry, host, David Perry & Associates. Aired August 4, 2010, on Comcast Hometown Network, San Francisco. https://www.youtube.com/watch?v=IjiemA_ExRo

Ties of Faith. Season 2. "Stefan Salinas" Ervin DeSmet, host, Shalom World. Aired July 4, 2016, on Shalom World TV, Rancho Cordova. https://www.youtube.com/watch?v=nCD_qFxuR4I

PRINT AND ONLINE PERIODICALS

Bean, Alan. "Last Call for Aging White Evangelicals." Friends of Justice blog, 12 January 2020. https://friendsofjustice.blog/2020/01/12/last-call-for-aging-white-evangelicals/

Biddick, Anamaría Scaperlanda. "Catholic Churches Big and Small, Introduction for Children." Sooner Catholic, 30, Nov. 2014, P. 10.

Bryson, Jennifer S., Ph.D. "What A Muslim Family's Chair for the Pope Teaches Children about Catholic-Muslim Relations" Public Discourse, the journal of the Witherspoon Institute 13 Aug. 2017. https://www.thepublicdiscourse.com/2017/08/19926/

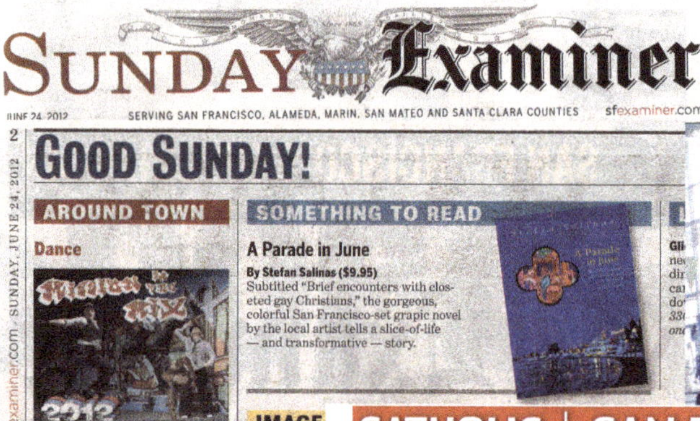

SUNDAY Examiner

JUNE 24, 2012 SERVING SAN FRANCISCO, ALAMEDA, MARIN, SAN MATEO AND SANTA CLARA COUNTIES sfexaminer.com

2 SUNDAY, JUNE 24, 2012

GOOD SUNDAY!

AROUND TOWN

Dance

SOMETHING TO READ

A Parade in June

By Stefan Salinas ($9.95)
Subtitled "Brief encounters with closeted gay Christians," the gorgeous, colorful San Francisco-set grapic novel by the local artist tells a slice-of-life — and transformative — story.

IMAGE

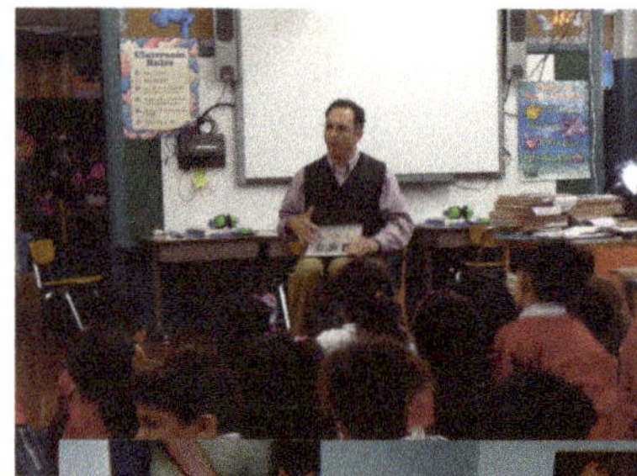

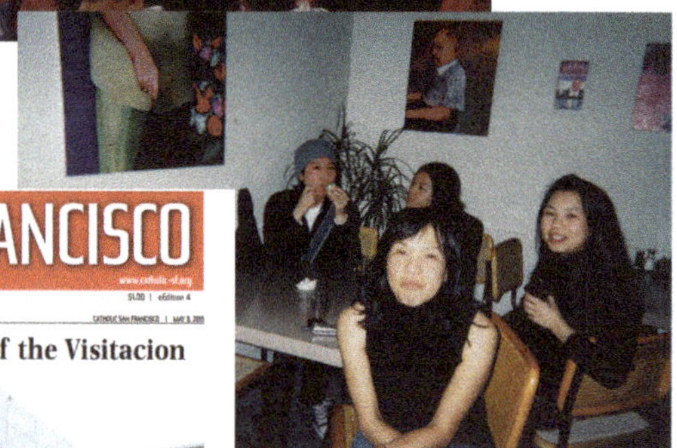

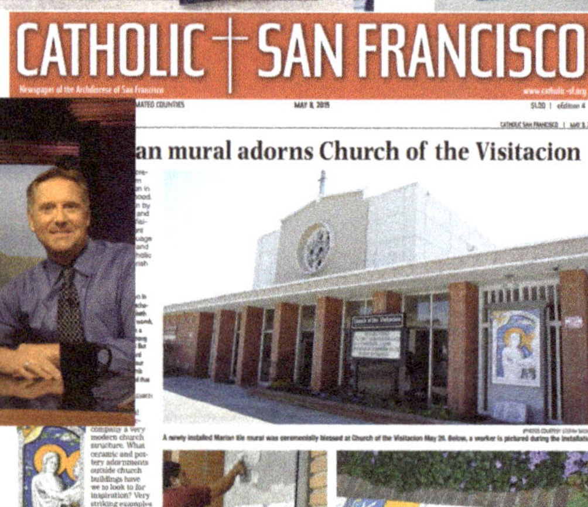

CATHOLIC † SAN FRANCISCO

Newspaper of the Archdiocese of San Francisco www.catholic-sf.org

MATEO COUNTIES MAY 8, 2015 $1.00 | eEdition 4

…an mural adorns Church of the Visitacion

A newly installed Marian tile mural was ceremonially blessed at Church of the Visitacion May 26. Below, a worker is pictured during the installation.

…company a very modern church structure. What ceramic and pottery adornments outside church buildings have we to look to for inspiration? Very striking examples…

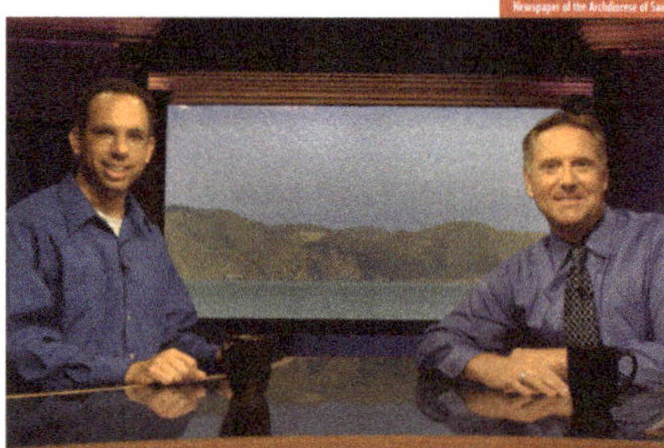

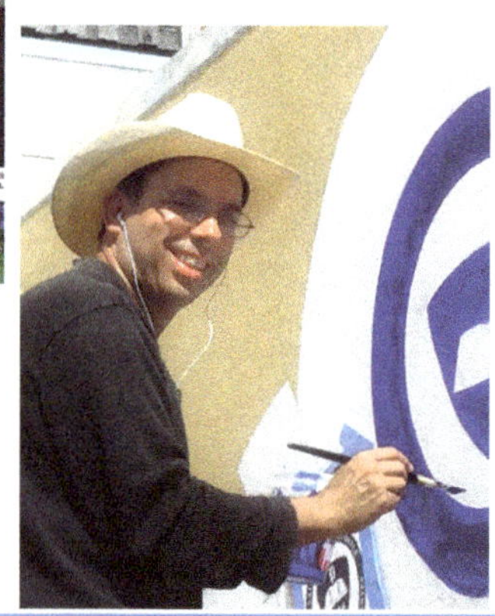

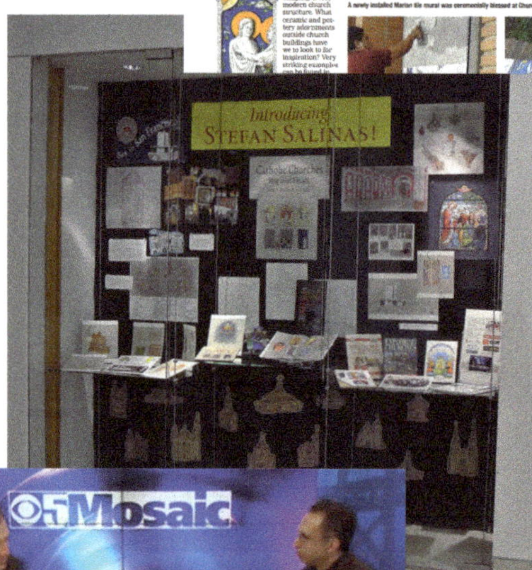

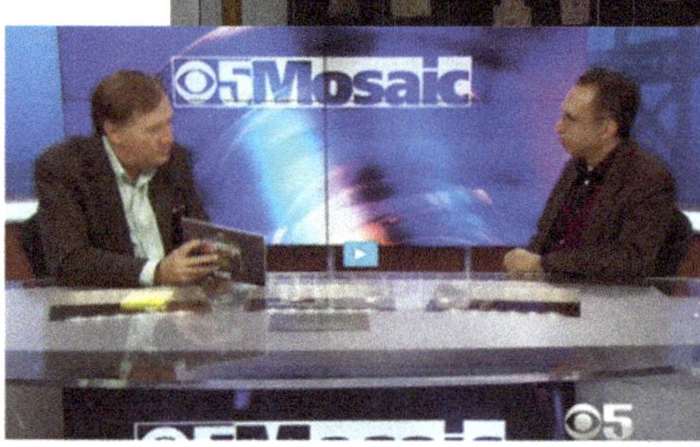

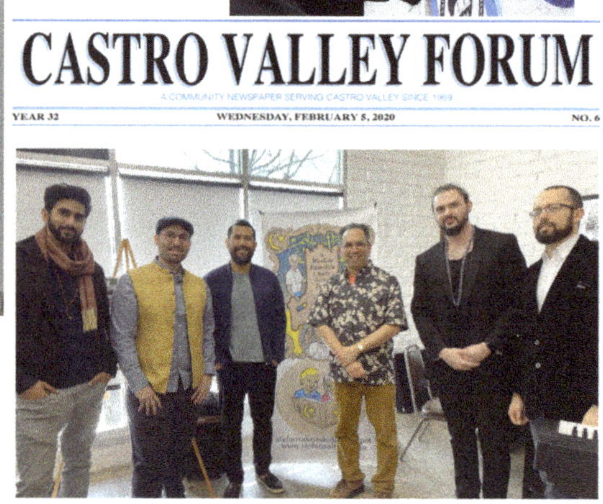

CASTRO VALLEY FORUM

A COMMUNITY NEWSPAPER SERVING CASTRO VALLEY SINCE 1969

YEAR 32 WEDNESDAY, FEBRUARY 5, 2020 NO. 6

Sufi Band 7 Stations and author Stefan Salinas of "A Muslim Family's Chair for the Pope" at last week's interfaith event at Smalltown.

Cherry, Kittredge, Rev. "AIDS spiritual resources: Art and books connect Christ, saints and HIV on World AIDS Day." Qspirit, 1 Dec. 2020. https://qspirit.net/aids-spiritual-resources/?fbclid=IwAR12hp31gzK4fcKne3dq5NxWvjK6fOKlqh2sGdBoRrzx9vj4apGv4zGnN8I

Cherry, Kittredge, Rev. "Top 30 LGBTQ Christian books of 2020 named." Qspirit, 9 Dec. 2020. https://qspirit.net/top-lgbtq-christian-books-2020/

Connection, NETWORK's quarterly magazine, July 2018, Back cover.

Cooney, Christine. "Book review: Catholic Churches Big and Small." Epiphanies of Beauty (Catholic Sense Media), 7 July 2012. http://epiphaniesofbeauty.com/2014/07/07/book-review-catholic-churches-big-and-small-by-stefan-salinas/

DelVecchio, Rick. "'MUNI Francis': Pope of the people inspires Catholic graphic artist." Catholic San Francisco, 12 April 2013, P. 2.

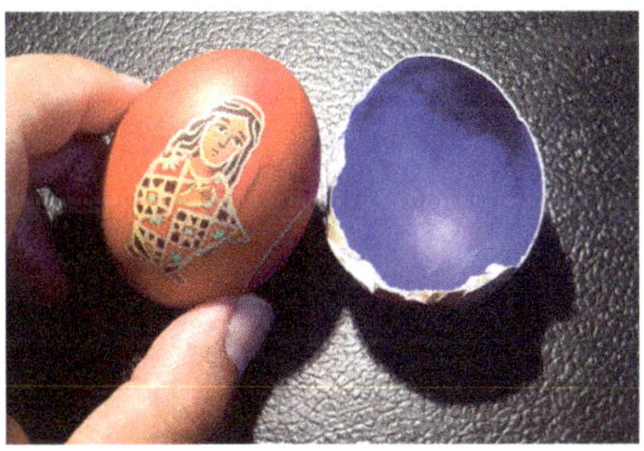

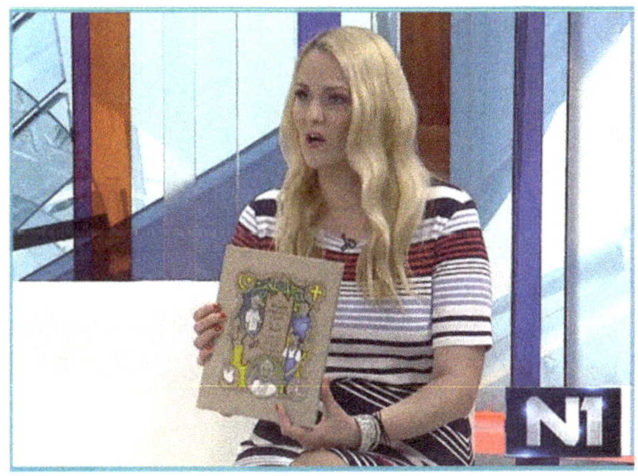

Channel N1, Sarajevo, 2017

Ehrenreich, Barbara. "Fixated on Growth." The Progressive, March 2008, P. 12.

Gray, Christina. "Abandoned Baptistery Reclaimed with Mural of Christ's Baptism." Catholic San Francisco, 13 Feb. 2020, P. 4.

Gray, Christina. "Convert Commissioned to Paint New School Mural." Catholic San Francisco, 14 August 2015, P. 24.

Gray, Christina. "Convert Creates Book on Church Architecture." Catholic San Francisco, 4 July, 2014, P. 3. Re-issued under the title "Where's Waldo for Catholics." California Catholic Daily, 22, July 2014. https://www.cal-catholic.com/wheres-waldo-for-catholics/

Gray, Christina. "Painter, Carpenter Create Altar Rails in Church of the Visitacion." Catholic San Francisco, 26 Sept. 2014, P. 21.

Gray, Christina. "Parishioner-Artist Publishes Book about Muslim Carpenters' Gift to Pope Francis." Catholic San Francisco, 7 Feb. 2017, P. 3.

"Independent Press Listings." New York Review of Books, Mar. 2014.

"Interfaith Event at Smalltown." Castro Valley Forum, 5 Feb. 2020.

Next page: From episode 66 of **The Sacramental Father Dom** ⟶
2020, Acrylic, pencil and ink on paper

Karen. "Book Review: Catholic Churches Big and Small." Karen's Adventures in Mommyland, 21 Jan. 2015. http://kareninmommyland.blogspot.com/2015/01/book-review-catholic-churches-big-and.html

Lordan, Regina. "This summer explore nature, poetry, saints with new children's books." Catholic News Service (also featured in The Boston Pilot, Catholic Courier, Catholic Philly & The Visitor), 2 June 2017. https://www.thebostonpilot.com/article.asp?ID=179951

Meat & *Skin*. "Art Crawl '99 review." Houston's Other, 7, Nov. 1999, P. 13.

"Nonfiction: The Buzz on Bees, Dipping into Chocolate | June 2017 Xpress Reviews." School Library Reviews, June 2017. http://www.slj.com/2017/05/reviews/books/nonfiction-the-buzz-on-bees-dipping-into-chocolate-june-2017-xpress-reviews/#_

Obrenović, Mladen. "Stolica za papu iz BiH motiv za dječiju knjigu u SAD-u (A chair for the Pope from BiH is a motif for a children's book in the USA)." Al Jazeera Balkans, 7, Feb 2017. https://balkans.aljazeera.net/teme/2017/2/7/stolica-za-papu-iz-bih-motiv-za-djeciju-knjigu-u-sad-u

Powell-Deschamps, Michael Orion. "Interview With Bay Area Catholic Author Stefan Salinas." Radical Second Things, 9 June 2017. http://radicalsecondthings.blogspot.com/2017/06/interview-with-bay-area-catholic-author.html , http://radicalsecondthings.blogspot.com/2017/06/interview-with-bay-area-catholic-author_8.html

"Priča o muslimanima koji su napravili stolicu papi Franji pretvorena u dječiju knjigu (The story of the Muslims who made the chair of Pope Francis turned into a children's book)." Klix Magazine, 7 Feb. 2017. https://www.klix.ba/magazin/zanimljivosti/prica-o-muslimanima-koji-su-napravili-stolicu-papi-franji-pretvorena-u-djeciju-knjigu/170207028

Salinas, Stefan. "The Path to Writing a Children's Book about Muslims and Christians" Medium, 30 May 2017. https://medium.com/@stefansalinas/this-is-ecumenical-this-is-sorely-needed-in-our-world-today-said-linda-the-gift-shop-manager-e7e49c97a27e

Shea, Mark. "A Muslim Family's Chair for the Pope." Patheos, 12 Aug. 2017. https://www.patheos.com/blogs/markshea/2017/08/muslim-familys-chair-pope.html

"Something to Read – A Parade in June." San Francisco Examiner, 24 June, 2012. P. 2.

Tierney, Kendra. "A Book You Should Know: An Interview and Giveaway with Stefan Salinas of Catholic Churches Big and Small." Catholic All Year, 10, Sept. 2014. https://catholicallyear.com/blog/a-book-you-should-know-interview-and/

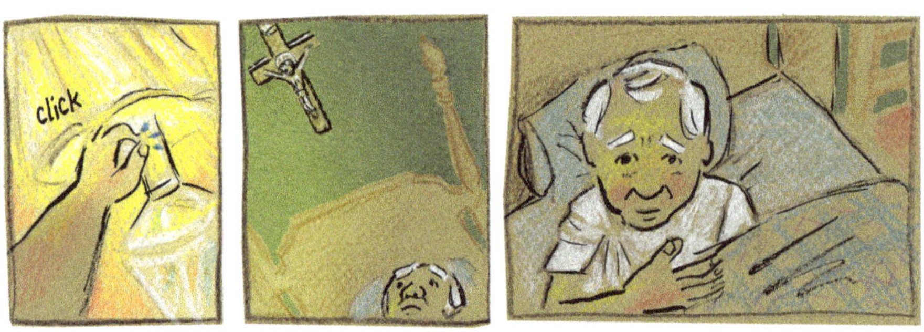

We have a busy day ahead, o Lord.

www.ingramcontent.com/pod-product-compliance
Ingram Content Group UK Ltd.
Pitfield, Milton Keynes, MK11 3LW, UK
UKHW061015020826
14090UKWH00046B/1426